D1478803

RELIGION IN CHANGING JAPANESE SOCIETY

RELIGION
IN
CHANGING
JAPANESE
SOCIETY

KIYOMI MORIOKA

UNIVERSITY OF TOKYO PRESS

This volume was published with the assistance of the
Publication Fund of the Japanese Ministry of Education

In warmest memory of
Jesse F. Steiner, eminent American sociologist,
and his wife, Ruth Steiner,
for their abiding affection toward Japanese students

CONTENTS

Preface   xi
Acknowledgments   xiii
Introduction
1. Contemporary Religions in Japan:
    Coexistence and Conflict   3
Folk Religion and Shinto
2. Religious Behavior and the Actor's Position in His
    Household   13
3. The Impact of Suburbanization on Shinto Belief and
    Behavior   39
Buddhism
4. Preferential Non-Mixed Marriage among Shin Buddhist
    Believers   75
5. Buddhist Sects and the Family System in Japan   89
6. The Changing Family and Buddhism in Postwar Japan   99
Christianity
7. Christianity in the Japanese Rural Community:
    Acceptance and Rejection   117
8. The Impact of Demographic Changes on Christian
    Churches   135
Conclusion
9. The Impact of the Physical Movement of Population
    on Japanese Religions after World War II   155
Appendices
10. Development of the Sociology of Religion in Japan,
    1900–1967   171
11. An Integrated Bibliography   185
Index   225

Maps

1. Niike and its vicinity   18
2. Areas along the Chuo Line   136
3. The city of Tokyo   137

Tables

1. Frequency of participation in neighborhood religious
   events   20
2. Frequency of participation in religious events at shrines
   and temples   30
3. Frequency of participation in household religious events 34
4. Interviewed households distributed according to period
   of arrival in Nozaki   44
5. Sense of parish membership correlated with period of
   arrival   46
6. Household religious behavior correlated with period of
   arrival   48
7. Religious behavior of parish households and sense of
   parish membership   49
8. Types of parishioners and/or parish households correlated with period of arrival   51
9. Distribution of Shrine Shinto facilities and symbols   52
10. Shrine Shinto behavior correlated with period of
    arrival   53
11. Importance of festivals and shrines   55
12. Opinions affirming importance of festivals and shrines 56
13. Reasons for importance of Shinto shrines   57
14. Participation in formal organizations   62
15. Participation in informal relationships   64
16. Factors conducive to participation in formal organiza-
    tions and informal relationships: I   66
17. Factors conducive to participation in formal organiza-
    tions and informal relationships: II   68

18. Temple membership of Kawanishi households   77
19. Local endogamous cases according to
    religious affiliation and subsections of Kawanishi   78
20. Class structure of Kawanishi   80
21. Occupational differentiation in Kawanishi   80
22. *Dōzoku* groups in Kawanishi   81
23. Traditional religious facilities and practices in Christian
    households   130
24. Distribution of churches by submission of annual
    reports   139
25. Distribution of churches by founding date   140
26. Changes in church membership, 1960–1964   142
27. Changes in church membership analyzed by causes,
    1960–1964   144
28. Natural increase and social increase in church
    membership, 1960–1964   145
29. Ratio of in-community resident officers of churches to
    total number of officers   147
30. Comparison of growth rates of church membership
    and district population   149
31. Population density by prefectures, 1950–1970   159

Figures

1. Social foundations of religions   157
2. Shift of migration ratio   158

x CONTENTS

Picture section

1. Kawanishi burial procession
2. Niike graveyard
3. Niike stone monuments
4. Niike
5. Shōganji
6. Mitaka
7. Mitaka
8. Kawanishi and Awakura

PREFACE

During the quarter-century since the Second World War, Japanese scholars have made numerous studies in the field of the sociology of religion. The language of the publications has been virtually confined to Japanese, and articles in European languages have been scarce. At the same time, religion in postwar Japan has widely attracted the attention of Western scholars: the considerable number of significant achievements by them are indicative of their deep interest in the subject. At this juncture, it seems to me that Japanese students of religion should strive to make the results of their scientific research available internationally. The present volume is an attempt to perform this task.

In this book I have collected several research reports and theoretical papers concerning changing religion in contemporary Japan. The articles included here were all written independently and span a period of some ten years since 1962. During these years Japan underwent major changes in various sectors of society including that of religion.

The essays are arranged under three headings, which represent the major streams of religion in Japan, that is, folk religion and Shinto, Buddhism, and Christianity. I studied Shinto in terms of the hamlet or community, Buddhism with special reference to the *ie* or household, and Christianity from the viewpoint of deviant behavior of the individual. Special attention was paid to the impact of migration and changes in the family system on these religions. There is no single chapter dealing directly with new religions, for the focus of my investigation has for many years been the established religions, both indigenous and imported. My recent study of a new religious movement has convinced me of the

usefulness of knowledge about the established religions as a basis
for a clearer understanding of their new postwar offshoots.

A brief description of what I attempted in the nine chapters
of the present text may be useful for readers. In the introductory
chapter, religions in Japan are discussed in terms of their coexistence and conflict, and special attention is called to the pattern of
dual or multiple membership to two or more religions at the same
time.

In Chapter 2, the relationship between religious practices and
the household position of the actor is analyzed, with a detailed
record by time-budget, taken in Niike, Okayama Prefecture, as
the basic data. Thereby, new light is shed on religious life at the
bottom stratum of contemporary Japanese society. In Chapter 3,
based on materials derived from intensive research in a suburb
of Tokyo, it is inferred that the greater the population growth in
an area due to immigration, the greater is the delocalization of a
Shinto shrine.

In Chapter 4, the tendency toward non-mixed marriage among
Shin Buddhist parishioners in the Noto Peninsula is identified and
possible factors responsible for the phenomenon are discussed. In
Chapter 5, using Shin sects as a case study, I attempt to show
how the social organization of Japanese Buddhism has been patterned after the *ie* system and how the former transformed itself
under the impact of political reformations over the past century.
In Chapter 6, the postwar transformation of Buddhist sect organization and the efforts on the part of sects to modernize themselves
in response to rapid social changes are analyzed with special
reference to Shin Buddhist sects.

In Chapter 7, I discuss how the behavior of Japanese Protestants in the Meiji Period, deviant by definition, became modal
through syncretization of religious practices and also through acceptance of the Christian culture by non-Christians and how this
change promoted a shift of Protestant groups from sect-type to
church-type. In Chapter 8, the effects of the population growth
on Christian churches in an area are examined, with contemporary data from Tokyo and neighboring prefectures.

In the concluding chapter, the social foundations of religions in
Japan are classified into three categories, and it is confirmed that

the greater the impact of migration on a particular foundation, the more the religion based on that foundation tends to change.

In preparing the present volume, I was assisted by many colleagues and friends. My grateful appreciation is extended first to Professor Tadashi Fukutake of the University of Tokyo for his warm encouragement and assistance in making arrangements for publication. My indebtedness to Joan L. Rieck of the University of Michigan for her critical reading and careful editing of the manuscript is immense, and I am also grateful to the University of Tokyo Press and Miss Elizabeth Powers for their editorial assistance. I appreciate deeply the assistance of Shigeru Nishiyama, a graduate student of Tokyo University of Education, in compiling the bibliography that has been greatly expanded with 1970–1973 additions. Lastly, many thanks go to my daughter, Kyoko, for her expeditious typing of the manuscript.

ACKNOWLEDGMENTS

Appreciative acknowledgment is made to the following publishers and journals for permission to publish slightly modified versions of copyrighted materials in the present work.

CONFÉRENCE INTERNATIONALE DE SOCIOLOGIE RELIGIEUSE for the article "The Impact of the Physical Movement of Population on Japanese Religions after World War II," by Kiyomi Morioka and Mitsuru Shimpo, from *Acts of the Eleventh Conference*, edited by CISR, 1971, pp. 189–211.

CONTEMPORARY RELIGIONS IN JAPAN for the article "Impact of Population Mobility on Christian Churches," by Kiyomi Morioka and Sonoko Kumagai, from *Contemporary Religions in Japan*, vol. 7, no. 3 (September, 1966), pp. 274–296, published by International Institute for the Study of Religion, Tokyo.

EAST ASIAN CULTURAL STUDIES for the article "The Changing Family and Buddhism in Post-War Japan," by Kiyomi Morioka, from *East Asian Cultural Studies*, vol. 11, nos. 1–4 (March, 1972), pp. 83–96, published by the Centre for East Asian Cultural Studies, Tokyo.

E. J. BRILL for the article "Development of the Sociology of Religion in Japan," by Kiyomi Morioka, from *The Sociology of Japanese Religion*, edited by Kiyomi Morioka and William H. Newell, 1968, pp. 3–12. Copyright 1968 by E. J. Brill, Leiden, Netherlands.

E. J. BRILL for the article "Religious Behaviour and the Actor's Position in His Household," by Kiyomi Morioka, from *The Sociology of Japanese Religion*, edited by Kiyomi Morioka and William H. Newell, 1968, pp. 25–43. Copyright 1968 by E. J. Brill, Leiden, Netherlands.

PRENTICE-HALL for the article "Contemporary Changes in Japanese Religion," by Kiyomi Morioka, from *Sociology and Religion: A Book of Readings*, edited by Norman Birnbaum and Gertrud Lenzer, 1969, pp. 382–386. Copyright 1969 by Prentice-Hall, Inc., Englewood Cliffs, N.J., U.S.A.

SOCIAL COMPASS for the article "The Impact of Suburbanization on Shinto Belief and Behaviour," by Kiyomi Morioka, from *Social Compass*, vol. 17, no. 1 (1970), pp. 37–65, published by Centre de Recherches Socio-Religieuses, Louvain, Belgium.

THE SOCIOLOGICAL REVIEW MONOGRAPH for the article "Christianity in the Japanese Rural Community: Acceptance and Rejection," by Kiyomi Morioka, from *The Sociological Review Monograph*, no. 10, *Japanese Sociological Studies*, edited by Paul Halmos, University of Keele, Staffordshire, England, 1966, pp. 183–197.

INTRODUCTION

1. CONTEMPORARY RELIGIONS IN JAPAN: COEXISTENCE AND CONFLICT

I

According to the latest governmental statistics (1972), there are 422 religious groups in Japan. These can be ordered into four major categories: 155 Shinto, 174 Buddhist, 61 Christian, and 32 miscellaneous groups. The largest among them, Shrine Shinto, claims 79,000 local bodies and 58 million parishioners; the smallest, by contrast, Tensokyo, is reported to have but one local unit and 4 adherents. Shinto is the indigenous religion of Japan. Buddhism came to ancient Japan through China and Korea. Christianity was also brought in from the outside, in the latter half of the sixteenth and again in the latter half of the nineteenth centuries. The miscellaneous groups have syncretic doctrines, containing elements derived from two, and sometimes more, religious traditions.

During the Second World War, the Japanese government compelled amalgamations between religious groups; it granted official approval to only thirteen Shinto, twenty-eight Buddhist, and two Christian bodies. After the war, however, the removal of governmental control over religion led to a rapid increase in the number of independent religious groups, most of which had been forcibly organized into larger ones or had gone underground during the war. Postwar confusion, deprivation, and inflation created anxiety and frustration in the Japanese, feelings that could not be handled adequately by existing religions with their emphasis on ritual. In response to these emergent problems there developed a large number of new religious movements.

How large is the religious population of Japan? The latest

statistics record 85 million Shintoists, 84 million Buddhists, 9 million adherents of miscellaneous religions, and 885,000 Christians, a total of circa 179 million. This total is 1.7 times the national population in 1972. How can we account for this great discrepancy?[1]

One reason is that each religious group tends to include even "dormant" (Fichter 1954: Ch. 2) and hypothetical adherents[2] in its estimate of the faithful, especially when publishing its statistics—despite its awareness of the fairly exact number of active members. For example, Sōka Gakkai, the largest of the tightly organized contemporary Japanese religious associations, claimed 8 million households in 1972, but was estimated to have 2 million active members. An even more significant factor is dual or multiple membership. If an individual belongs to two or more different religious groups at the same time, the national total of adherents is likely to exceed the actual population, even if reports to the Agency for Cultural Affairs (which deals with religious statistics) are entirely accurate.

Dual membership is most typically and widely observed in Buddhism and Shrine Shinto. The government formerly regarded Shrine Shinto not as a religion but as the Japanese national ideology, with rituals to be observed by every citizen regardless of his personal religious creed. In reality, the special position given to Shrine Shinto did not deny but accentuated its religiosity, which culminated in the Emperor Cult. After the war, institutional ties between the state and Shrine Shinto were abolished overnight so that today its position is the same as that of any other religious body; thus concurrent affiliation with Shrine Shinto and another religion constitutes dual religious membership in the full sense of the term.

---

[1] According to the Japanese National Character Survey (1968) made by the Institute of Statistical Mathematics, only about 30% of Japan's adult population is estimated to have a religious faith. If we take this fact into consideration, the discrepancy becomes much greater (Tokei Suri Kenkyujo Kokuminsei Kenkyu Iinkai, 1970:45).

[2] By hypothetical adherents I mean members of a shrine community or members of a believer's household who are not believers themselves but who, it is presumed by the authority of a religious body, will convert sooner or later.

II

The National Union of Shrine Shinto consists of nearly 79,000 local shrine communities, each of which has a shrine as its center.[3] The enshrined deities are believed to protect the community, and it follows that all residents of the community are regarded as parishioners of the shrine. At the same time, however, virtually all the residents are affiliated with a particular Buddhist temple. The temples in question are not necessarily located within the community. Further, not all the Buddhists in a single community belong to the same temple; rather, neighbors may belong to different temples of varied sect affiliations, whose parishioners are drawn from several communities.[4] A Buddhist temple has no territory, whereas a Shinto shrine does. Temple affiliation contains an element of choice. Although both are tradition-bound, and the membership unit is the household rather than the individual, they differ in group structure. The Shinto shrine—to follow Joachim Wach's terminology—is based on a natural (territorial) group; the Buddhist temple is a specifically religious group (Wach 1944: 109). This significant difference between a shrine community and a temple parish suggests that dual membership means much more than mere duplication.

It now seems reasonable to ask why most Japanese hold dual membership in Shinto and Buddhism. First, there is little possibility of doctrinal conflict. Shrine Shinto, based upon traditional folk belief, has no doctrinal system worthy of the name. Japanese Buddhism, on the other hand, has created a special doctrine that proclaims the ultimate identity of Shinto deities and Buddhist holy figures. Japanese history does contain a few cases, however, that are exceptions to this generalization. Shin Buddhism, which is monotheistic, came into serious conflict with Shinto during a period of rapid growth and extension in the fifteenth century. But because it was an integral part of community life, Shinto survived

[3] In Japan, "shrine" means always a Shinto building of worship, while "temple" signifies its Buddhist counterpart.
[4] Temple affiliation rarely reflects the class structure of the community, but often reflects the existence of several lineage groups and other forms of sectional differentiation.

the Shin Buddhist attack. During the opening years of the Meiji period (around 1870), aggressive Shintoists persecuted Buddhist priests and temples, but this persecution remained on the level of clergy and local government and failed to win popular support; the common people needed both temple and shrine, Buddhism and Shinto, in either mixed or separate forms.

Second, the functions of Shrine Shinto and Buddhism are generally coordinated and complementary. Buddhism was accepted by the people at large in a way that involved no serious conflict with their traditional religion; the division of labor or harmonious coexistence of the two produced no doctrines that could legitimize any antagonism. How, then, are their functions differentiated? As John F. Embree has shown, the festival calendar of the Shinto shrine reflects events of social value for the community and expresses the wish for community welfare, thus serving to maintain the solidarity of the local group and to keep alive its common beliefs and sentiments. By contrast, a Buddhist priest deals with the ultimate frustration and social dislocation caused by death; he helps his parishioners to a sense of security and protection by conducting funeral services and the subsequent rituals of ancestor veneration (Embree 1941:184–189). The ritual of the shrine is for the whole community; the Buddhist service is for parishioner households. The former is for this-worldly prosperity; the latter is of other-worldly concern. The sense of security fostered by the former invokes the interdependence of living neighbors; that afforded by the latter rests on the continuity of the family over generations.[5]

Conflict can occur among Buddhist groups or between Buddhist priests of the same or different sect affiliation, particularly in the course of proselytization. The impracticability of a division of labor among the Buddhists accounts for this sort of conflict. However, a group such as Shugen in the Edo period (1603–1867) and some famous temples like Narita-san near Tokyo have functioned in the intermediate area between Shinto shrines and ordinary Buddhist temples. Their main aim has been prayer for the worldly

---

[5] This contrast may be an oversimplification of the reality, but it helps in understanding the general picture of the division of labor between Shrine Shinto and Buddhism in the local community. See also Chapter 2.

prosperity of the individual household. In these cases, a certain division of labor between temples is apparent; the one organizes funeral services and the other prayer.[6] (The tie between a prayer temple and its worshipers is loose, and contact is infrequent and rather impersonal; I have excluded the prayer temple from the discussion of dual membership.) It is among funeral temples, therefore, that a division of labor is impracticable, not between funeral temples and prayer temples, or even between prayer temples that specialize in different prayers. In view of the open and covert conflict among funeral temples, the Tokugawa Shogunate prohibited priests from competing for more adherents. In order to eliminate Christianity, the Shogunate assigned priests to be registrars, officials who registered birth, marriage, and death for the parishioners; this made a change of temple affiliation extremely difficult. After the Meiji Restoration (1868), when governmental protection and interference were withdrawn, the Buddhist groups themselves agreed to refrain from competing with one another.

Lack of competition and efforts to avoid possible conflict reflect a high evaluation of personal harmony, which is one of the characteristics of Japanese culture. This is not a reflection of that sort of tolerance that might emerge after centuries of brutal warfare among religions. By maintaining the boundaries of their domains, religious groups and priests escaped the possible consequences of excessive competition, but there ensued, necessarily, a compartmentalization and rigidification on the levels of both doctrine and organization. The universalistic elements in Buddhism were excluded, and Buddhism's vital ability to free people from community and tradition was almost totally lost. A Buddhist ethic did not develop; instead, Buddhism became a mere prop to the existing social order and to the traditional value system.

Dual religious membership, observable everywhere in rural and traditional Japan, is reflected in the religious objects found in individual households. A household keeps a family Buddhist altar, where Buddha and the family's ancestral spirits are enshrined, and a family Shinto altar for charms distributed by the local

[6] This division of labor corresponds to the distinction between *bodai-ji* and *kitō-ji*. See Chapter 6.

shrine and the Ise Grand Shrine; in addition, charms issued by prayer temples are posted on the walls and pillars of the house. Although these three kinds of religious objects have different meanings, on the whole they are felt to have a protective role in the household and thereby support the traditional family system.

III

New elements entered the religious scene in the course of Japan's modernization, beginning in the 1870's. One was Christianity. The propagation of Catholicism began again, mainly in Kyūshū, and Protestant missions, largely from the U.S., developed vigorously in the cities. The spread of Christianity created serious tensions between it and Shinto and Buddhism. Although Christians assumed in the 1880's that the whole country would be converted to Christianity before long, the idea of a transcendent God was quite foreign to the Japanese and prevented a widespread acceptance of Christianity. Its converts were limited to a small number of intellectuals, professionals, and students.

Another new element was the new religions that appeared at the end of the Edo period and came to be approved by the Meiji government as independent groups under the category of Sectarian Shinto. They claimed the right to officiate at the burial services of their converts, thereby coming into conflict with the Buddhist clergy. They tried to respond to the peoples' desire for salvation in this world, which both a community-bound Shinto and a fossilized Buddhism failed to satisfy. With the acceleration of Japan's industrialization and urbanization, Tenrikyo, a leading Sectarian Shinto group, won converts rapidly from the lower classes. One major characteristic of Sectarian Shinto was the founder's healing power, which attracted many followers under the stress of conflict, poverty, and illness. As these groups grew and stabilized, they became bureaucratic and made patriotism and loyalty to the emperor part of their ethical creed in order to solicit favorable reaction from the government.

IV

After the peace treaty of 1951, a marked increase in the rate of industrialization and urbanization changed some aspects of Japanese religious life. In the cities, the notion that a Shinto shrine has a territory of its own is still held only by the old-timers who have lived in their neighborhood for generations and who participate in the shrine's annual festivals. The majority of immigrants to the neighborhood, who commute to work outside it, are generally indifferent toward the shrine; all that can be asked of them is a modest financial contribution. The old-timers are affiliated with particular Buddhist temples that perform funeral services; immigrants, especially newcomers, have no temple affiliation except in their place of origin. The shrine community does not make much sense for those whose loyalty has been shifted from the community to the place of work; similarly, the temple is meaningless for those who lack ancestors requiring priestly services. Urban Buddhist priests, despite the minimal possibility of conflict, do not approach the migrants—chiefly due to the priests' lack of experience in active proselytization. Cities and even suburbs with their rapidly growing populations have become religious deserts; it is in this vacuum that new postwar religions have been successful in making converts.

Risshō Kōsei Kai and Sōka Gakkai, offshoots of Nichiren Buddhism, may be considered representative of the new postwar religions, in the sense that they have expanded astonishingly since 1950. They provide a doctrine of salvation that is considered a modern interpretation of Buddhism. The values they assert appeal to the ordinary Japanese who suffered the loss of long-cherished values following Japan's surrender in 1945. As a result of rapid expansion, they have a huge organization from which a believer can derive a sense of security. They also provide small face-to-face discussion groups that satisfy psychological needs for expression and response. These organizational characteristics are particularly significant for those who are uprooted from their native places and who do not belong to large organizations, such as business corporations or labor unions. It is not surprising that these new religions seem to cater mainly to housewives and to owners and employees of middle- and small-scale businesses who are easily disturbed by economic fluctuation.

In the course of their expansion, these groups necessarily disturbed the vested interests of existing Buddhist groups. Sōka Gakkai and Risshō Kōsei Kai represent two contrasting attitudes in this situation. The former is condemnatory of other religions and demands of its converts that they discard their former religions completely. The latter manifests a compromising attitude and allows its followers to keep their ties with their former religions. This attitude is continuous with Japanese tradition, and the more exclusive one is rather atypical, if not entirely new. In this sense, it is worthy of note that Sōka Gakkai, in 1972, formally proposed the possibility of cooperating with other religions in attacking social evils, thereby softening its aggressive attitude toward other faiths.

FOLK RELIGION
AND
SHINTO

2. RELIGIOUS BEHAVIOR AND THE ACTOR'S POSITION IN HIS HOUSEHOLD

Problem

The aim of this chapter is to elucidate the tendency for a particular sort of religious behavior to be performed by a person in accordance with his particular position in the household. In this presentation I will make an intensive use of materials from one agricultural neighborhood in western Japan.

Some preliminary clarifications are necessary before analysis of the materials. First of all, the term "religious behavior" is defined operationally as the performance of religious rituals. This definition implies that my investigation is confined to overt behavior, specifically to the overt behavior patterned by local customs and regulations of religious bodies. In other words, my observation sets aside such covert behavior as religious attitudes and those religious actions that are not highly patterned but permit a wide range of individual variation (Kishimoto 1961). This limitation does not reflect the author's understanding of religious behavior, but simply the nature of the materials used.

Second, it is evident that some religious actions are performed by actors with no reference to their position in the family, but from their individual frustration or desires or from their wishes for a better society and consciousness of social responsibility. I will, however, observe only religious behavior that has any connection with an actor's position in his family. Although it is undeniable that the so-called universal religions have the power to emancipate believers from the control of the family group, among the Japanese most significant religious actions are directly or indirectly regulated by the actor's position in his family. This argument gains support from consideration of the prime importance of family life for human beings in general and for the Japanese in particular. In the Japanese rural community where there has not been any noteworthy differentiation between the household as consumption unit and the enterprise as productive unit, the *ie* (family household) is the fundamental unit of social life. Therefore, the view that religious behavior is regulated by one's position in the family is especially applicable to the rural community. It is admitted that religious behavior has a certain relation to the developmental stages of an individual, with some religious behavior being attributed in particular to old people, for example. However, I will emphasize that religious behavior associated with a particular stage of psychological development is performed by a grandparent, a son, or a daughter, rather than by an old man, a young boy, or a girl.

Then, why not speak about the relation of one's position in the family to one's religious role? Or how is religious behavior distinguished from religious role? The term "role" is used to designate, as R. Linton defines it, "the sum total of the culture patterns associated with a particular status. It thus includes the attitudes, values and behavior ascribed by the society to any and all persons occupying this status . . . In so far as it represents overt behavior, a role is the dynamic aspect of a status" (Linton 1945:77). Thus, it seems to be legitimate, or even recommended, to employ the term "religious role" instead of "religious behavior." However, the term "religious behavior" has been adopted on the following grounds.

Some scholars interpret "role" performance as fulfillment of any function of the group. It follows from this that the religious role is an assignment of the religious function of the family. Of course, there are many kinds of religious behavior that are regarded as performance of a religious function of the family, but all religious behavior does not necessarily have such a meaning. Some religious behavior arises apart from functional requirements of the family. Since this kind of religious behavior is to be included in my examination, the term "behavior" is preferred to "role" in order to avoid possible misunderstandings.

Then, what range of behavior can properly be regarded as

religious? Religious behavior does not always manifest itself in a pure form; often it is blended with recreational and social elements, and at times the latter are dominant over the religious elements. Therefore, it is necessary to set up an operational criterion whereby the range of religious behavior is limited. I will consider all performances of rituals as religious behavior regardless of the admixture of other elements, in so far as they are performed in or before religious facilities, such as Shinto shrines, Buddhist temples, family Shinto altars, family Buddhist altars, and gravestones, in accordance with the purpose for which each religious facility has been established. Having thus defined the term, I shall attempt to investigate what sort of religious behavior tends to be performed by which member of the family.

My basic data are time-budgets recorded by eight households[1] in Niike, an agricultural neighborhood consisting of twenty-four households, in Takamatsu Town, Okayama Prefecture. Among the eight, five households took a record of daily events for two years (from April 1957 to March 1959), and the rest for one year (from April 1957 to March 1958). The time-budgets are recorded so as to show in detail how each family member spends each unit of fifteen minutes during the period of one day. They enable me to identify "religious behavior," find its seasonal distribution, and

---

[1] The households of Niike are well represented by our sample except those with farms of one acre or less and one-couple households with the addition of one parent of the household head. For detailed information about Niike, see Beardsley et al. 1959.

Acreage	All households	Households in the sample
One acre or less	5	1
One to two acres	11	4
Two to three acres	8	3
Total	24	8

Composition	All households	Households in the sample
Two-couple	9	4
One-couple with one parent	7	1
One-couple	6	3
Broken family	2	0
Total	24	8

(Niike households as of August 1959)

determine convergence and dispersion of behavior among family members. It is perhaps the first time that as many as one-third of the total households of a neighborhood participated in recording such a detailed time-budget over a period of one year or more.

On the other hand, I must admit several drawbacks to my data. First, daily religious behavior that is performed within ten minutes or less, such as worshipping at the family Shinto altar or the Buddhist altar or the clapping of hands facing the rising sun in the morning, tends not to be recorded in the time-budget. Second, some households recorded in a less-detailed manner than others, and one cannot conclude that behavior appearing on a detailed time-budget did not occur in a household with a less-detailed time-budget lacking the entry of the behavior. It is possible that the recorder may have forgotten to make an entry of a certain religious act, and as a result the time-budget would fail to reveal the occurrence of the particular behavior. Therefore, the prerequisite for comparing records of different households is that they are precise and minute records. One may presuppose an equal minuteness of recording when one compares the behavior of two individuals or more in the same household. A third drawback is that households with less-minute time-budgets may have recorded events for a few days in a lump in spite of instructions to make daily recordings. It is impossible, however, to compensate for this drawback completely, though there are some items that can be adjusted by referring to the same items on detailed time-budgets recorded by other households.

In spite of all these drawbacks, I regard the time-budget method as fruitful in the sense that analyses of the records make a long-term "pseudo-observation" possible. Field observation of actual behavior is superior to a field interview whereby one secures information that concerns behavior patterns only. But casual observation fails to reveal long-term tendencies in religious behavior. Hence, one feels compelled to undertake a long-term observation. This technique is quite a demanding one to employ, however, so that it becomes necessary to devise a research technique that can be substituted for long-term observation. The time-budget technique was devised to meet this demand. Since one can secure detailed, sequential information covering a long time with the aid of the time-budget, this technique is called a long-term "pseu-do-observation." One cannot maintain that the time-budget technique is always the best, but I think it is definitely superior to any other approach to the aforementioned subject. In this sense, the present analysis is an attempt to validate the usefulness of this new research technique.

Participation in Religious Events of the Neighborhood

Most religious behavior recorded in the time-budget is cus-tomary behavior performed through participation in annual re-ligious events. Therefore, a classification of annual religious events should lead to a classification of religious behavior. Annual reli-gious events can be classified in a variety of ways. The classifica-tion adopted here is: (1) religious events to which every constituent household of a neighborhood has to send a participant; (2) reli-gious events that take place in temples and shrines in the form of Shinto festivals or Buddhist services; and (3) religious events that take place in individual households in connection with, or in-dependently of, (1) or (2). These three sorts of annual religious events will be studied to discover the relationships between the kinds of events and the familial positions of the participants in them.

This section deals with participation in religious events of the Niike neighborhood, which include *mura-gitō* (neighborhood prayer), *jishin-matsuri* (land god festival), *Nichiren-sama* (Saint Nichiren festival), and *tsukinami-kanki* (monthly sutra-chanting).

Three times a year, in the first, fifth, and ninth months of the lunar calendar, the villagers of the Niike area are expected to visit Kōjingū Shrine on the hilltop of Tsukuriyama to partici-pate collectively in a service called *mura-gitō*. This service is offici-ated over by the head priest of Honryūji Temple at Yamane. Five neighborhoods adjacent to Niike also perform this ceremony in order to worship their tutelary deity at Kōjingū Shrine, but on different days in the first, fifth, and ninth months. Since May is the busy season, the service in the shrine is all that is performed. In January and September, however, the service is followed in the evening by a collective chanting of sutras in the house of the member household on duty that month and by a communal dinner prepared according to a fixed menu. In previous days the *mura-gitō* was more complicated: before World War II, the participants used to stay up all night, and at sunrise they visited the shrine once again before breaking up. Wooden amulets symbolizing prayers for safety and a good harvest are given out by the head priest of the Honryūji Temple after the service in the shrine, to be placed for a time in the alcove of the household whose turn it is to provide a meeting place and prepare the dinner. After that, they are placed on bamboo stands at the south and north entrances of the hamlet and are believed to keep out bad luck. The social function of the *mura-gitō* is manifest in the religious implications attributed to the amulet.

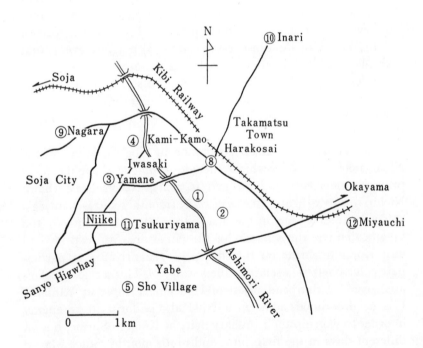

Map 1. Niike and Its Vicinity
(Numbers refer to places mentioned on pp. 26–28 of text.)

The land god festival takes place on those days called *shanichi* around the time of the spring and autumn equinoxes when no one should cultivate the ground. The object of worship at this festival is a stone monument engraved with the Chinese characters for land god, which stands in a corner of the front yard of the public hall of the neighborhood. In the evening, neighbors assemble before the monument and chant sutras with an elder as the leader. Then they go into the public hall for a communal dinner of red rice and a few dishes prepared by the household on duty.

In this area, every hamlet has a stone monument of the land god and one of Saint Nichiren, placed side by side. The stone called *Nichiren-sama* (Saint Nichiren) has the seven characters for *nammyōhōrengekyō* (Lotus Sutra) carved on it. In Niike there is a third stone monument engraved with the name of the Head Priest Daikaku. Daikaku was a Nichiren priest who is said to have made a preaching trip in this area more than 600 years ago. On the same day in September, both Nichiren and Daikaku are worshipped in the same way as the land god is. It is worthy of note that these rituals are performed as a neighborhood event and not as a sectarian service of Nichiren Buddhism. This is probably because all households in Niike are parishioners of Buddhist temples belonging to one of the Nichiren sects.

The monthly sutra-chanting is also a neighborhood event with the sectarian color of Nichiren Buddhism.[2] It takes place, as a rule, on the twelfth day of the month to commemorate the day of Nichiren's death 700 years ago. Nichiren Buddhism has penetrated into this area so thoroughly that almost all residents are Nichiren believers. If the size of a neighborhood observing this monthly ritual is large, it is divided into several sutra-chanting groups (*kanki-kō*). Each group not only holds the monthly meeting, but also assists with the funeral service when there is a death in a member household. Niike is a small hamlet composed only of twenty-four householders, however, and comprises only one group for chanting sutras. The group member whose turn it is offers his house for the meeting place. Formerly he also prepared a com-

---

[2] *Tsukinami-kanki* (monthly sutra-chanting) is very similar to the *oyorikō* gathering in a Shin-sect neighborhood. Examples of *oyorikō* are given in Morioka (1962:130–131).

munal dinner. This custom was abolished a few decades ago, and members now assemble after supper. It is a rule that one person from each member household attend the service, but usually several households fail to send a delegate unless advance notice is given that there will be some important announcements after the service. An elderly participant proficient in chanting sutras officiates at the service, marking time with a drum and a wooden gong. The service takes place in front of a sacred calligraphic scroll (*omandara*) hung in the alcove and is finished within half an hour. It is followed by announcements and discussions of a totally secular nature that have become an integral part of the *tsukinami-kanki*. The post-service meeting proceeds without following a formal pattern: sometime during the conversation following the service one of the leaders will call for the attention of those present in order to make an announcement or advance a proposal. Though highly informal, this part of the *tsukinami-kanki* is very important as a monthly occasion for promoting communication. It can be argued that the collective chanting of sutras prepares those present for discussion by stimulating their *esprit de corps*. Consequently, the *tsukinami-kanki* may be regarded as a monthly hamlet meeting of a secular nature as well as a religious event.

Now let us study Table 1, which shows frequency of participation according to the familial position of participants and the kinds of neighborhood religious events. The capital letters that

Table 1

Frequency of Participation in Neighborhood Religious Events

| Farm Household (acreage) | Household Composition | Age (as of 1957) | Neighborhood Prayer | | Land God Festival | Saint Nichiren Festival | Montly Sutra-Chanting |
			Service at the Shrine	Chanting of Sutras			
A (2.96 acres)	Household head	64					
	Wife	62					
	Daughter's husband (Farm manager)	42	1		4		15
	Daughter	39					
	Grandson	14					
	Granddaughter	11			1	1	
	Grandson	9			1	1	

P (1.35 acres)	Household head	76		(1)			
	Wife	64	4		2	2	7
	Daughter's husband (Farm manager)	43	2	4	2		17
	Daughter	38					
	Granddaughter	16					
	Granddaughter	12					
Q (1.18 acres)	Household head	62	4	4	3	2	(1)
	Wife	53		(1)			(1)
	Son (Farm manager)	29	2	(1)	1		18
	Son's wife	25		(1)			(1)
	Grandson	3					
	Daughter	17					
E (2.95 acres)	Household head	38	2	4	3	2	23
	Wife	33			(1)		(1)
	Father	64	3		(1)		
	Mother	60					
	Son	9	(1)		2	2	
	Daughter	6			3	2	
	Mother's brother	46					
D (2.84 acres)	Household head	46	2	4	3	2	21
	Wife	41					(1)
	Daughter	17					(1)
	Son	14					
	Son	10					
	Daughter	7					
I (1.79 acres)	Household head	32	1	2	1	1	6
	Wife	30					
	Son	5	1 (1)		2	1	
	Mother	54					1
K (1.76 acres)	Household head	37	2	2	2	1	6
	Wife	30		(1)			(1)
	Son	10					
	Son	8					
T (0.81 acres)	Household head	31		2	2	1	12
	Wife	29		(1)			(1)
	Son	5					
Maximum participation			6	4	4	2	24

stand for each farm household are the same as those that were adopted in a report on agricultural mechanization in Niike (Okada and Kamiya 1960). The figures in parentheses under the letters represent farm acreage. Households A, P, Q, E, and

D made a time-budget for two years, and I, K, and T only for the first year. As Table 1 shows, Households A, P, Q, and E are comprised of two couples of different generations, while the other three have only one couple, thus forming nuclear family households. The remaining one, I, includes the mother of the household head and thus is an incomplete stem family household. Special attention will be called to the differences in patterns of participation in religious events between the two-couple and the one-couple households.

Neighborhood prayer meetings were held six times during the two-year period. Therefore, if a member of a household had participated in every meeting and if the participation had been recorded each time without fail, the total would be six. (In the case of Households I, K, and T, the total would be three, since their record is confined to one year.) The land god festival was held four times, the Saint Nichiren festival twice, and the monthly sutra-chanting twenty-four times. (Again, for I, K, and T, the numbers would be one-half of these.) The total number of times a religious event was held serves as the base line against which frequency of participation by each household is examined.

Let us begin with the monthly sutra-chanting. It can be maintained that participants are limited largely to household heads, or to farm managers in cases where the positions of household head and farm manager are occupied by different persons. Of course, there are exceptions. For example, in the households whose turn it was to provide a meeting place and serve dinner to the participants, family members other than the household head or farm manager also participated in the event since they were obliged to be there in order to entertain the neighbors with tea and cakes. The figures in parentheses in Table 1 show this kind of participation. Also, the participation of the wife of the head of Household P is unusually frequent. This can be explained by the fact that the farm manager, a primary school teacher in Soja City, was sometimes prevented from attending the meeting by school business, and the household head, his father-in-law, was sick. These exceptions do not conflict with the assumption that it is mandatory for the household head or farm manager to be present at the meeting. Such a rule seems to be necessitated by the secular aspect of the monthly sutra-chanting, that is, it is a general meeting of the hamlet.

Why does the farm manager and not the household head participate in the events, in cases where the two positions are occupied by different persons? One reason is that the items to be discussed at the monthly sutra-chanting belong to the domain of the farm manager rather than to that of the household head who controls household finances but leaves the responsibility for farm management to the younger generation. Another reason is the social expectation that young farm managers take the burden of attending the meeting, which is held later in the evening, from their aged fathers. But the most significant reason is that the farm managers of Households A, P, and Q were officers of the Cooperative for Agricultural Mechanization and were responsible for making announcements and leading discussions at the monthly sutra-chanting. (In E, the remaining two-couple household, the head himself was the farm manager.)

The neighborhood prayer meeting can be divided into two parts: collective visits to Kōjingū Shrine and collective chanting of sutras at the household designated to provide the meeting place and food for the participants. My analyses will start with the latter part. It is a salient tendency for the household head or farm manager only to participate in the chanting of sutras except in the case of the host household whose ordinary members, too, attend the service. When the household head is a different person from the farm manager, it is usually the latter who participates. Household Q is the only exception, due probably to its characteristic pattern of division of work: the father, household head, attends the service and enjoys the communal dinner when no important information is given, while the son, farm manager, remains back home to take a rest. With regard to collective visits to the shrine, participants are a little varied in terms of their position in the household. Frequent attendants are the household head or farm manager. But, sometimes father, mother, or even children visit the shrine as proxies, so that the farm manager can work in the fields during the daytime. Even in cases of vicarious participation in shrine services, the farm manager himself attends the sutra-chanting in the evening after the daytime work is finished.

Household heads or farm managers participate in the land god and the Saint Nichiren festivals rather frequently, but attendance by other household members is also considerable. Adult members other than the household head participate in the festival when the household has the duty of preparing the communal dinner. In addition, children of primary school age or under who come from households both on an off duty frequently attend. This is because the festival takes place before dark in the front yard of the public hall and because children are given rice balls specially made for the festivals. It is debatable, therefore, whether their attendance can be regarded as genuine participation in the events. However, children are permitted or even expected to assemble in the yard where the festival takes place. It is through such occasions that they are socialized in the traditional ways of feeling and acting in the hamlet. One can regard children's attendance as an incipient form of participation in the events.

To sum up, first of all, the facilities for neighborhood religious events are not limited to Shinto shrines or other Shinto establishments. Some are closely related to Buddhism. However, the distinction between Shinto and Buddhism is itself not fundamental at the local community level: it is a distinction made for convenience. Such a distinction indicates the coexistence of beliefs of different origin, but the mere knowledge of coexistence can contribute little toward a deeper understanding of the religious life of the ordinary Japanese. The point is that villagers collectively worship spiritual, superhuman beings that are believed to affect the welfare of the neighborhood and pray for the safety and prosperity of their own households and neighborhood. The second item, which follows from this, is that one representative from each household should be present at neighborhood religious events, regardless of the number of household members available at a given moment. Total absence is disapproved even in the case of one-couple households, which often suffer from a shortage of family labor.

Third, the actual participants in annual religious events consist mainly of household heads or farm managers. This tendency is most evident at the monthly sutra-chanting and the neighborhood prayer meetings. A little more variety is found among participants in the land god and Saint Nichiren festivals. It is in two-couple households where vicarious participation tends to occur: the father or mother of the household head (or farm manager) often attends the events on his behalf. On the other hand, multiple participation by one person is marked in the case of one-couple households. Sometimes they may send a young child to the services, but the latter can hardly be regarded as a representative of the household.

Fourth, the assumption (Morioka 1964a and Yanagawa 1959) that old people most frequently attend annual religious events is not supported. The most frequent participants are households heads rather than old people, and young farm managers rather than old household heads.[3]

Participation in Religious Events at Shrines and Temples

The centers of neighborhood religious events are Shinto shrines or stone monuments and family Buddhist altars that can be considered incipient forms of shrines and temples. The fundamental factors connecting each household to these centers and promoting participation in the religious events that take place in or before

[3] The placing and removal of large pennants in the hamlet at the time of the autumn festival at the Shinto shrines may be added to the list of neighborhood religious events, but these are carried out exclusively by the households on duty. The people of Niike together with the residents of five adjoining neighborhoods worship the deity of Kōjingū Shrine in Tsukuriyama as their tutelary god. These six hamlets also worship, with six others along the Ashimori River, at Kami-Kamo Shrine on the north bank of the river. Kami-Kamo Shrine is the main shrine, and Kōjingū Shrine its branch. Obviously, the former is superordinate to the latter, but it is the latter that is much closer to the people of Niike, not only geographically but also in a social-psychological sense. Festivals at both shrines take place on the same days, 12 and 13 of October. Formerly, on October 11, young people used to put up two poles with pennants within the hamlet. Nowadays, the decreasing number of young people staying in the neighborhood has made it necessary for older villagers to carry out this communal work. During the two years of recording the time-budget, the head of Household D placed the pennants and the head of Household I removed them. The heads of Households A and E were among the three representatives from Niike to the shrine communities, but they were not recorded on the time-budgets as having attended the shrine festivals during the two years.

these centers are: (1) a kind of social pressure exerted by the neighborhood itself, and (2) the attitudinal characteristics of local people, that is, group-directed mingled with tradition-directed attitudes. In the case of religious events at shrines and temples, neither group pressure nor group-directed attitudes operate effectively. Participation is largely undertaken by each household or by individuals when the religious faith of each participant is the prime factor. For instance, a neighborhood prayer meeting at Kōjingū Shrine is a neighborhood religious event, but the New Year visit to the same shrine is, on the contrary, regarded as a shrine religious event.

From the time-budget records, one can identify the following shrines and temples as centers of religious events characterized in the foregoing parapraph. (Consult the map on page 18.)

1. Sōrenji Temple, belonging to the Nichiren sect, situated in Tsudera, Takamatsu Town, on the east side of the Ashimori River. It has about 120 households as parishioners, among whom are 16 Niike households with the surname of Hiramatsu, including Households A, P, Q, D, and K. The heads of Households A and P are among the four representatives from Niike to the parish. Parishioners are expected to visit the temple on the occasion of annual festivals honoring *Kishimojin* (goddess of children) and *Sanjūbanshin* (thirty guardian deities), and of the *Segaki* (hungry-ghosts-feeding) rite that is performed during the week of the spring equinox.

2. Renkyūji Temple, also belonging to the Nichiren sect, located in Tsudera. This temple has about 230 households as parishioners, among whom are 8 Niike households with the surname of Yuasa, including Households E, I, and T. The father of the head of Household E is among the two representatives from Niike to the parish. The major annual event of the temple that parishioners are expected to attend is the rite of *Segaki* held during the week of the autumn equinox.

3. Honryūji Temple, district cathedral belonging to the Hommon school of the Hokke sect, situated in Yamane. The approximately 230 parishioner households are located in all the neighborhoods of Shinjō-kami and Shinjō-shimo except Niike. As already mentioned, the head priest of this temple officiates over the Niike

neighborhood prayer meeting at Kōjingū Shrine. He is also the caretaker of Kōshindō Minor Temple.

4. Kōshindō Minor Temple, located on a hilltop in Iwasaki and maintained by all the neighborhoods in Shinjō-kami and Shinjō-shimo including Niike. Festivals are held here three times a year, in January, May, and September. The faithful visit the temple on the specified days allocated to each neighborhood and ask the priest to pray for their good luck and prosperity. Special festivals of *Bonten* (Brahma-Deva) and of *Taishakuten* (Sakra Devānām Indra) enshrined in the minor temple are held every thirteen years. Only on these occasions is the door of the sanctuary opened, so that during these festivals the precincts are crowded with a constant flow of worshippers and sightseers.

The head of Household A and the father of the head of Household E are among the three representatives from Niike to the Kōshindō cult. The Niike neighborhood group may sometimes direct the behavior of these representatives. On the whole, this is not the case, however, since the connection between Niike and the Kōshindō cult is loose, and the representatives who are in charge of liaison are volunteers rather than official delegates from Niike to the cult. Kōshindō Minor Temple is subordinate to Honryūji Temple. The people of Niike are not parishioners of Honryūji Temple and previously had no relations with the Kōshindō cult. Later, they came to be involved in the cult as a result of shrewd canvassing by the temple priest, but the relation of the neighborhood to the cult has not been firmly established.

5. *Bishamonten* (god of treasure) Minor Temple, situated in the precincts of the Hizashi Temple, Yabe, Sho Village, Tsukubo County. On the first day of the tiger in the almanac, about 10,000 people visit this temple to pray for good luck and a prosperous New Year.

6. Daikaku Minor Temple, belonging to the Nichiren sect and located in Daikaku, Kiyone Village. This temple is dedicated to the Head Priest Daikaku.

7. Myōhonji Temple, district cathedral of the Nichiren sect, popularly known as Noyama-sama, located in Kita, Kayo Town, Jobo County. It claims 77 subordinate temples, but neither Sōrenji Temple nor Renkyūji Temple are among them.

8. Rempukuji Temple, commonly called Jizōin Temple, belonging to the old school of the Shingon sect, and located in Harakosai, Takamatsu Town. The popular name comes from *Ksitigarbha-bodhisattva* (guardian deity of children) to whom this temple has been dedicated. On the festival day of the deity, the compound of the temple is crowded with visitors.

9. Konkō Preaching Center, located in Nagara, Soja City, 2.5 miles north of Niike. This center belongs to the Konkōkyo sect of Shinto, the headquarters of which are situated in Konkō Town, Asaguchi County.

10. Myōkyōji Temple, known popularly as Inari Temple, located in Inari, Takamatsu Town. Previously, it belonged to the Nichiren sect, but it became an independent body called the Saijō-Inarikyo sect in 1954, an example of postwar separation of a prosperous body from its mother association.

11. Kōjingū Shinto Shrine in Tsukuriyama mentioned in the previous section.

12. Kibitsu Shinto Shrine, situated in Miyauchi, Takamatsu Town. In the feudal age it was ranked highest among all the shrines in the three provinces of Bizen, Bicchu, and Bingo, and has kept its prestige up to the present. However, its relation with the people of Niike is slight and indirect.

13. Honryūji Temple, popularly known as Myōken-sama, located in Nose Town, Toyono County, Osaka Prefecture. After World War II it became an independent body called the Myōken sect. It is visited by a great number of people from distant places on New Year's Eve.

14. The Izumo Grand Shrine in Shimane Prefecture.

15. Headquarters of the Tenrikyo sect of Shinto in Tenri City, Nara Prefecture. Like the Izumo Shrine, this is a sacred place well known all over Japan.

Participation by members of the eight farm households in Niike in the religious events at shrines and temples mentioned above is recorded in Table 2. Let us first look at the ways of participation that vary according to the centers of the religious event. People participated in religious events at Sōrenji Temple and Renkyūji Temple as parishioners. They visited Honryūji Temple to ask the priest to officiate over the neighborhood prayer meeting at Kōjingū Shrine. Visits to Kōshindō Minor Temple were paid during the period of the special festival held in early May 1957. People of Niike visited *Bishamonten* Minor Temple on the first day of the tiger in the year. Daikaku Minor Temple, Noyama-sama, and Jizōin Temple were visited by aged believers or children. The Konkō Preaching Center was visited by a faithful old lady and her grandchildren. Inari Temple and Kōjingū Shrine were visited on New Year's Day. Kibitsu Shinto Shrine was visited by a household head and his son on its spring festival day. People went on a leisurely trip to Myōken-sama and the Izumo Grand Shrine on New Year's Eve or New Year's Day. Tenri Headquarters were visited on a group trip organized by the sect.

Let us correlate the frequency of participation in religious events at shrines and temples with the position of household members based on the two-year records. First, participation is, on the whole, not monopolized by a household head, but shared by other members. The household head is the major visitor only to the parish temple and to Honryūji Temple, particularly in one-couple households. Two-couple households share this tendency, but the meaning seems to be different. That is to say, the reason why the aged head rather than the young farm manager participates more frequently probably lies in the fact that the young manager is busy in the fields, and not in the social expectation that the head visit the temples. This assumption is supported by the case of Household E where visits to the temples are exclusively made by the father rather than by the young head and manager. A similar tendency is observed in the visits to Kōshindō Minor Temple, but participation by household members other than heads is more noticeable than in the case of visits to a parish temple and Honryūji Temple. This is due probably to the fact that the special festival at Kōshindō Minor Temple has an element of show, which attracts both old and young, men and women. Being responsible for the festival as representatives, the heads of Household A and E visited the temple unusually often.

Visits to *Bishamonten* Minor Temple, Daikaku Minor Temple, Noyama-sama, and Jizōin Temple do not appear to be made as representatives of a household. Jizōin Temple is visited by children, whereas visits to Daikaku and Noyama are regarded as a

Table 2

Frequency of Participation in Religious Events at Shrines and Temples

Farm Household	Household Composition	1 Sōrenji	2 Renkyūji	3 Honryūji	4 Kōshindō	5 Bishamonten	6 Daikaku	7 Noyama	8 Jizōin	9 Konkō	10 Inari	11 Kōjingū	12 Kibitsu	13 Myōken	14 Izumo	15 Tenri
A	Household head	2			6											1
	Wife				2	1	1	1		9	1					1
	Daughter's Husband										1			1		
	Daughter															
	Grandson				1											
	Granddaughter	1			2	1			1	1						
	Grandson	1			2	1				1	1					
P	Household head									1						
	Wife	1			2		1	1		1	2					1
	Daughter's Husband										2	2				
	Daughter	1			1	1			1		2					
	Granddaughter				1						2					
	Granddaughter				2				1		2	1				
Q	Household head			2												
	Wife											2				
	Son										1					
	Son's wife										1					
	Grandson											2				
	Daughter										1					
E	Household head				1					2				2		1
	Wife									1	1					1
	Father		4		6	1		1		1						
	Mother		1			1	2									
	Son				2											
	Daughter		1		2											
	Mother's Brother															
D	Household head	2			1									1		
	Wife				1				1		1					
	Daughter										1					
	Son										1					
	Son				1				1							
	Daughter				1				1							
I	Household head	2												1	1	
	Wife				1								1			
	Son				1									1		
	Mother	1			1		1				2					

K	Household head	1			1
	Wife	2		1	1
	Son				
	Son				
T	Household head				
	Wife	1			
	Son				

religio-recreational activity for the aged, particularly women around sixty years old. Pilgrimages to the headquarters of Tenrikyo by old couples also have a strong element of recreation rather than religious practice. The single instance worthy of the name of religious devotion may be visits to the Konkō Preaching Center by the wife of the head of Household A.

Nearby Kōjingū Shrine is frequently visited for the purpose of worship on New Year's Day and on other occasions as well. The most popular place to visit, however, is Inari Temple. Even young farm managers who seldom visit temples pay homage to Inari during the New Year holidays, accompanied by their wives and children. Young farm managers in a congenial group also visit grand shrines and famous temples in distant places on New Year's Eve.

Among the eight households studied, participation in the religious events at shrines and temples is infrequent with Q, a two-couple household, and T, a one-couple household. One reason may be that these two households were careless in recording the time-budget, but that is not the main reason. Rather, it may lie in the newness of these households, which leads to the lack of incentive to attend events at the shrines and temples. Household T is the newest branch family in Niike, established in 1953, only four years prior to the year when the time-budget study began. Household Q is also a new branch, established in 1945. The very fact that frequency of visits varies according to households reveals that participation in these kinds of religious events is not enforced by social pressure from the neighborhood, but that it is left to the convenience of each household and to the personal interest of individuals. Lack of social pressure is the basic factor that leads to a pattern of multi-participation by household members.

What is conspicuous, next, is frequent participation by old people. Their participation has various social implications: some participation, such as visits to a parish temple, is regarded as performance of their family role, while other visits are only to satisfy their personal needs for recreation or religion. Third, the tendency exists for places visited to be differentiated according to sex-age categories of the visitors. Old people, women, and children pay visits to nearby shrines and temples on New Year's Day and on festival days of the gods. Farm managers who are in the prime of life pay homage to grand shrines and famous temples, mostly in distant places, on New Year's Day. Consequently, a three-generation household consisting of grandparents, parents, and children discloses more varied and more frequent visits to centers of religious events than a two-generation household composed only of parents and children. In short, the religious events at shrines and temples are attended by household members of various positions and age categories, but especially by old people. The places visited are more or less differentiated according to the sex and age of the participants. This differentiation is in striking contrast with the pattern of participation in neighborhood religious events which are attended mostly by farm managers or young household heads.

Participation in Household Religious Events

Table 3 presents data on frequency of participation in household religious events. Religious rituals included here are those performed in each household before the family Shinto and Buddhist altars and at graves. The rituals concerned are those on the occasion of the Bon Festival, New Year's, the spring and autumn equinoxes, and the fall festival of Kōjingū Shrine.[4] This limitation of events is made on the assumption that the most important family rituals would be practiced at these five times. Significant

---

[4] Besides these, funeral ceremonies and anniversary services may be included as household religious events. Since these ceremonies are attended by relatives and dōzoku members, however, they cannot be called purely household religious events. For this reason they are omitted from the present analyses.

1. Burial ceremony procession led to the grave by an assistant priest. Close relatives are in white costumes. Kawanishi, November 1953. (See Chapter 4.)

2

3

4

5

2. Communal graveyard. Niike, November 1953. (See Chapter 2.)

3. Three stone monuments. From left to right: *Daikaku-sama, Nichiren-sama, Jishin-sama*. Niike, October 1956. (See Chapter 2.)

4. Kokubunji, an ancient temple near Niike, from the distance. October 1956.

5. Shōganji, a country temple with 290 parishioner households. A hereditary assistant priest and his family live in the flat house at the left. July 1952. (See Chapter 4.)

6

7

6. Mitaka, June 1956. (See Chapter 3.)
7. Mitaka, June 1956. (See Chapter 3.)

8. Kamanishi in front, Awakura in the distance. November 1953. (See Chapter 4.)

rituals are identified with each of the five events and listed under the respective headings in the top column of Table 3. Among them, the ritual called *tatehana*-fetching, which appears under the Bon Festival and New Year's, designates the custom of fetching a branch of the *kusasaki* tree that grows on a hill in the neighborhood. The branch is offered to the gods and ancestral spirits. The original purpose of the ritual was to attract the spirits of ancestors from the hill with an evergreen branch. The circular symbols in Table 3 indicate practices recorded during the fiscal year of 1957, and the squares those during the fiscal year of 1958. The figures attached to visits to graves and sutra-chanting under the Bon Festival heading describe frequency of practices performed.

As in the case of religious events at shrines and temples, various members of a household perform the rituals connected with the five events. There are differences, however. It is not often that household members visit shrines and temples together, whereas the collective performance of household rituals is inferred through the coincidence of time and kind of religious behavior recorded for each member and from the likelihood that the coincidence is synchronous rather than autonomic. In other words, household members perform the same kind of religious behavior collectively rather than independently but at the same time. In this sense, too, the term "household religious event" seems appropriate.

Next, it is noticed that grave-visiting is the most popular among household religious rituals. Virtually everyone visited graves during the Bon Festival; many visited the graves twice or three times during the three days of the festival. An arrangement is apparently made that the graves are visited by one or more of the household members at least once a day throughout the whole Bon period.

The next most popular ritual is the one called *hotoke-okuri* (seeing-off of the ancestral spirits), which takes place on the final day of the Bon Festival. Late in the evening, all members of the household go out to a drainage creek flowing from a small pond to see off the spirits of their ancestors who were believed to be visiting the household during the Bon period. There were only a few households, Q, T, and K in our sample, that did not perform the popular ritual. This is because Q and T were new branch households recently established and hence did not have any dead an-

Table 3

Frequency of Participation in Household Religious Events

Farm Household	Household Composition	Bon Festival							Autumn Equinox		Festival of neighborhood shrine: Shinto altar-clearing	New Year				Spring Equinox	
		Grave clearing	Tatehana-fetching	Offerings-presenting	Visit to graves	Sutra-chanting	Spirits seeing-off	Altar-clearing	Grave-clearing	Visit to graves		Tatehana-fetching	Sacred festoons	Deities-worshipping	Bonfire-making	Grave-clearing	Visit to graves
A	Household head	○			①①	②③	○□						□○				
	Wife	○			①	①③	○						○				
	Daughter's husband			○	①①				○								
	Daughter		○		①			○		○							
	Grandson				②①			○		○							
	Granddaughter																
	Grandson		○		②①		○										
P	Household head	○			①①	①①	□○○			○	□	□	○	□○	□	□	□○
	Wife				①		○○		□	○							
	Daughter's husband				①①	11	○□										
	Daughter				①②	11	○□										
	Granddaughter				①②		○										
	Granddaughter				①②		○										
Q	Household head		○	○	③③	11				□□□□	○			□□□□	□	□	□□
	Wife			○	③②	1											□
	Son				①③												
	Son's wife				3	1											
	Grandson				②②												
	Daughter																

E Household head
   Wife
   Father
   Mother
   Son
   Daughter
   Mother's brother

D Household head
   Wife
   Daughter
   Son
   Son
   Daughter

I Household head
   Wife
   Son
   Mother

K Household head
   Wife
   Son
   Son

T Household head
   Wife
   Son

NOTE: ○ participation during the fiscal year of 1957.
       □ participation during the fiscal year of 1958.

cestors of their own. Household K had two close relatives sick at that time, and the head and his wife were attending them at the hospital.

Third, it is evident that the old people play a leading part in household rituals, such as grave-clearing, *tatehana*-fetching, *shime-kazari* (hanging of sacred straw festoons), presenting of offerings at the family Buddhist altar, and cleaning of the family Shinto altar. They also take the lead in the chanting of sutras in front of the Buddhist altar. On the other hand, farm managers and young household heads participate in household rituals only infrequently. They are engaged almost exclusively in rice and rush cultivation and in the collective work of the neighborhood, leaving ancestor festivals and other household rituals to the care of their aged parents. Thus, the old people with the assistance of women and children assume the main reponsibility for household religious events, which are organized around ancestor veneration as the core ritual. It follows that the task of socializing the younger generation into these household rituals is done mainly by old people. In time, when the old people die, a two-couple household will become a one-couple household and some religious rituals performed by the old people, for instance, grave-clearing, *tatehana*-fetching, and cleaning of the family Buddhist altar, may be either simplified or abondoned. Other rituals, such as visits to graves, seeing-off of the ancestral spirits, and hanging of sacred straw festoons, are so essential that they will be maintained by the younger generation. Thus, a young household head will begin to be involved deeply in religious events of the family. However, the total volume of participation by the household at this stage of the family cycle will decrease when compared with the stage it was at while the old were still alive. This tendency is demonstrated by my data on one-couple households.

It has been alleged by some that women are the main performers of religious rituals in the household. The case of Household T is in accord with this popular proposition. On the whole, however, women do not play a leading part. If daily services to gods and ancestral spirits are largely confined to preparing and presenting offerings to them and these tasks are carried out almost exclusively by women, they should be regarded as the most important performers of household rituals. But material supporting positively the theory of women's predominance in household religious events is scarce, because the time-budget technique employed did not record daily religious behavior that was finished in less than ten minutes, and one rarely spends more than ten minutes in presenting daily offerings at the family Buddhist altar.

Conclusion

I have classified religious behavior into three categories and have considered the relation between the kind of religious behavior and the main actor's position in his family. In this final section some major findings pinpointed in the three foregoing sections will be reviewed.

In neighborhood religious events, the principal participants are farm managers and young household heads, whereas participation of the old people is predominant in religious events at temples and shrines and in the household. This division reveals expected spheres of activities of the older and the younger generations. It can be assumed that excessive interference by older people in the ways of farm management would be avoided by this division.

It is mainly old people who discipline the youngest generation in religious rituals and events. Therefore, in one-couple households lacking old people, not only does the volume of religious practice decrease but the religious training of young people also tends to be neglected. One can assume from the present material that the increase in the number of one-couple households in cities may be a powerful factor in promoting secularization.

Religious participation by women is not especially noticeable. The dominance of old people in religious participation and the longer life expectancy for women could lead to the hypothesis that participation by old women is predominant, as is exemplified in the case of Household I. It is hard to maintain, however, that women's participation is in general highly noticeable. If the cooking of food on the occasion of religious events is regarded as a kind of religious participation, then women's participation naturally occupies a large part. The cooking of food for festival days used to be an important religious act, but nowadays it cannot be regarded as religious. Only the cooking of sacred food to be offered to gods and ancestral spirits can be included in the category of religious behavior. However, this kind of cooking was not specified in the time-budgets, for it is done concurrently with preparation of meals for the living members of the household. Hence, I cannot positively argue that women's participation in religious events is especially noticeable.

Since my analyses are based primarily on time-budgets of farm households, the religious behavior studied is restricted to such patterned behavior as participation in annual religious events and performances of rituals. Even when religious behavior is defined as performance of rituals, supplementing the time-budgets with information secured through other techniques was necessary to achieve deeper understanding of the subject. The present chapter has been produced from long-term "pseudo-observation" aided by panel interviewing and field observation.

Generalization of these findings may have some regional limitations. It is hoped, however, that the present chapter is a sociological contribution that highlights one important, though so far badly neglected, aspect of the relation between family and religion in Japan.

3. THE IMPACT OF SUBURBANIZATION ON SHINTO BELIEF AND BEHAVIOR*

Introduction

The geographical mobility of the Japanese population since the end of World War II, especially since the beginning of Japan's rapid economic growth in the 1960's, has increasingly become a focus of attention among social scientists. This mobility signifies, in brief, a concentration of population in urban areas. Population flow away from farm and mountain villages has led, on the one hand, to the phenomenon of so-called overscarcity and, on the other, to the phenomenon of overdensity in major cities.

How are the major religious bodies, particularly their constitutive units, the local religious organizations, responding to this geographical mobility of the population? Religious bodies that take population mobility trends into consideration and frame policies accordingly are not lacking, but by far the great majority are merely drifting along, letting things take their natural course and formulating no policies whatever. In areas with decreasing populations, the activities of Shinto shrines, Buddhist temples, and Christian churches are stagnating, and some of these institutions are finding it difficult to maintain themselves. On the other hand, in the major cities, while the so-called new religions are actively engaged in spreading their faith to the torrential influx of people, the shrines are losing their ties with parishioners, and

* This chapter is a slightly modified abridgment of an article originally coauthored by Kiyomi Morioka and Masazaburō Hanashima (1968), which was a report on two communities, whereas the present one reports only on the one studied by Morioka. The translation was made by Dr. David Reid, Professor of the Study of Religion at Japan Biblical Seminary, Tokyo, and to him the author wishes to express his grateful appreciation.

the temples, not knowing what techniques to employ in the face of the great throngs of new residents, are largely ignoring the problem.

At this juncture, it is more appropriate to ask what effect population mobility is having on religious organizations[1] than how religious organizations are responding to population mobility. With the former question in mind, Sonoko Kumagai and I made a study of Christian churches in areas that contrast with each other as regards population mobility, namely, four areas in Tokyo, Yamanashi, and Nagano Prefectures. On the basis of statistical information relative to the Christian churches and to these areas of population mobility, an analysis was made of their interrelationship (Morioka and Kumagai 1966). The conclusion was reached that, while there are variations from area to area in the spatial distribution of church members and in the characteristics of the population (viewed in terms of social strata, age ranking, etc.), on the whole, there is a close relationship between population movement in a particular area and the growth or loss of church members in that area. Population influx into an area generally brings about an increase in church membership, and the greater the influx, the greater will be the tendency for church statistics to reflect this state of affairs. This is not true of Shinto shrines, however.

Until the end of World War II, whatever population increase occurred in a given area was absorbed into the community or village councils (*chōnai-kai, buraku-kai*), and, since such councils were integrated into the Shinto shrine organization, notable population influx was generally attended by rising prosperity of the shrines. But since November 16, 1946, when the GHQ's instruction entitled *Chōnai-kai, tonari-gumi tō ni yoru Shintō no kōen oyobi shiji no kinshi* (Prohibition of Shinto backing or support by community councils, neighborhood associations, and the like) was issued, all legal organizational structures that would make incoming people part of the existing shrine organization have vanished. Moreover, the character of the local councils has changed. Now that they have

---

[1] The first to undertake research of this kind was Genchō Fukui, who reported on his investigation of 107 temples in and around the city of Tsuruga in 1941 (Fukui 1942).

become optional associations, the proportion of non-participants among the incoming population has gradually increased. Thus, the greater the increase in incoming people who do not participate in the local councils or who, even if they participate, have no interest in the local shrines, the more the fortunes of the shrines tend to decline while the ties between the shrines and their parishes become increasingly tenuous. The influence of population influx on the shrines therefore involves, at the present juncture, a problem of quite a different kind from that which the Christian churches confront.

In the agricultural society of an earlier day, Shinto shrines enjoyed a position of security and stability, and they exercised a unique social function. But in today's urban society the stability of the shrines has been undermined, and the uniqueness of their role is no longer certain. The present inquiry is concerned with a Tokyo suburb in which the rate of population increase is now extremely high; it attempts to analyze the situation of one local shrine[2] in a suburban area that is presently reeling under the impact of population influx.

The suburb selected for study is named Nozaki, a part of the city of Mitaka, which is located immediately to the west of Tokyo proper. The local shrine of Nozaki is known as Hachiman Shrine. I chose Nozaki because I had already completed a similar study in 1962 in the same locality on the effects on the shrine of changes in the social structure due to suburbanization (Morioka 1964), and I anticipated that interesting results might be obtained by carrying forward the 1962 study and by comparing the two situations.

Sample

A sample was chosen by taking the residents of the area as the universe and using a random selection method. However, inasmuch as the three categories worked out in the former study of

[2] By "local shrine" (*shūraku jinja*) is meant a shrine that has its roots in a particular settlement as a community shrine. In most cases the shrines called "people's shrines" (*minsha*), including the former prefectural shrines (*fukensha*) and shrines of lesser status, correspond to what are here referred to as local shrines.

Nozaki are again represented here, it should be anticipated that the selection rate for certain strata of the population may turn out to be somewhat higher due to an additional sampling, which will shortly be explained. The three categories and their explanations, as presented in the previous study, can be summarized as follows:

1. The core group of worshipers and parishioners. There are somewhat less than 140 households in this category. As may be inferred from the fact that they annually receive an amulet from Ise Grand Shrine, this group constitutes the stable stratum of shrine supporters. In addition this group also constitutes, for the most part, the backbone of the community council (*chōkai*). Comprised of the oldest households (*jimoto setai*) and next-oldest households (*jun-jimoto setai*), new households are almost entirely excluded from this category.

2. Other worshipers and parishioners. About 150 households. Households of newly arrived residents are in the majority, but this category also includes households newly constituted from among the local people. They have no particular interest in receiving an Ise Grand Shrine amulet, but, because they pay the monthly community council fee, an amulet of the local shrine is distributed to them. Passive as regards religious observances at the shrine and in their support for it, they doubtless include some who, though they pay the monthly community council fee, do not regard themselves either as worshipers or even as parishioners.

3. Non-participants in the community council. Approximately 240 households. Though more growth takes place in category 2 than in category 1, the growth in category 3 is by far the most remarkable, newly arrived households being absorbed for the most part into this group. As may perhaps be anticipated, households that have recently moved into the area preponderate. The majority of them look on Nozaki as merely a temporary place of residence, and their mobility rate is high. Since they do not participate in the community council, they do not have even an indirect relationship with Hachiman Shrine. They may participate in the council someday, but are likely to remain in the position of outsiders as far as religious observances at Hachiman Shrine are concerned (Morioka 1964: 90–91).

Of the total of 1,339 resident households registered in Nozaki as of July 1967, 603 one-person households and 101 deficient households (lacking either husband or wife) were excluded, the remaining 635 households being taken as the universe. On the basis of a regular-interval selection method, one out of seven households was chosen by random sampling procedure, yielding a sample of 91 households. One-person households and deficient households were eliminated from the outset for two reasons: first, because it was assumed, given the investigation of religious behavior with which we were concerned, that there would probably be a different outlook in such households in contrast with complete households; and, second, because we suspected that, in comparison with the latter, such households would involve us in much greater difficulty when it came to carrying out interviews. However, when the 91 households thus obtained were divided into groups according to the time they moved to Nozaki, the oldest households and what should perhaps be called the next-oldest households (i.e., households that had moved to Nozaki no later than the end of 1945) totaled 20. In view of the ratio of oldest and next-oldest households to the universe, this figure is about what we should expect. But for the purpose of analyzing the previously mentioned category of "the core group of worshipers and parishioners," this number was too small. Accordingly, from the oldest and next-oldest households not included in the original sample of 91 households, an additional 40 households were selected by random sampling. Thus, a total of 131 households was obtained, and it was to these households that the interviewers were sent.

The survey itself was carried out intensively in November 1968.[3] A 77-item questionnaire was prepared for the survey, and, taking into consideration the convenience of conducting the interviews during the daytime, it was decided to concentrate entirely on housewives. In the case of households containing more than one couple (elderly parents and married son or daughter),

[3] To the 22 students of International Christian University who cooperated in carrying out this survey, to the 119 Nozaki households that participated in the interviews, and to the members of the Civic Affairs Department of the Mitaka City Hall who made possible the sampling, the author wishes to express his sincere gratitude.

it was decided to take the wife from the younger generation because of our desire to deal with the most recent trends. As it turned
out, five households had moved, nobody was at home at five more
despite repeated visits, and two were revealed to be deficient upon
inspection. Eliminating these twelve, a survey of 119 households
was completed. When the 119 households are classified in accordance with the time they moved to Nozaki, a distribution like that
indicated in Table 4 results.

Table 4
Interviewed Households Distributed According to
Period of Arrival in Nozaki

Classification	Number	(%)
I. Oldest households	27	(22.7)
II. Next-oldest households	27	(22.7)
III. 1946–1955	7	(5.9)
IV. 1956–1960	10	(8.4)
V. 1961–1965	23	(19.3)
VI. 1966 and after	25	(21.0)
Total	119	(100.0)

It may be useful to explain at this point the main ideas underlying the distinction between oldest and next-oldest households.
"Oldest households" were defined as households that have existed
in Nozaki since the beginning of the Meiji period, this information
being accessible in the Nozaki Family Register of 1872, or as
branch households thereof. In the case of branch households,
however, only those in which the first generation had already died
were to be counted. "Next-oldest households" were defined as
households that had moved to Nozaki after the end of the Meiji
period (1912) and before the end of World War II (1945). Branch
houses of oldest households in which the first generation was still
alive (at least one partner of the founding couple) were included
among the next-oldest households. Because of the subsequent addition of an extra sample to supplement the oldest and next-oldest
households, these two groups constitute approximately 4/7 of the
total number of such households. The other four groups comprise
about 1/7 of the remaining households. From the distribution
pattern of the total number of households that were surveyed,

it may be inferred that the real suburbanization of Nozaki belongs to the period beginning about 1961. Since the two groups immediately prior to 1961 are few in number, they will be combined in the analysis that follows.

Sense of Parish Membership
and Religious Behavior of Parish Households

As a starting point, let us begin by examining differences in the sense of parish membership according to period of arrival. By "sense of parish membership" (*ujiko ishiki*) is meant that one regards the deity enshrined in the local shrine as one's patron deity (*ujigami*) and oneself as a parishioner of that deity (*ujiko*). The term may equally well be taken to mean a sense of belonging to the local shrine. But how can such a sense of parish membership be detected? Our method was to collate the responses to three questionnaire items.

Question 53. Where is your household's patron deity (or birthplace tutelary deity) (*ubusunagami*) located? Respondents who gave the Nozaki Hachiman Shrine as the location were designated by a plus sign, others by a minus.

Question 55. Where do you feel your household's patron deity is enshrined, at the shrine in the area where your husband was born or the shrine in Nozaki? Respondents who indicated that the deity of the Nozaki shrine was their patron deity, or that the Nozaki shrine was their birthplace shrine, or that both deities were their patron deities, were identified by a plus sign, while respondents who said that their patron deity was located at their birthplace shrine, or that they regarded neither as their patron deity, were given a minus.

Question 56. Does your family belong to the Nozaki shrine? Those who answered that they were members were designated by a plus sign, while those who said that they were not, or did not know, were designated by a minus.

After assigning pluses and minuses to all responding households in this way, we classified those respondents who gave positive answers to all three questions as A, "well-defined sense of parish membership." Respondents who gave negative answers to all three were classified as C, "no sense of parish membership," whereas those with a mixture of pluses and minuses were classified as B, "ambiguous sense of parish membership." The distribution of A's, B's, and C's by period of arrival in Nozaki is indicated in Table 5.

Table 5
Sense of Parish Membership Correlated with Period of Arrival

	I	II	III–IV	V	VI	Totals
A. Well-defined	27 (100.0)	24 (88.9)	5 (29.4)	4 (17.4)	1 (4.0)	61 (51.3)
B. Ambiguous		3 (11.1)	6 (35.3)	6 (26.1)	6 (24.0)	21 (17.6)
C. None			6 (35.3)	13 (56.5)	18 (72.0)	37 (31.1)
Total	27 (100.0)	27 (100.0)	17 (100.0)	23 (100.0)	25 (100.0)	119 (100.0)

As may be seen from Table 5, the earlier the arrival, the greater the number of respondents with a well-defined sense of parish membership, whereas the later the arrival, the greater the number of respondents with no sense of parish membership. Of group I 100% have a clear sense of parish membership, of group II 89%, group III-IV drops suddenly to 29%, group V to 17%, and group VI to 4%. Diminution occurs with each successive period. By the same token, while the "no sense of parish membership" classification is not represented at all in groups I and II, there is a sudden increase after group III-IV, so that group VI goes as high as 72%. It must be concluded, therefore, that the sense of parish membership gives evidence of a systematic development that accords with time of arrival.

Yoneo Okada once divided parishioners into "real parishioners" (*jisshitsu ujiko*), "festival parishioners" (*sairei ujiko*), and "spectator parishioners" (*bōkan ujiko*), going on to characterize them as follows:

1. Real parishioners—people who, by force of long-established custom, regularly pay the parishioners' fee in full. Generally this classification refers to people who have lived in the area since before the end of World War II.

2. Festival parishioners—people who pay only the festival

fee at festival times for the sake of good relations in the community. This classification involves people who have moved into the area after the Second World War and have lived there about ten years.

3. Spectator parishioners—recent arrivals in the area, almost entirely lacking any sense of community attachment (Okada 1964:10–20).

Assuming that among these three types there would be a correlation between the number of residents who paid the shrine fee and time of arrival in the community, he conjoined these two factors and carried out his inquiry accordingly.

In my research I also asked respondents whether they made a contribution to the shrine on the occasion of a festival; for the purpose of defining a sense of parish membership, however, this item proved to entail so many defects that I was finally forced to abandon it. If, in place of the shrine fee payment, we can classify parishioners on the basis of their sense of parish membership as defined above, even though this is not directly connected with shrine fee payments, then the previously mentioned classification A can be taken as a parallel to real parishioners, B to festival parishioners, and C to spectator parishioners. Setting aside the matter of money paid to the shrine, Okada's characterization of parishioners by time of arrival corresponds remarkably well to our ABC classifications and their distribution by period of arrival. Families resident in Nozaki from before the end of World War II are all or nearly all A and may appropriately be called "real parishioners"; families that moved to Nozaki after the war are a composite of A, B, and C, but, if they are thought of as represented generally by B, the term "festival parishioners" will apply to them; while among those who have moved to Nozaki since 1961, C respondents are by far the most numerous and may be spoken of as "spectator parishioners."

Besides the sense of parish membership, the religious behavior of parish households was considered. The term "religious behavior of parish households" (*ujiko kōdō*) as here employed embraces not such unusual behavior as might be typified by membership on the board of parish representatives (*ujiko sōdai*), especially devout households, or people with a special dedication to the shrine, but rather what ordinary parish households customarily do that links them with the shrine. The items in the questionnaire relative to the religious behavior of parish households are the following:

Question 57. When the Nozaki shrine has a festival, does your household make a contribution? The three kinds of answers were: (1) Yes, (2) No, and (3) Sometimes.

Question 58. On a festival day at the shrine does your family have a meal somewhat out of the ordinary (dishes that are, or once were, sacred foods)? Answers: (1) Yes, (2) No.

Question 59. Does your household keep a Nozaki shrine talisman? Answers: (1) Yes, (2) No.

Question 63. When the Nozaki shrine has a festival, do you or does somebody from the house go there to worship? Answers: (1) Yes, (2) We go not to worship but as spectators, (3) We neither go to worship nor as spectators.

Question 64. Do you or does somebody from the family go to worship at the Nozaki shrine at the beginning of a new year? Answers: (1) Yes, (2) No.

The question asking about contributions proved to be defective not only for inquiring about a sense of parish membership but also for examining religious behavior, so our attention will be directed to the remaining four.

Taking these four items together, I assigned an α meaning "complete religious behavior" to households that gave affirmative answers to all four, a γ meaning "no religious behavior" to those that responded negatively to all four, and a β meaning "incomplete religious behavior" to those that gave partly affirmative and partly negative answers. When correlated with periods of arrival,

Table 6
Household Religious Behavior Correlated with Period of Arrival

	I	II	III–IV	V	VI	Totals
α, Complete	16 (59.3)	14 (51.9)				30 (25.2)
β, Incomplete	11 (40.7)	12 (44.4)	14 (82.4)	17 (73.9)	5 (20.0)	59 (49.6)
γ, None		1 (3.7)	3 (17.6)	6 (26.1)	20 (80.0)	30 (25.2)
Total	27 (100.0)	27 (100.0)	17 (100.0)	23 (100.0)	25 (100.0)	119 (100.0)

these three types fall into the distribution pattern found in Table 6.

Type α is concentrated entirely in groups I and II. Type β is found in all groups but most frequently in groups III-IV and V. Type γ is missing entirely in group I, makes a hesitant appearance in group II, and continues to rise until in group VI it goes as high as 80%. It may be clearly perceived, therefore, that α characterizes groups I and II, β groups III-IV and V, and γ group VI.

Earlier it was pointed out that, depending on the period of arrival, a definite pattern could be observed in the degree of distinctness with which the sense of parish membership was expressed. In the same way it has now become clear that a noticeable pattern exists, relative to period of arrival, in the degree of completeness of religious behavior. This being the case, it becomes possible to think that there may be a parallel relationship between the degree of clarity in the sense of parish membership and the degree of completeness in religious behavior. In addition, from the angle of theory it is to be expected that the clearer the sense of parish membership, the more complete the religious behavior will be, and vice versa. However, as was mentioned above, while the sense of parish membership has reference to the interviewee or wife, religious behavior refers to the household, and it is understandable that there may well be a gap between the two. My next task, therefore, will be to examine the relationship between them.

Let us consider the relationship between the degrees of clarity in the sense of parish membership and the degrees of completeness

Table 7
Religious Behavior of Parish Households and Sense
of Parish Membership*

	A	B	C	Totals
α	100.0 (49.2)			100.0 (25.2)
β	50.9 (49.2)	23.7 (66.7)	25.4 (40.5)	100.0 (49.6)
γ	3.3 (1.6)	23.3 (33.3)	73.4 (59.5)	100.0 (25.2)
Total	51.3 (100.0)	17.6 (100.0)	31.1 (100.0)	100.0 (100.0)

* In this table all numbers are percentages, representing the result of taking a sense of parish membership on the one hand, and the religious behavior of parish households on the other, as independent variables.

in household religious behavior as derived from collating the answers to the four questionnaire items cited above. As may be seen from Table 7, the more well-defined the sense of parish membership, the more complete the religious behavior, and, conversely, the more complete the religious behavior, the more distinct is the sense of parish membership. On the other hand, because respondents identified as possessing a strong sense of parish membership and parish households identified as giving evidence of incomplete religious behavior comprise nearly one-half of the total, the inference is plain that just as a clear sense of parish membership does not necessarily imply complete religious behavior, so, too, incomplete religious behavior does not necessarily imply an ambiguous sense of parish membership. The connection between these two includes both correlative and discontinuous aspects. ($R = +0.682$, if we give A and α a score of $+1$, B and β 0, and C and γ -1.)

If, in the light of this binary character of correlation and discontinuity, the sense of parish membership and the religious behavior of parish households are conjoined, it should be possible to distinguish between different types of parishioners and/or parish households. They have been brought together as follows:

Sense of parish membership	A	A B	$\frac{A}{B}$ C	C
Religious behavior of parish households	α	α β β	α γ β	γ
Numbers	30	44	23	22
Types of parishioners and/or parish households	Nuclear (combination of A and α)	Modal (does not combine A with α, and also excludes both C and γ)	Marginal (including either C or γ)	Dormant (a combination of C and γ)

The names given to these types of parish members and/or parish households, namely, nuclear, modal, marginal, and dormant, have been borrowed from Fichter (1954: Chap. 2). The average or modal parishioners constitute, as it turns out, the largest group.

If applied to Okada's threefold classification, the nuclear and modal types would correspond to the "real parishioners," the marginal type to the "festival parishioners," and the dormant type to the "spectator parishioners."

Table 8
Types of Parishioners and/or Parish Households
Correlated with Period of Arrival

	I		II		III–IV		V		VI		Totals	
Nuclear	16	(59.3)	14	(51.9)							30	(25.2)
Modal	11	(40.7)	12	(44.4)	10	(58.8)	8	(34.8)	3	(12.0)	44	(37.0)
Marginal			1	(3.7)	5	(29.4)	11	(47.8)	6	(24.0)	23	(19.3)
Dormant					2	(11.8)	4	(17.4)	16	(64.0)	22	(18.5)
Total	27	(100.0)	27	(100.0)	17	(100.0)	23	(100.0)	25	(100.0)	119	(100.0)

When period of arrival is correlated with this classification of parishioners and/or parish households (Table 8), the distribution which results shows that groups I and II fall into the nuclear or modal types of parishioners (group I tending more toward the nuclear), while groups III-IV through VI span the modal, marginal, and dormant types. However, most respondents in group III-IV are of the modal type, most in group V are of the marginal type, and most in group VI belong to the dormant type. Thus, the relationship of Nozaki residents to the shrine is expressed in a form, relative to periods of arrival, more comprehensive than anything we have had hitherto.

Ideas and Behavior Relative to Shrine Shinto

The subject of ideas and behavior having to do with the local shrine in the area under investigation was taken up in the preceding section. Here attention will be directed toward a wider range of ideas and behavior relative to Shrine Shinto generally, analysis proceeding as before by reference to periods of arrival. The questionnaire items dealing with this matter were five in number: (1) Shinto facilities, both inside and outside the house, such as the Shinto altar (*kamidana*) and a small shrine for house-site deities (*yashikigami*), (2) Shinto symbols, such as a talisman from the Ise Grand Shrine or other amulets, (3) worship at a shrine outside the community at the beginning of a new year, or at festival times, or, again, worship at any shrine after the birth of a child, (4) putting up the traditional pine-branch decorations for the New Year season, and (5) ideas as to the importance of having shrines and festivals.

The first two items will be taken as a starting point. As an overall tendency, it was found that the more recent the period of arrival, the less frequent are family altars and household god shrines present. Within the framework of this general tendency (Table 9), the Shinto altar is maintained by 96% of the households in group I and by 85% of those in group II, a noticeably high proportion in both cases. In the III-IV group it drops suddenly to 29%. With regard to families maintaining shrines for house-site gods, there is already a sharp difference between the 59% of group I and the 7% of group II, while from groups III-IV on, the fact that no households whatever maintain such shrines is worth noting. As for keeping a talisman from the Ise Grand Shrine or other Shinto amulets, apart from group V, which seems slightly out of line, it turns out that, the more recent the period of arrival, the less numerous the households that keep these symbols. Just as in the case of the percentage of households that maintained family altars, so in the case of households that keep an Ise Grand Shrine talisman there is a sudden drop from group II with its 59% to group III-IV with its 24%. It may be that if there is no Shinto altar in the house, it is difficult to find an appropriate

Table 9
Distribution of Shrine Shinto Facilities and Symbols

	I	I	III-IV	V	VI	Total
1. Have a Shinto altar	26 (96.3)	23 (85.2)	5 (29.4)	5 (21.7)	3 (12.0)	62 (52.1)
2. Have a house-site god shrine	16 (59.3)	2 (7.4)				18 (15.1)
3. Keep an Ise Grand Shrine talisman	18 (66.7)	16 (59.3)	4 (23.5)		2 (8.0)	40 (33.6)
4. Keep other amulets	23 (85.2)	13 (48.1)	3 (17.6)	6 (26.1)	3 (12.0)	48 (49.6)

place to keep a shrine talisman. It is not surprising to find exactly the same kind of sudden drop in the case of the Hachiman Shrine talisman.

The third item deals with shrine visits, and we will start with visits at the beginning of a new year and at festival times (Table 10). Omitting from consideration the rather high percentage of both kinds of visits among the households of group I, we find that analysis in terms of periods of arrival leads to no clear gradient pattern. Of ten households, one or two out of every group take these opportunities to visit a shrine. Though one should probably not go so far as to speak of the practice of paying a visit to a shrine at New Year's or at festival time as "popular," it does occur, not exclusively in particular groups but in a diffuse way, in every group from II on. Among shrines chosen for the first visit of the new year (*hatsumōde*), Meiji Shrine was selected by an overwhelming majority, 27 cases (82%) out of 33. Thus the diffuseness seen in the pattern of visiting a shrine outside the community for the first shrine visit of the new year correlates with the fact that a predominant majority of households pay this first visit to Meiji Shrine, the two being opposing sides of the same coin.

Table 10
Shrine Shinto Behavior Correlated with Period of Arrival*

	I	II	III-IV	V	VI	Total
1. Shrine visit at New Year's	12 (44.4)	6 (22.2)	4 (23.5)	6 (26.1)	5 (20.0)	33 (27.7)
2. Shrine visit at festival times	7 (25.9)	3 (11.1)	2 (11.8)	5 (21.7)	3 (12.0)	20 (16.8)
3. Shrine visit with newborn child	26 (100.0)	23 (92.0)	9 (52.9)	12 (63.2)	10 (66.6)	80 (78.4)
4. Pine-branch decorations	18 (66.7)	20 (74.1)	6 (35.3)	18 (78.3)	11 (44.0)	73 (61.3)

* In calculating percentages for item 3, only households with children were included.

As for shrines visited at festival times, in 12 (60%) of the cases the shrines visited were those of adjoining communities, showing that people do not usually go very far away. Only 20% (4 cases) went to Meiji Shrine. The pattern of shrine visitation that one sees here is not of concentration on the big-name shrines but, with a diffuseness that covers all periods of arrival, a pattern of limitation to shrines in the immediately surrounding area. Such shrine visits should probably be characterized not so much as religious acts but more as social and recreational acts in which the children are taken along for the purpose of festival sightseeing.

Turning to the matter of shrine visitation with a newly born child (Table 10), we find a remarkably high rate of observance, amounting to 100% and 92% respectively, in groups I and II, probably because families in these categories live near Hachiman Shrine and thus can easily visit the place where the tutelary deity of their birthplace dwells. However, even from groups III-IV on, there is evidence of an observance rate of approximately 60%, which means that no gradient pattern relative to periods of arrival is to be found. In brief, the pattern of shrine visitation is a diffuse one. Hachiman Shrine is most frequently cited as the place chosen for shrine visits of this kind, but in the case of people who have moved in from outside, it should also be understood that this observance may involve taking the child to the shrine of the area where the parents were living at the time the child was born.

Item 4, concerning pine-branch decorations for the New Year's season, might be expected to be similar in character to items 1 and 2 in Table 9, inasmuch as all concern Shinto components relative to the house, but it is handled separately here because of a remarkable diffuseness in the responses (Table 10). The rate of observance is high enough to be compared to that of shrine visitation with a newly born child, and in the same way no pattern of decreasing observance rate corresponding to periods of arrival can be discovered. It appears, therefore, that the practice of putting up pine-branch decorations at New Year's time is a diffuse one that has no relation to period of arrival.

The final item—concerning ideas as to the importance of having Shinto festivals and, more basically, ideas as to the importance of having Shinto shrines at all—is likewise to be viewed in relation to periods of arrival. The distribution of opinions prior to correlation with period of arrival shows (Table 11) that 56% thought it better to have the festivals than not to have them and 60% thought it better to have than not to have the shrines. The

Table 11
Importance of Festivals and Shrines

	Festivals		Shrines	
1. Absolutely essential	10	(8.4)	11	(9.3)
2. Better to have them	66	(55.5)	71	(59.7)
3. Makes no difference	34	(28.6)	28	(23.5)
4. Better not to have them	8	(6.7)	6	(5.0)
5. Don't know	1	(0.8)	3	(2.5)
Total	119	(100.0)	119	(100.0)

opinion next in order of support was the passive opinion, "whether we have them or not doesn't matter," about 25% of the respondents expressing this view. Those who held that both festivals and shrines were absolutely essential came to somewhat less than 10%, while the negative opinion that it would be better not to have either elicited even less support. The most generally found opinion, therefore, is the quite positive one that it is better to have both. If opinions as to the importance of festivals and shrines are distinguished and compared, the percentage of those affirming the importance of the shrines is somewhat higher. Festivals constitute the core of shrine activity, but, needless to say, shrine functions are not exhausted thereby.

Let us see now what kind of distribution pattern results when the number of respondents affirming the two opinions "absolutely essential" and "better to have them" are added together and viewed in relation to periods of arrival (Table 12). Apart from the fact that there is one order-reversal, group II being higher than group I in responses to the first and the third items, it turns out that, the older the group, the higher the percentage of respondents who think of festivals and shrines as important. The difference, however, between the older and more recent groups is not great. In effect, opinions affirming the importance of shrines and festivals come to expression here in the form of a rather mild degree of diffusion.

The question arises, therefore, as to why the distribution pattern found in the case of respondents who hold a positive view of the importance of shrines and festivals is a more or less diffuse one. In order to explain this point it will be useful to present the results of an analysis of reasons advanced for affirming this importance.

Table 12

Opinions Affirming Importance of Festivals and Shrines

	I	II	III–IV	V	VI	Total
1. Festivals are important	20 (74.1)	22 (81.5)	12 (70.6)	12 (52.2)	10 (40.0)	76 (63.9)
2. Shrines are important	25 (92.6)	22 (81.5)	10 (58.8)	16 (69.6)	9 (36.0)	82 (68.9)
3. Both are important	18 (66.7)	21 (77.8)	9 (52.9)	11 (47.8)	8 (32.0)	67 (56.3)

We may begin by looking at the four reasons suggested by respondents for the importance of Shinto shrines, grouping those
who proposed them according to their periods of arrival (Table
13). Even though "for community solidarity" is given least frequently, occurring in only about 13% of the cases in groups I
and II and not at all among more recent arrivals, as a tendency it
involves something worth noticing. This is the phenomenon of
what should perhaps be spoken of as a weakness of community
attachment evidenced in the reasons for shrine importance. An
attempt to account for this phenomenon will be made in a subsequent section. The reason next in line, "for religious rites and
worship," also shows a tendency to occur with decreasing frequency in proportion to recentness of arrival. Even if visits to the
Nozaki Hachiman Shrine and visits to other shrines are considered
together, the diminishing number of respondents who advanced
this reason corresponds to the finding that, the more recent the
arrival, the lower the rate of shrine visits.

In contrast to the foregoing two reasons with their declining
rates of frequency, the other two reasons occur at a rather consistent rate. That is to say, the percentages of respondents who
merely referred to "custom" in affirming the importance of shrines
display no particular increase or decrease. Accordingly, it seems
appropriate to speak of these percentages as consistent. The con-
sistency of the percentages of respondents who gave as their reason
"something to rely on" is even clearer. But one caution that needs
to be borne in mind is that among the newcomers there are some
whose way of putting this reason was somewhat detached and
meant not that they included themselves among those who rely

Table 13

Reasons for Importance of Shinto Shrines*

	I	II	III–IV	V	VI	Total
1. For religious rites and worship	5	8	3	3	1	20
2. Because of custom	12	4	1	6	3	26
3. For community solidarity	3	3	1			7
4. As something to rely on	5	7	5	7	5	29
Totals	25	22	10	16	9	82
1. For religious rites and worship	18.5 (20.0)	29.6 (36.4)	17.6 (30.0)	13.0 (18.8)	4.0 (11.1)	16.8 (24.4)
2. Because of custom	44.4 (48.0)	14.8 (18.2)	5.9 (10.0)	26.1 (37.5)	12.0 (33.3)	21.8 (31.7)
3. For community solidarity	11.1 (12.0)	11.1 (13.6)	5.9 (10.0)			5.9 (8.5)
4. As something to rely on	18.5 (20.0)	25.9 (31.8)	29.4 (50.0)	30.4 (43.7)	20.0 (55.6)	24.4 (35.4)
Totals	92.6 (100.0)	81.5 (100.0)	58.8 (100.0)	69.6 (100.0)	36.0 (100.0)	68.9 (100.0)

* The upper half of Table 13 gives the distribution in numbers, the lower half in percentages. In the lower half, numbers outside parentheses represent percentages in relation to the total number of respondents in any given group (see Table 4); the numbers within parentheses represent the percentages that result when the totals in the upper half of Table 13 are assigned a value of 100.0.

on the shrines, but rather that, while they do not, some people do, so for them the shrines are important. Be that as it may, the mild degree of diffusion indicated above in opinions as to the importance of shrines in general is doubtless a reflection of the diffuseness of affirmations of the two opinions that shrines are necessary "as something to rely on" or "because of custom"—these two together accounting for 67% of the responses under the heading of reasons for shrine importance. Again, the decrease in the percentage of opinions that affirmed shrine importance by reason of "community solidarity" or "religious rites and worship" is a commentary on the weakness of community attachment to Shinto shrines, or, more generally, on the decline of the shrine in its role as a point of unification for community life. The shrines are losing touch with their communities, and shrine importance is affirmed, in a pattern diffused among all Nozaki residents, either by reference to time-honored custom or by reference to religous tradition.

In the ideas as to the importance of shrines and festivals there is no clear-cut gradient pattern that correlates with periods of arrival. Detailed examination has shown quite clearly that, while one part of the data can appropriately be represented by the gradient pattern, there is another side that coexists with the first and that has to be regarded as more diffuse in character. Again, though a definite gradient pattern was discovered in the percentages of respondents who maintained a Shinto altar, a household god shrine, and shrine talismans, when it came to items that concerned traditional customs in which local feeling was minimal, such as putting up pine-branch decorations at New Year's, visiting a shrine with a newly born child, or visits to shrines other than the local shrine, it was noted that the responses tended to be diffuse. In brief, it may be said, therefore, that it is the coexistence of the gradient pattern and of the state of diffuseness which, when contrasted with the clear-cut gradient patterns found in the sense of parish membership and in the religious behavior of parish households, constitutes the distinctive feature of ideas and behavior relative to Shrine Shinto in general.

If only the gradient pattern were taken into account, it might be possible to throw some light on the indifference of recent arrivals toward the local shrine, but to explain why such a large number of people make their first shrine visit of the new year to Meiji Shrine or other big-name shrines would be impossible. In addition to the gradient pattern, however, we have found that another principle—diffusion—is also at work. Because of the diffusion of Shinto customs in Japanese life, despite the weakness of community attachment, or, rather, in direct proportion to the weakness of local attachment, there arises the phenomenon of great throngs of people descending on the big-name shrines.

Ideas and Behavior Relative to Other Religions

In relation to the local shrine and in correlation with periods of arrival, a definite gradient pattern was observed, while in relation to Shrine Shinto in general, as distinct from the local shrine, the coexistence of a gradient pattern and of a state of diffuseness was indicated. Our next task will be to consider the main items concerned with non-Shinto religious behavior. Grouping responses by period of arrival, we shall try to see what kinds of tendencies can be discerned and to determine their similarities to and contrasts with the tendencies previously identified.

All kinds of questionnaire items could have been thought up in connection with non-Shinto religious behavior, but since it is reasonable to suppose that the most fundamental questions are likely to be those associated with funeral rites, items were prepared relative to: (1) possession of Buddhist altars, (2) ownership of a cemetery plot, (3) funeral experience (whether there has ever been a funeral in the household), and (4) observances on Buddhist All Souls' Day (*Bon*), such as preparing a *Bon dana*[4] or lighting a *mukae-bi*.[5]

In the responses to these four items, a clear gradient pattern emerged, such that the earlier the period of arrival, the higher the rates of Buddhist altar possession, cemetery plot ownership,

[4] *Bon dana* is a term used to refer to a special stand erected for Buddhist All Souls' Day on which the ancestral mortuary tablets are placed and offerings made. The stand may be simple or elaborate, inside the house or out. In some areas instead of building a special stand, people use the Buddhist altar. (Translator.)

[5] A *mukae-bi* is a fire lit to welcome the ancestral spirits on All Souls' Day. It is ordinarily lit either at the home or at the family grave. Its counterpart is the *okuri-bi*, the fire lit to see the ancestral spirits off at the close of this special period. (Translator.)

funeral experience, and All Souls' Day observances. Particularly striking is the fact that precisely the same tendency observed in parish-oriented ideas and behavior and in religious behavior relative to Shinto facilities and symbols also comes to expression here. That is to say, if arrival in the community is recent, not only is there a tendency for a household to have an ambiguous sense of parish membership, to register an incomplete in its intraparish religious behavior, and to be inactive with reference to Shrine Shinto religious behavior (much of which normally takes place within one's community), but it also becomes evident that such households tend to neglect the religious practices relative to funeral rites, which ordinarily involve numerous ties with a Buddhist temple.

Among these four questionnaire items, the most basic is probably the one concerning the percentage of households that have had funeral experience, because only through such an experience is a household likely to find it necessary to have a cemetery plot, obtain a Buddhist altar, and carry out All Souls' Day observances. In addition, the strength or weakness of neighborhood and household customs relating to possession of a Buddhist altar and to All Souls' Day observances, the presence or absence of elderly parents in the home, opportunity for obtaining a cemetery plot—these and other factors all have their effect, and, as a result, it is likely that items relative to Buddhist altars, cemetery plots, and All Souls' Day observances will each have their own distinctive gradient patterns.

The gist of my findings in this area may be reiterated as follows. More recent arrivals not only display a tendency to turn away from the local shrine and its rituals, as was seen in relation to the sense of parish membership and in relation to the religious behavior of parish households, but they also turn away from the Buddhist post-funeral rites.[6] It is in this connection that conspicuousness

---

[6] The term "funeral rites" as used in Japan involves not only the funeral itself but also the whole series of subsequent rites theoretically held on the forty-ninth day after death and on the first, third, seventh, thirteenth, seventeenth, twenty-third, twenty-seventh, thirty-third, and fiftieth annual anniversaries. The "neglect of funeral rites" that the author discovered refers, I believe, to these subsequent rites. Accordingly, the Japanese term *sōsō girei*, which would normally be translated "funeral rites," has here been expressed as "post-funeral rites." (Translator.)

attaches to the practice of paying one's first shrine visit of the new year to Meiji Shrine or one of the big-name shrines—and to do so with a partly recreational intent. It is also in this connection that members of households that have recently moved into the area are, as it appears, being drawn into Buddhist-oriented "new religions." If this were not the case, they would form a stratum in society that would be utterly indifferent to religion and religious observances.

The oldest and next-oldest households, however, are withdrawing neither from the shrine services nor from the Buddhist rites. The reason they are not breaking away from the existing religions is not so much that they are fervently committed to religion as that they are deeply involved in the social life of the community. Conversely, the reason that more recent arrivals are turning away is, it would seem, that they are not putting roots down into community life. The rites and festivals of a community shrine like the Hachiman Shrine of Nozaki are very closely connected with the cooperative patterns of existence in the locality, the Buddhist funerary rituals likewise being deeply rooted in the cooperative life of the community by means of the gravediggers' circles and by visits and condolence gifts. In the next section it will be my task, therefore, to examine from various angles the respondents' degree of participation in the cooperative structures of the community.

Involvement in the Cooperative Life of the Community

My examination of involvement in the cooperative life of the community will proceed by dividing such involvement into two kinds: participation in formal organizations and participation in informal relationships.

Beginning with participation in formal organizations (Table 14), let us take up first the matter of joining the community council (chōkai). The Nozaki community council is an organization of residents whose main functions are to distribute disinfectant for mosquito control in the summertime, to keep street lights in operating condition, to collect contributions for the community

Table 14
Participation in Formal Organizations

	I	II	III–IV	V	VI	Total
1. Council participation	27 (100.0)	27 (100.0)	15 (88.2)	18 (78.3)	9 (36.0)	96 (80.7)
2. Kō participation	21 (77.8)	11 (40.7)				32 (26.9)
3. Union participation	25 (92.6)	18 (66.7)	4 (23.5)		1 (4.0)	48 (40.3)
4. Participate in all three	21 (77.8)	11 (40.7)				32 (26.9)
5. Participate in none			2 (11.8)	5 (21.7)	16 (64.0)	23 (19.3)

chest, to keep up the shrine, and to carry out the festivals. It hardly need be mentioned that there is, of course, nothing compulsory about participation.

In contrast to the households in groups I and II, which without exception participate in the council, the participation rate declines in groups III-IV and V, until in group VI only one-third of the households is represented. Approximately half the families in group VI live in apartments, this group having a higher proportion of apartment-dwelling households than any other, and the noticeably low participation-rate of families that live in apartments means that the participation-rate of group VI as a whole is also remarkably low. In any event the pattern observed here takes the form of a gently descending gradient.

Next to be considered under the heading of formal organizations are the kō.[7] In Nozaki there exist the *Haruna-kō*, the *Mitake-kō*,

[7] *Kō* are usually referred to in English translations as "voluntary religious associations," but while the English phrase connotes a group of devoted individuals who decide to meet together for religious purposes, the Japanese *kō* is ordinarily neither voluntary nor religious in the same sense. *Kō* membership is usually reckoned not by individuals but by households, and, once a household has joined a *kō*, it is generally expected that some representative from the household will participate in the meetings, which range in frequency from once a month to once a year. Consequently, the actual content of household members' religious beliefs or ideas rarely if ever comes up for discussion. The main sense in which *kō* are religious is that once a year, perhaps, they send a few representatives, with travel funds provided through a levy on each household, to visit a major shrine outside the immediate area, perform an act of worship there on behalf of the entire membership, and bring back some shrine talismans and distribute them to the member households. The above applies, however, only to religious *kō*, or to *kō* in their religious capacity. It does not include, e.g., recreational, tourist, or savings-club *kō*. (Translator.)

the *Kobugahara-kō*, and other *kō* of the type that sends representatives to visit a more or less distant major shrine on behalf of the entire membership (*daisan-kō*). Households that participate in more than one *kō* of this kind are found only in groups I and II, but the sharp difference in the participation rates between these two groups should be noted.

In contrast to these exceedingly traditional religious organizations stand the secular, economically oriented unions (*kumiai*) which have come into existence more recently than the *kō* and of which many kinds are to be found in Nozaki. For example, the Nozaki unions include the Agricultural Cooperative Union, the Agricultural Affairs Union, the Pig Breeders' Union, the Poultry Farmers' Union, the Horticultural Union, the Asparagus Growers' Union, the Tobacco Trade Union, the Fish Merchants' Union, the Bathhouse Keepers' Union, the Real Estate Business Union, the Scaffold Workers' Union, and the Nozaki Storekeepers' Association (the above examples were taken solely from the unions in which households of group I participate). The majority of such unions do not begin and end within the confines of Nozaki, but since they operate in a particular geographic area that includes Nozaki, in a broad sense they clearly provide an opportunity for entering into the cooperative life of the community. The percentage of households that participate in the unions, distributed according to period of arrival, again forms a clear gradient pattern.

In order to examine in more detail the subject of participation in these three kinds of organizations, if the percentage of households that participate in all three is set alongside the percentage of those that participate in none of the three, it turns out that the only groups containing households that participate in all three are groups I and II, group I having 78% and group II 41%—again a significant percentage difference existing between these two. Households that participate in none of the three exist only in groups III-IV and on, the percentage of non-participation showing a gradual increase from the 12% of groups III-IV and the 22% of group V to the 64% of group VI. If pluses were assigned in accordance with the percentage of participating households and minuses in accordance with the percentage of nonparticipating households, a strikingly clear difference, ranging from the +78 of group I to the −64 of group VI, would be perceived between the respondent households when they are grouped by period of arrival.

We turn now to the subject of participation in informal relationships (Table 15). To guide the investigation, the following four criteria were set up: (1) whether a household maintained relationships with more than six households of relatives living in Nozaki; (2) whether a household kept up relationships with more than six households of relatives in the area embraced by Mitaka City excluding Nozaki; (3) whether a household maintained relationships with more than six neighborhood households, relationships of such a kind that the respondent, when calling at one of these households, would go into the garden or house to chat; and (4) whether a household was a main family (*honke*) or branch family (*bunke*) and in one of those capacities maintained relationships with other households. Actually, it is possible for the fourth criterion to elicit responses that will duplicate those in the first, but duplication will not necessarily result.

Table 15
Participation in Informal Relationships

	I	II	III-IV	V	VI	Total
1. With Nozaki relatives	16 (59.3)	13 (48.1)	1 (5.9)			30 (25.2)
2. With Mitaka relatives	12 (44.4)	10 (37.0)	2 (11.8)			24 (20.2)
3. With neighbors	17 (63.0)	14 (51.9)	3 (17.6)	3 (13.0)	2 (8.0)	39 (32.8)
4. As main or branch family	24 (88.9)	19 (70.4)				43 (36.1)

For all four criteria, it was perceived that when responses were tallied in accordance with period of arrival, a definite gradient pattern appeared. Most pronounced was the percentage of households with main or branch family relationships, followed by relationships with relatives in the community, then relationships with relatives in Mitaka excluding Nozaki. The most diffuse form was that which emerged in the responses to the question on relationships with neighbors, but in no case was the regularity of the gradient broken. The oldest households of group I, followed by the next-oldest households of group II, have the highest concentration of relationships with relatives, neighborhood contacts, and main or branch family relationships in the area. Both may be regarded as having a deep involvement in local society. In contrast, the households of groups V and VI, households, that is, which moved to Nozaki after January 1, 1961, when measured against the same criteria, have little opportunity to enter deeply into the community. It can probably be said that this is an indication of their mobile, highly transient character and lack of community attachment.

The result of my observations thus far is, therefore, that both with regard to participation in formal organizations and to maintaining informal relationships with relatives and neighbors, a distinct gradient pattern can be seen in the sample as a whole when households are grouped by period of arrival. It is evident that there are quite definite differences between these groups of households in their involvement in the cooperative life of the community. I now propose to introduce some factors that may be regarded as having given rise to these differences, to see what kind of distribution occurs when these factors are correlated with periods of arrival, and to examine them as conducive to the gradient pattern found in the various degrees of participation in formal organizations and informal relationships with neighbors and relatives.

At one time Nozaki was a purely agricultural community. Its farm households consequently have a long history of cooperative relationships. Admittedly, the many forms of mutual aid that once obtained between farm households have today fallen into disuse, but even now opportunities for mutual aid are provided through the interrelations between people who have developed a particular specialization, such as asparagus-growing or pig-raising. It seems reasonable to suppose, therefore, that, the more a household is involved in agriculture, the easier it is for it to enter into formal organizations and to sustain informal relationships. Today there are many kinds of farming households, particularly among those located in the suburbs, but it was decided that the first factor would be whether the main breadwinner was engaged in agricultural work. However, even if the main breadwinner was not in agricultural work, as long as his main work was some kind of self-employment within the area, such as commerce or construction, he must have a base within the community. By the same token, even though one was not self-employed, if one's place of work was within the locality, one's relationships with the community would probably be quite close. Accordingly, the second factor was to determine whether the main breadwinner was either self-employed or employed within the community. For the third factor, I assumed that if a household had lived for a lengthy period of time in the community, it would be easier for it to join in the organizations and enter into informal relationships. But since no clear trend could appear if the time division were faulty, it was decided to take only the figures on households that were in their second or later generation in Nozaki. Fourth, because households in which either the interviewee (wife) or her husband was born in the community may be regarded as finding it easier than other households in joining organizations and entering into informal relationships, figures on households of this kind were included. Fifth, the fact that the immediate community was given

Table 16

Factors Conducive to Participation in Formal Organizations and Informal Relationships: I

	I	II	III-IV	V	VI	Total
1. Main bread-winner in agri-cultural work	15 (55.6)	6 (22.2)	1 (5.9)			23 (19.3)
2. Self-employed or locally employed	21 (77.8)	15 (55.6)	6 (35.3)	7 (30.4)	6 (24.0)	55 (46.2)
3. In second or later generation in Nozaki	27 (100.0)	8 (29.6)				35 (29.4)
4. Husband or wife born in Nozaki	29 (107.4)	27 (100.0)	2 (11.8)			58 (48.7)
5. Nozaki official permanent dom-icile	27 (100.0)	27 (100.0)	8 (47.1)	2 (8.7)	3 (12.0)	67 (56.3)

as the officially registered place of permanent domicile (*honseki chi*) may also be considered as at least a partial indication of a sense of belonging to the community.

The gradient pattern that results (Table 16) from considering responses in accordance with periods of arrival is most striking in the responses to item (3), the item identifying households that are in their second or later generation in Nozaki. Next comes item (4) on whether husband or wife was born in Nozaki, then item (1) on agricultural work, item (5) on the officially registered place of permanent domicile, and item (2) on self-employment and so on, the last-mentioned showing the most pronounced degree of diffusion. Yet even in item (2) the clear gradient pattern continues unchanged. The fact that the earlier the period of arrival the higher the proportion of households that participates in formal organizations and maintains informal relationships links up, as is perfectly natural, with the observation that the distribution of factors that can be thought of as supporting such participation and such relationships is greater among the older groups.

To carry the inquiry forward a step further, it is conceivable that whether a family intends to live permanently in the area may also have some connection with its participation in organizations and informal relationships. But while this factor may support such involvement, there are no doubt cases in which it is instead a result of such involvement. In connection with a family's intention to live permanently in the community, it seems reasonable to examine whether the family owns or rents its home and also whether the residence is of adequate size. The standard of adequate residence size was set tentatively at six or more rooms on the one hand, or twenty-six or more *tatami* mats[8] on the other, and the analysis was conducted on this basis.

As regards all the four factors on Table 17 the proportion of households in group I was highest, and a clear gradient pattern was observed that extended from group I through group VI. Housing conditions in the III-IV group were particularly bad, but

---

[8] The heavy woven-straw mats used as a floor covering in Japan are of a standard size, approximately $6' \times 3' \times 2''$. Rooms are therefore commonly referred to as 6-mat rooms, 8-mat rooms, etc. (Translator.)

apart from that one zigzag in respect to factor (4), the gradient pattern obtained everywhere else.

Table 17
Factors Conducive to Participation in Formal Organizations
and Informal Relationships: II

	I	II	III-IV	V	VI	Total
1. Intend to live permanently in Nozaki	25 (92.6)	25 (92.6)	12 (70.6)	14 (60.9)	3 (12.0)	79 (66.4)
2. Own their residence	27 (100.0)	27 (100.0)	9 (52.9)	12 (52.2)	3 (12.0)	78 (65.5)
3. At least 6 rooms	14 (51.9)	11 (40.7)	3 (17.6)	1 (4.3)	1 (4.0)	30 (25.2)
4. At least 26 *tatami* mats	21 (77.8)	12 (44.4)	2 (11.8)	4 (17.4)	2 (8.0)	41 (34.5)

As a result of examining each of these aspects, a distinct gradient pattern was observed, relative to periods of arrival, in the overall involvement in the cooperative life of the community. It seems quite possible that not only the gradient pattern already pointed our under sense of parish membership and the religious behavior of parish members, but also the gradient pattern of the religious behavior associated with funerary rites, can be almost entirely explained on the basis of the gradient pattern found in the degrees of local involvement. In order to confirm this point, if one examines the data to determine whether a clear gradient pattern in degrees of involvement in community life emerges when parish residents are classified into nuclear, modal, marginal, and dormant groups, it will be found that a prominent gradient comes into view. Seen as a whole, there is a sharp and unmistakable gap between any two categories. As far as the difference between nuclear and dormant parishioners or households are concerned, in contrast to what was observed when parish households were grouped by period of arrival, the percentage differences here are generally greater, and in consequence the gradient pattern is even more conspicuous. It may be said, therefore, that a cause-and-effect relationship exists between the degree of local involvement and the degree of religious commitment among the parishioners.

Conclusion

In this study of a small Tokyo suburb called Nozaki the primary focus of attention has been the problem of the impact of suburbanization on Shinto belief and behavior. Several matters related to this problem have been analyzed in terms of the residents' period of arrival.

The first result to which our attention was drawn was that a gradient pattern could be seen when the period-of-arrival classification was employed. A certain diffuseness of response was seen, however, when it came to such matters as shrine visitation at New Year's or at festival times, visiting a shrine with a recently born child, decorating the household entrance with pine branches, and so on, actions, that is, which can exist quite apart from having a connection with the local shrine. This same diffuseness also occurred when it came to the idea that shrines were important as a matter of custom or as something to rely on. In this suburb, which is currently experiencing an inrush of population, Shinto belief and behavior display not only the gradient pattern but also a more general diffuseness, and both aspects are typical of the phenomenon. It is precisely the coexistence of these two aspects that constitutes the real nature of the transformation that is taking place in Shinto belief and behavior.

The gradient pattern exhibits a tapering-off tendency commensurate with periods of arrival (or one could equally well say that it exhibits an augmentative tendency with respect to minus responses), but the diffuseness discovered shows of course no such tendency. It seems, therefore, that these two conceptions contradict each other. Can it be that these two mutually contradictory tendencies are part and parcel of the trends that characterize modern Shinto belief and behavior? Or, alternatively, can it be that what at first glance appear to be contradictions are actually different aspects of a single tendency?

I am inclined to regard them as differing aspects of a single tendency, which should perhaps be spoken of as a tendency toward the delocalization of Shinto belief and behavior. The more recent a household's arrival, the weaker does its sense of parish membership tend to be and the fewer are its religious practices. (This exemplifies the gradient pattern.) It appears, therefore, that in localities where population influx is great and the number of incoming households high, the local shrine will tend to lose its roots in local community life and take on a new form of existence. It is this that gives rise to the phenomenon of community shrine delocalization. At the same time, however, there are certain Shinto customs and ways of thinking which, when they have lost their local ties and come to exist in their own right independently of neighborhood life, or rather precisely because they have been able to drop their local ties and exist independently of neighborhood life, can be maintained in diffuse form as social customs. In short, diffuseness is born of the delocalization of Shinto belief and practice.

The gradient pattern, under the influence of the postwar situation in politics, society, and ways of thinking, evidences a decline that has taken place in the suburban community shrines, which offer nothing unique in the way of religious services and have no sizable geographic area whose inhabitants can be counted on as parishioners. The decline that Nozaki Hachiman Shrine is presently undergoing and its lack of new lines of development are to be understood against this background. Conversely, the diffuse formation has stimulated a condition of prosperity in the big-name shrines in that they are now able to count on a wide range of worshipers, exemplified by the crowds of people who throng to Meiji Shrine at New Year's. Thus, the trend toward delocalization is bound up, on the one hand, with the declining fortunes of the community shrines as evidenced by the gradient pattern, while it is linked, on the other, with the growing prosperity of one fraction of the shrines as evidenced by the diffuse formation. Prosperity for one segment, however, does not necessarily signify an advance for Shinto belief and practice as a whole.

This analysis has been concerned with only one suburban shrine, but the information I have drawn from it may be thought of not merely as indicative of a unique state of affairs at this particular shrine but also as reflecting the situation of local shrines in suburbs generally and even as permitting us to foresee what course Shinto shrines are likely to take in urban society in the years to come. At the risk of being a bit overbold, if we take the information gained thus far out of its limited frame of reference and think of it in broader terms, a certain number of hypotheses can be proposed.

Reflection on how the Shinto shrine developed makes it possible to suggest that it first came into existence to enshrine the guardian deity of a clan (*ichi mon no ujigami*) and that subsequently, with the collapse of the clan system and the participation of people who had once been outsiders, the guardian deity became the tutelary deity of an area. Admittedly, there were probably some shrines that existed from the beginning as dwellings of guardian deities of local areas, and perhaps some shrines that continued to exist as symbolic embodiments of clan deities. But if we confine ourselves to the overall trend, it can probably be said that the development that took place was one from clan deities to guardian deities of local areas. From the perspective of the worshipers, this coincided with the transition from clan members (*ujibito*) through village elite members (*moroto*) to parish members (*ujiko*). At the present time, however, due to the urbanization of society, the guardian deities of local areas are in the process of becoming delocalized and their shrines too are drawing worshipers from increasingly extensive areas. At one time, when shrine ties with a clan were being severed, some shrines rode out the wave and continued to develop, while those that could not fell into oblivion. In the same way, now that the tutelary deities of local areas are becoming delocalized, it seems probable that shrines that have the capacity to extricate themselves from their particular areas and become shrines that draw worshipers from larger areas will grow, while those that cannot will experience declining fortunes. "Shrines that draw worshipers from large areas" (*kōiki no sūke-isha*) will be those that rely on spiritual ties as differentiated from the clan shrines, which relied primarily on kinship ties (though not to the exclusion of local and spiritual ties), and the locally oriented shrines, which relied primarily on ties with a specific area (though not to the exclusion of spiritual ties). Consequently, they must be able to attract worshipers from near and far. Their attractiveness may consist of a manifestation of miraculous power, of beautiful and impressive festival rites, or even of the magnificent construction and superb arrangement of the shrine and what lies within its precincts. But the most significant feature of all may be one that is presently neglected by Shinto—its teachings.

BUDDHISM

BUDDHISM

4. PREFERENTIAL NON-MIXED MARRIAGE AMONG SHIN BUDDHIST BELIEVERS

Introduction

For most present-day Japanese Buddhists, a denominational difference means hardly more than a difference in the rituals that characterize each specific denomination (Beardsley et al. 1959: 466). An exception is the case of adherents of the Shin sects[1] whose daily and seasonal customs, both sacred and secular, are more or less distinctive from those of other Buddhist denominations. Information concerning this group suggests the possibility that religious affiliation is a matter of crucial importance for Shin adherents in the selection of mates. Through a case study of a local neighborhood, I will attempt in the present chapter to examine whether and to what extent there is a tendency toward religious homogamy among the contemporary followers of Shinran, founder of the Shin sects, and which factors are responsible for the maintenance of this tendency, if its existence is proven.

Generally speaking, an organized religion that stresses the spiritual training of its members tends to discourage interfaith marriage in one way or another. A good example is the Catholic Church. According to the official records of the Nagasaki Catholic Church, there was only one mixed marriage among the 842 marriages contracted during the five years from 1945 to 1950 (Schull 1953). My hypothesis is that the Shin sects also tend to avoid interfaith marriage. One should not overlook, however, an im-

---

[1] The Shin sect, or group of sects, is the largest group of Buddhist sects, claiming nearly 30% of all temples and 20% of all Buddhists in Japan (1972). In the United States of America, it is the only Buddhist body of considerable influence in the Japanese-American community.

portant difference between these two religious bodies in this
respect; unlike the Catholic Church, Shin Buddhism has never
formally prohibited mixed marriage of any sort. Since Shin adherents have some peculiar social traits that are not merely due to
local custom but that seem to be an outward manifestation of an
inner faith, it is reasonable to assume that a tendency toward
religious endogamy should occur among Shin believers. Or, to
put it reversely, the ratio of religious endogamy can be regarded
as a sort of barometer for measuring the vitality of the faith of
Shin adherents.

The present analysis of religious endogamy has been based upon
an intensive field study of one small community, since the method
of statistical mass observation was unfeasible for the author. In
choosing a community, an area where the tendency is conspicuous
seemed to be more easily submitted to a detailed examination, and
hence better for my purposes than others, even though it does not
represent a modal state of affairs. Thus the Hokuriku district,
which is predominantly populated with Shin adherents, was
picked as the area in which my community should be located. It
was also decided that the community should have a mixed population of Shin and non-Shin believers because, if the group consists
almost exclusively of Shin adherents and there is little chance of
religious exogamy, one may easily point out the *fact* of religious
endogamy but be unable to prove its *tendency*. Consequently the
ideal community should have a considerable number of non-Shin
parishioners living side by side with Shin followers, and there must
be ample opportunity for mixed marriage to occur. With these
considerations in mind, I eventually selected a hamlet called
Kawanishi in the interior Noto Peninsula as the locality for my
field research, which was conducted in 1952.

Fact—The Tendency Observed

The households in Kawanishi, which numbered 94 in August
1952, are classified into two groups in terms of religious affiliation:
53 belong to the Shin Ōtani sect, and 39 to Kogi Shingon sects
(i. e., old or orthodox Shingon), the remaining two being un-

known.[2] The Shin faithful, who are in the majority, belong to five temples, Kyōgan-ji, Shōgan-ji, Chōkō-ji, Honkaku-ji and Shōkō-ji, while almost all of the Shingon adherents are parishioners of Konzō-ji.[3] Nowadays there is no temple in Kawanishi, but those mentioned above are located in neighboring hamlets or are close enough to visit and return within half a day. Table 18 shows temple membership according to the three subsections of Kawanishi.

Table 18
Temple Membership of Kawanishi Households as Divided
by Three Subsections of Hamlet (August 1952)

	Hiro	Sakuragi	Tanagai	Total
Shin				
Kyōgan-ji	1	16	4	21
Shōgan-ji	11	9		20
Chōkō-ji	3	7		10
Honkaku-ji	1			1
Shōkō-ji	1			1
Total	17	32	4	53
Shingon				
Konzō-ji	16		21	37
Takada-ji		1	1	2
Total	16	1	22	39
Unknown	1		1	2
Total	34	33	27	94

Temple membership remains unchanged over generations except in cases where a serious interpersonal conflict occurs or migration makes temple attendance extremely difficult. One should also keep in mind that in the traditional sections of Japan marriage occurs between households rather than between the individuals concerned. In other words, marriage does not mean the establishment of a new household unit but simply the addition

[2] They are newcomers and because a death has not yet occurred in the family since their arrival, their religious commitment is still pending. Buddhist religious affiliation is ordinarily determined by the family's choice of a temple to conduct funeral services.

[3] An interesting question is how hetero-religiosity and diversified church membership came about in this village, but existent materials fail to provide any satisfactory answers. One thing apparent in my present sample is the irrelevancy of social class to religious affiliation.

of an adult female or male to an existing household that is in need of a spouse for one of its younger members. Therefore, it makes sense to classify marriage cases by the religious affiliation of the household and also by the direction of the transmission of an adult member, that is, by two types of endogamy (Shin to Shin, Shingon to Shingon) and two types of exogamy (Shin to Shingon, Shingon to Shin). A third factor to be considered is the tendency for a household to stay in the same hamlet for a long period without moving away, and the ensuing closely knit network of social interactions among households within the hamlet. Thus, it is meaningful to divide marriage cases into two groups, namely, local endogamy where both parties are households within the same hamlet, and local exogamy where one party is a household outside the hamlet.

The total number of marriages involving household heads or successors in Kawanishi during the period from 1870 to 1952 was 193, and 36% of these were locally endogamous cases. When we analyze these 67 endogamous cases in terms of religious affiliation, we find 62 non-mixed marriages (34 Shin-to-Shin and 28 Shingon-to-Shingon), in striking contrast to only 5 cases of mixed marriage (2 Shin-to-Shingon and 3 Shingon-to-Shin). The five cases are, however, all intra-subsection marriages, as shown in Table 19. We can discern two kinds of forces at work, tendencies toward religious endogamy and tendencies toward local endogamy. These two are contradictory to one another, as seen in the examples of mixed marriage, but at the same time harmonious with each other, as seen in the fact that more than two-thirds of the non-mixed cases are intra-subsection marriage.

Table 19
Local Endogamous Cases According to
Religious Affiliation and Subsections of Kawanishi

To \ From		Shin			Shingon		
		Hiro	Sakuragi	Tanagai	Hiro	Sakuragi	Tanagai
Shin	Hiro	4	8		1		
	Sakuragi	1	18				
	Tanagai	1	2				2
Shin-gon	Hiro	2			9		
	Sakuragi					1	
	Tanagai					1	17

We can conclude that there is a tendency toward religious homogamy in Kawanishi but, must now question whether it is accidental or a manifestation, though fragmentary, of an existing preferential marriage pattern. This question can be answered by a careful examination of the situations in which marriages occur.

Analysis—Social Background

1. *Religious endogamy may be a function of class endogamy.* My first question was whether I could find the reasons for religious endogamy in the social position of Shin believers relative to that of Shingon believers. In Kawanishi, households can be ranked according to three categories—upper, middle, and lower— depending upon the three kinds of standardized terms of address for household heads, that is, *oyassama, ototo,* or *pappa.* Nearly one household head out of ten is called *oyassama* (the same as *oyaji-sama,* honorary name for the patriarch) and is of a family that in the past belonged to the landed class of the hamlet. One out of four is called *ototo* (*o-toto,* honorary name for the father). *Ototo* make up the middle class and are from families who were landowner-operators for a long period of time. Heads of households that were tenants in the preland-reform period[4] are called *pappa* (seemingly of Western origin but actually no relation at all) and are given the lowest status in the class structure of the hamlet. They are in the majority, seven out of ten household heads belonging to this category. This rather conservative pyramid-like structure is still maintained despite the impact of major economic changes in the wake of the last war.

I therefore sorted the Shin and Shingon believers into these three categories and compared them for social class and religious affiliation (Table 20). No significant class difference between the two groups was observed, however. In order to check the findings, a young, well-educated *oyassama* was requested to rank all of his neighbors as upper, middle, or lower class in terms of that aspect

---

[4] The land reform was carried out in the period shortly after Japan's surrender and reduced the ratio of tenants from 26.7% to 5.5% and that of leased land from 46% to 12%.

of household status which would be most seriously considered when selecting a mate. The pyramid-like structure that resulted from this procedure confirms our observations (see the lower half of Table 20). Although Shingon has a little greater ratio of *pappa* and lower-class families, neither Shin nor Shingon families as a whole have a superior status in the hamlet. Rather, we are impressed by the similar distribution of Shin and Shingon households among the three classes.

Table 20
Class Structure of Kawanishi

Class	Shin	Shingon	Total
Oyassama	5	3	8
Ototo	18	5	23
Pappa	30	31	61
Upper class	5	2	7
Middle class	26	13	39
Lower class	22	24	46
Total	53	39	92*

* Two unknown cases of Table 18 are discarded.

2. *Religious endogamy may be a function of occupational endogamy.* If occupational differences existed between Shin and Shingon parishioners, we could assume that religious endogamy would naturally ensue. However in Kawanishi this is not the case. The single main occupation is farming. Since the average acreage is only 6.5 *tan* (1 *tan* equals 0.25 acres), the majority of peasants have to engage in some other work as well. Although the ratio of full-time farmers to part-time farmers is not the same for the two groups, as seen in Table 21, the difference observed is not significant enough to be positively related to the tendency toward endogamy.

Table 21
Occupational Differentiation in Kawanishi

	Shin	Shingon	Total
Full-time farmer	25	9	34
Part-time farmer	25	30	55
Non-farmer	3		3
Total	53	39	92

3. *Religious endogamy may be a function of genealogical cleavage between the two.* The outcasts in feudal Japan were almost invariably Shin parishioners, but all Shin believers are not necessarily their descendants. If the Shin parishioners in Kawanishi were outcasts, no mixed marriages would have occurred. We can ask, then, if there are any serious cleavages along household lines that would figure as important factors in social segregation. This question must be answered negatively. Though households belonging to the same extended household group (*dōzoku*)[5] have membership in the same parish, neither the Shin nor the Shingon adherents of Kawanishi belong to one of a few large *dōzoku* groups but are rather divided into a number of small *dōzoku* (Table 22). The largest *dōzoku* group consists of six households, but the modal cases are very small in size. All formal mutual aid among member households has died out except for cooperation in funeral services, and any substantial mutual aid is confined to close kinsmen. In a word, the average *dōzoku* is so poorly developed both in size and in function that it is by no means a social force influential enough to create a tendency toward endogamy.

Table 22
Dōzoku Groups in Kawanishi

Number of member households	Surnames	
	Shin	Shingon
6	Sumi*	Higashi**
5		Tagata
3	Inoshita, Kitada Takayasu, Yachi	
2	Furuya, Hida, Inoue, Manju, Nagi, Nakaya, Tamura	Hironaka, Shimada, Tanbata, Toshiya, Yasuhiro

* However, Sumi is exceptional. The Sumi *dōzoku* is divided into two faiths, namely, 5 Shin and 1 Shingon household.

** Six households with the same surname of Higashi form one *dōzoku* group and belong to the same parish. Other surname groups should be interpreted in the same way.

[5] The scholar's term *dōzoku* applies to the extended household group composed of a main house and its branch houses acting in corporate solidarity in various ceremonial and other significant situations.

4. *Religious endogamy may be a function of local endogamy.* If the Shin adherents' residential section were spacially segregated from that of Shingon believers, the widely recognized tendency toward local endogamy or the propinquity principle of mate selection would result in religious endogamy. But this is not the case as can be clearly seen in Table 18. Shin believers show a remarkable concentration in Sakuragi, the central subsection of Kawanishi, and Shingon parishioners in Tanagai, but there is not sufficient evidence to conclude that Shin forms one section and Shingon another. Therefore, local endogamy cannot be regarded as the factor that led to religious endogamy, though both are positively or negatively interrelated.

The foregoing examination suggests that there must be religious factors responsible for the tendency toward endogamy since non-religious factors have proved to be incapable of explaining it.

Analysis—Religious Background

The teachings of the Shin patriarch Rennyo (1415–1499)[6] are kept alive and meaningful among the Shin faithful in Kawanishi. According to Rennyo, a daughter should not be married into a non-Shin household, although adoption of a non-Shin girl as a sons's bride is allowed (Inaba 1948:241). Accordingly Shin believers try to avoid marrying a daughter to the heir of a non-Shin household. To do so would change her religious affiliation and deprive her of predestined salvation. When such a case does occur, social censure follows, and elders, especially, frown upon such marriages. On the other hand, it is permissible to receive a bride from a non-Shin household, on the grounds that salvation is now extended to one who otherwise would not be saved. This mirrors the latter part of Rennyo's rescript.

Keigo Seki reports that in a fishing village near Nanao-shi, capital city of the Noto Peninsula, people say that the tutelary deities dislike population decreases in the parish and therefore do

---

[6] Rennyo, the eighth abbot of Hongan-ji, made it the most prosperous and influential temple in Japan.

not permit moving out by marriage although moving in by marriage is welcomed (Seki 1965). This folkway has something in common with the norm that exercises a controlling influence in the minds of Shin believers in Kawanishi. A common cultural ground seems to exist beneath the strata modified by Shin teachings, but, at the same time, one difference is worthy of special mention: in Kawanishi, combined with a sort of territorial consciousness is the notion of the loss or gain of salvation. This notion is not peculiar only to Kawanishi but can also be found in other hamlets of the area. In Kanakura, a neighboring hamlet, they say that a Shin girl will go to hell if she is married into a Shingon household, and a Shingon girl, if married into a Shin household, will go to paradise. The folklorist Hirayama says that in Gōroku, a hamlet in the same area, Shin households do not hesitate to accept a non-Shin girl as their heir's bride, but cases of Shin daughters being married into non-Shin households are very few (Hirayama 1955:137). These reports, which are based on information obtained through personal interviews rather than on statistical data, reveal the prevailing ideal pattern of mate selection as well as its factual tendency.

A causative relationship should not be hastily alleged, however, from the parallelism between Rennyo's teachings and contemporary preferential marriage among Shin believers. In order to determine the role of Rennyo's teachings in the mate-selection process among Shin believers, it is advisable to examine how his teachings remain influential in other facets of neighborhood life. Rennyo urged his followers to hold small meetings among themselves frequently to share experiences in faith, guide each other, and cultivate faith in Amida (Inaba 1948:84). He told them to talk without hesitation when they meet and to express whether their confessions are of faith or of doubt, for when a person talks his thoughts are conveyed to the group, and if he is in error he can obtain advice from others (Inaba 1948:75). Such meetings are held regularly in present-day Kawanishi and play a vital role in the training of believers, just as Rennyo, five hundred years ago, had hoped they would. These meetings are called *oza*[7] and are

---

[7] *Oza* is an honorary expression for a seat, then a group of seats, and finally a meeting.

attended by at least one person from each Shin household in Kawanishi, irrespective of local temple membership. I do not have enough information to determine whether the *oza* takes its origin directly from Rennyo's teachings or whether it was inaugurated less than two centuries ago as a local version of a meeting held at Hongan-ji Temple in Kyoto, the national headquarters of Shin Buddhism. Still it is important as a collective phenomenon that reminds us of Rennyo's teachings.

Although we can regard the teachings of Rennyo as a causal, or at least a reinforcing or justificative factor of the tendency toward endogamy, they are not the single cause, for endogamy is more prevalent than would be expected if Rennyo's teachings were followed perfectly. As mentioned above, Rennyo permitted men to take brides from non-Shin households. This tolerance, if put into practice, would blur the tendency toward endogamy that Rennyo's prohibition against having one's daughter marry into a non-Shin household would produce. But in reality endogamy is very marked as shown in Table 19. Thus, we must seek for other religious factors that can satisfactorily explain this tendency.

1. *The latent function performed by the Shin believers' association in the hamlet.* Shin believers in Kawanishi form an association called the *Nijūhachinichi-kō*,[8] and hold monthly and annual meetings of which the *oza* is the most important. Shingon adherents also have collective activities of their own, though definitely less frequent and much more recreational than those of Shin followers. Religious segregation in this hamlet, therefore, can hardly escape the eyes of a careful fieldworker. Nonetheless, it is doubtful whether religious segregation is so decisive a factor as to be conducive to endogamy, for it is not accompanied by economic or political segregation. Thus, while it is hard to establish a causal relationship, a parallelism, at least, can be recognized.

2. *An institutionalized opportunity for social contact among Shin believers from a wide area.* Shin believers in Kawanishi participate in

---

[8] Literally, an association of the 28th day of the month. Since the 28th is the day that Shinran, the founder of Shin Buddhism, died, the name of the association indicates the nature of the association, i.e., a group of Shinran's followers.

the religious activities held at their parish temple. The most important yearly meeting is called *Hōonkō*, or Memorial Day of Shinran, and is attended by a large number of the faithful, including voluntary participants from other parishes. Hence, *Hōonkō* provides an institutionalized opportunity for social contact among the participants whose range of daily social intercourse is narrowly limited within their own hamlet. Noteworthy in this connection is the final service of *Hōonkō*, which is attended by young unmarried women dressed in their most colorful clothes. They are scattered here and there amidst the congregation that consists mainly of old men and women in subdued dress. Mothers take their daughters of marriageable age to the service with the clear intention of displaying them, and female relatives of unmarried youths who are looking for a bride take advantage of this opportunity to observe them. School sports events and Shinto shrine festivals are also convenient occasions for the same purpose, but *Hōonkō* is preferable because attendance at *Hōonkō* itself is regarded as evidence of excellent home discipline. We can assume that in former days *Hōonkō* also provided unmarried youngsters with the opportunity for heterosexual association that eventually led to marriage.

3. *Differences in the pattern of annual functions between Shin and Shingon households.* Shingon adherents observe the complicated, generations-old pattern of worshipping household deities, ancestors, and the guardian deities of agriculture. Shin believers, on the contrary, tend to simplify the traditional ways or reinterpret them in the context of Shin doctrine. Consequently, there is an evident difference in the way the two groups worship that presumably hinders mixed marriage between Shin and Shingon believers. For example, when a Shingon household takes a bride from a Shin household, the strict observance of annual religious functions tends to be neglected, for in most cases an adult female is one of the important performers of household religious duties. On the other hand, if a Shin household accepts a Shingon girl as a bride, the family's attendance at temple services tends to decrease. Therefore, Shin households, particularly Shin elders, prefer non-mixed marriages. Although Shingon households are more tolerant of

religious heterogeneity than Shin households, the practices of Shin believers naturally result in religious homogamy.

Class Endogamy

As pointed out before, local endogamy is an important tendency that can be discerned along with religious endogamy. A third tendency I will now consider is class endogamy. Our case studies demonstrate that the majority of affinals of Kawanishi households are not only of the same faith but also of the same social status. It is not easy to weigh the relative importance of the two factors: the one strengthens the other in most cases, but in a few cases the two come into conflict.

Let us examine this general tendency according to social class. As shown in Table 20, the lower class makes up 50% and the middle class 42% of the total population of Kawanishi. For lower- and middle-class families, therefore, religious endogamy is not a force that limits the range of possible mates so narrowly as to make selection from within their own class difficult. For upper-class households, however, their low proportion and small number make it necessary to take one or more of the following measures: (1) selection within the upper class but from a wider geographical area than that of ordinary households; (2) selection not only from within the upper class but also from the middle class in Kawanishi; (3) selection from the upper class only but including both Shin and Shingon households. Usually two or more of these measures are applied in combination. Thus, it is among the upper-class households that religious endogamy gives way to class endogamy when conflict occurs. In actuality, the upper-class households in Kawanishi are all related to each other directly or indirectly through blood ties or marriage, irrespective of their Shin or Shingon affiliation.

Conclusion

The tendency toward endogamy is remarkable among Shin

believers in Kawanishi. It is obviously due to a number of factors, among the most important of which are the lasting influence of Rennyo's teachings, the collective activities of Shin adherents in the hamlet, social contact among Shin believers from a wide area at such functions as *Hōonkō*, and the differences between Shin and Shingon households in the manner of observing annual religious functions. The full realization of religious endogamy is hindered by the interference of local endogamy, which is marked among the lower and middle classes, and of class endogamy, which is conspicuous among the upper class. Although the manifestation of religious endogamy is incomplete, it is safe to conclude that there is a cultural pattern of non-mixed marriage among Shin believers, in so far as the phenomenon is guided by the consciousness of "ought to." The religious endogamy observed is persuasive evidence of the extent that religious belief has been incarnated in the daily life of Shin adherents in Kawanishi and possibly throughout the Noto Peninsula where a great majority of the residents belong to the Shin sects of Pure Land Buddhism.

5. BUDDHIST SECTS AND THE FAMILY SYSTEM IN JAPAN*

Introduction

The *ie*, or traditional family (or household), system was the pervasive pattern of Japanese social organization, not only familial, but also commercial (Nakano 1964), industrial (Matsushima 1962; Hazama 1964), artistic (Shimazaki 1953–54; Kawashima 1957; Nishiyama 1959), and religious. To some extent, it still remains so. Hence, the *ie* system must be seriously taken into consideration in any scholarly discussion of Japanese social structure.

Buddhism was originally a religion calculated to free people from secular bonds, including that of the familial tie. But, as it became firmly established among the Japanese populace, its practices became closely associated with ceremonies in honor of the dead and of ancestors. Ancestors are not necessarily one's own biological forebearers, but predecessors in the household line. Ceremonies in honor of deceased family members and ancestors are an essential obligation of descendants, a means to secure ancestral assurance for household prosperity and good fortunes. As a result of this accommodation, Buddhist practices now precisely meet the religious needs of the traditional stem family in Japan. But Buddhism in Japan did not merely tolerate special interpretation on the part of laymen or make concessions in its tenets. Social organization within Buddhist sects themselves became markedly patterned after the *ie* system. The present chapter calls attention to

* This chapter was read at a symposium of the Tenth Pacific Science Congress in Honolulu, August 1961. The author is especially indebted to Professor Richard K. Beardsley of the University of Michigan for critical reading of the manuscript and time-consuming editorial assistance.

this aspect of Japanese Buddhism, which has been relatively neglected, even by Japanese scholars.

The Temple, or the Sociological Unit of Buddhism

Every Buddhist sect has a clergy and laity, its priests and parishioners, but as individuals they are not the sect's main components. Rather, the local temples to which priests and people affiliate are the primary components of a Buddhist sect. Therefore, our attention will be directed first of all to the temple.

The *tera* or *jiin* of Japan, usually translated into English as "temple," has several connotations:

1. The *tera* as a set of structures in a Buddhist compound. As such, it comprises various Buddhist halls and a rectory.

2. The *tera* as a juridical person or an incorporated body. As such, the *tera* comprises property and persons: the above-mentioned Buddhist structures, Buddhist statues enshrined in halls, priests living in a rectory and taking care of altars, and parishioners who apply for the priests' services and are responsible for the upkeep of buildings. In this sense, the *tera* is the primary element of a sect. This second meaning has gained both clarity and importance as the result of modern religious laws that applied the concept of a juridical person to local religious bodies and to their national federation as well. In pre-modern periods, before the Meiji Restoration in 1868, this connotation was left rather vague and obscure.

3. The third connotation centers on persons, namely, the *tera* as a residence group of clerics. It is a group of priests and apprentices living together in a single Buddhist compound and taking care of altars in the halls. This connotation was clear even in pre-modern times and continues to be important as the core of the juridical-person concept outlined above.

From the priest's viewpoint, *tera* has all three connotations simultaneously. It is his residence (the first meaning), his family or household (the third meaning), and the business incorporation of his household (the second meaning). To go back to the term *ie* (pronounced ee-ye and translated "household" or "house"), the *tera* (unlike the Christian minister's church) is the priest's *ie*, for *ie* in identical fashion has three connotations: residence, household as a social group, and house as a semi-legal entity.

A number of lines of evidence substantiate my conceptualization. For example, in the pre-Meiji periods Buddhist priests did not publicly carry a family name, but used their temple name as a substitute for it. Later, in the opening years of Meiji, the national government ordered them to take their temple name as their family name, for as long as they stayed in that temple. To take another example, as the *ie* continues to exist for generations, so the temple is expected to exist from generation to generation. Just as a son of the house head, commonly the eldest son, succeeds to the family headship, so is the position of the head priest of a temple taken over by his first disciple. The relationship of a teacher-priest to his disciples is that of a man to his adopted sons. Therefore, succession to the headship and continuance of the institution through succession are concepts shared in common by both the *ie* and the *tera*.

Buddhism as an Organized Religion

If we regard a *tera* as an *ie* for priests living there, the sect to which the *tera* belongs may be considered to be a sort of federation of *ie*. Now, what organizational form does this federation take in the case of a Buddhist sect?

Temples are ranked within a sect; at the top is the main temple (*honzan*), headquarters of a sect, and below it are subordinate temples (*matsuji*). Their relation neatly parallels that of a main household (*honke*) to its branch or subordinate households (*bunke* or *makke*) in the secular world. Of course there are some differences. First of all, the majority of those who founded branch houses in a *dōzoku* were actual junior sons of the main households, whereas the founder of a subordinate temple was only very rarely actual kindred to the head priest of the central temple; instead such priest-founders were only his disciples or fictive sons. Moreover, the relationship between a main household and its branches in the secular world is personal, face-to-face and intimately informal, whereas that in Buddhism is by and large formal and impersonal both because of the absence of a kinship tie and because of the social and geographical distance that separates branches from the central temple. These are minor and inevitable discrepancies, but it is clear that there is a strong resemblance or basic pattern common to the secular and the Buddhist organizations.

The parallel we allege goes even further in the Shin sects where priests have always married and raised families, and where the office of head priest of a temple is transferred from father to son. Organizations within the Shin sect are, therefore, especially worthy of note.

The Shin Sects and the *Ie* System

Nowadays, almost all Buddhist priests irrespective of their sect affiliation (Shin or not) marry and transmit their office to one of their sons. These are not only de facto procedures, but are even sanctioned by the canon law of certain sects. In most sects, however, the abbots of the *honzan* and other upper-ranking temples do not inherit their office; they are elected from among high-ranking priests of the sect. In the Shin sect, on the contrary, the abbot's office, whatever the rank of his temple, is hereditarily transmitted from father to son. Hereditary succession is one of the cardinal principles of the Shin sect organization, which has always permitted married life for its priests, beginning with its founder, Shinran (1173–1262).

The hereditary abbot of the Shin *honzan* is the head of his sect on the one hand, and the head of his household on the other. In the same way the priest of a *matsuji* is the representative of his temple to the sect on the one hand and the head of his household on the other. Since the inheritor is simultaneously the household successor and the temple successor, as explained above, the *honzan* and the abbot's household are identical, just as are the hereditary *matsuji* and the households of their priests.

Since temple coincides with household, the organizational superior-subordinate relation between a *honzan* and its *matsuji* establishes the same kind of relation between the abbot's household and priests' households. In other words, the leader-follower relation between a *honzan* as the source and origin of religious authority and its *matsuji* as receptor is accompanied by a lord-and-vassal relation between the abbot's household and lesser priests' households. This was particularly true in the Tokugawa period when the *honzan* was vested officially with the power to govern its subordinate temples.

Up to the beginning of the Meiji era, there were district temples, or *chūhonji*, that were under control of their national central temple and at the same time governed their own subordinate temples, usually called *mago-matsuji* (grandchild *matsuji* of the *honzan*). A sect was thus crowned with the central temple at the very top, furnished with district temples half way down the hierarchy, and based firmly upon local temples at the bottom. Needless to say, some temples were directly under control of the central temple without mediation of any district temples, while others had two or more hierarchically superior temples between themselves and the *honzan*. The social structure of a sect, as described here, was not only a precise copy of the *dōzoku* group consisting of a main house, branch houses, and grandchild branch houses (*honke, bunke*, and *mago-bunke*); but it was also a reflection of Tokugawa society, which was constructed with the *shōgun* at the top, *daimyōs* (local lords) under him, *daimyōs'* retainers next, and, finally, commoners at the very bottom. While dualism of the secular and ecclesiastical hierarchies was a major characteristic of Western feudal society, in Tokugawa Japan the secular hierarchy was the basic component of social structure. The ecclesiastical order, subjugated to secular power and beholden to it for existence, was forced to copy secular polity. This held true for every Buddhist sect at that time. To control Buddhism, the Tokugawa Shogunate systematized the *hon-matsu seido* (system of *honzan* and *matsuji*), vesting *honzan* with the political power to govern temples under them, and using this system as an important axis of religious administration.

Although Shin sects were conditioned by the polity of Tokugawa society in the same manner as other sects, its *hon-matsu* relation differed more or less from that of others. I spoke earlier of district temples, intermediate in the sect hierarchy. In sects other than Shin, the district temples were literally sub-centers of their sects and held minor authority in both religious and administrative matters. On the contrary, in the Shin sects they were hardly more than intermediate agencies between the *honzan* and its *matsuji*. Each was a local center, it is true, but only in the sense that it served as the local administrative branch of its *honzan*. It enjoyed higher prestige than ordinary temples, but it was rarely vested with greater religious authority than others. Religious authority emanated exclusively from the *honzan* and was transmitted to common temples through the intermediation of a district temple. This character became more and more notable during the Tokugawa period. In the opening years of Meiji, the Tokugawa hierarchy was disestablished overnight and every person became a subject of the emperor without having any intermediary lord between. The Shin sect consequently annulled the generations-old institution of district temples and made every *matsuji* directly subordinate to the *honzan* regardless of its former status and prestige. Other sects, however, did not undertake so drastic a reform even long after the Restoration.

The real intent of the Shin sects in simplifying the *hon-matsu* relations by abolishing the district temple was to assimilate to the new polity of Meiji Japan and, by a thorough concentration of power and further bureaucratization, to modernize the sectarian organization. But the alleged justification was that, in Shin doctrine, the abbot alone was teacher of all priests of the sect. The proof was his prerogative of presiding over each ordination ceremony through which sons of priests were invested in the priesthood. By contrast, in other sects any teacher-priest was entitled to preside over this ceremony. Therefore, it was concluded, the *hon-matsu* relation should be cut to the pattern of the teacher-disciple relation in the Shin sects, that is, one teacher above all the rest, who were his disciples, on the one hand, and one *honzan* above all the rest, which were its *matsuji*, on the other. Temples, in short, came to be organized in a fashion identical to that of the clergy.

A candidate for priesthood, who usually is the son of a priest, applies for the ordination ceremony about the time he has reached his fifteenth year. The ceremony, called *tokudo*, is the most important rite of passage for a priest, because it symbolizes his departure from the secular and his entry into the sacred world.

In traditional Japan, each boy of around fifteen years of age went through a rite of passage called *gempuku*, the ceremony initiating a boy to manhood. *Tokudo* is undoubtedly the Buddhist version of *gempuku*. And as the *gempuku* ceremony was presided over by the ritual father (*gempuku-oya*) of the boy concerned, so the *tokudo* ceremony, conducted for a group, is presided over by the abbot. He has the hair shaven off the candidates' heads and gives a priestly robe and a Buddhist name to each of them. This means that he publicly accepts them as his disciples and assures their status and privilege in his domain of Buddhism. The same procedure with the same connotation was followed in the case of the *gempuku* ceremony. The parallel we have observed here suggests that the abbot is not only the teacher but also the ritual father of the new priests. If so, the coalescence of the fictive father-son relation and the *honzan-matsuji* relation corresponds nicely to the theoretical coincidence of the *oyabun-kobun* relation between individuals (Ishino 1953) and the *honke-bunke* relation between households, which has been reported from various parts of traditional Japan, both rural and urban (Beardsley et al. 1959:34, 261–275). Like the hereditary tie of *honke-bunke*, and the ritualized life-long tie of *oyabun-kobun*, the *honzan-matsuji* relation and its individual counterpart fitted well with the stable, minimally mobile society of traditional Japan. The son of a priest was destined to become a priest of whatever rank was appropriate to the status of his father's temple, and he was a trustee of the temple's hereditary relationships to the *honzan*.

Organizational Transformation

After the Meiji Restoration, with the progress of modernization in Japan, the time-honored *honzan-matsuji* institution also underwent reform. The first blow to the system was the raising to the peerage of six abbot-households of the Shin sects and the accompanying creation of family names for them as nobles (1872). Before long, ordinary priests were also ordered to take family names to be recorded in the nationwide register of families (*koseki*). Since this new appelation applied only to members of the priest's household, gradually the name of his temple was understood to denote the temple as an incorporated body, an entity distinct from the priest's household; the former indivisibility of temple from priest's household began to dissolve as a result of this separate nomenclature. The second assault on the *honzan-matsuji* institution was a transfer of administrative responsibility over the sect, completed in 1884, that took this responsibility from the *honzan* and gave it to the abbot. Under the Tokugawa Shogunate, the *honzan* had been authorized to govern subordinate temples; now it had no such legal power, and the abbot was assigned the administrative function. Thus, the superior-inferior relation between a *honzan* and its *matsuji* as entities ceased to be legal and was maintained only as a traditional and moral relation, supported as it was by the lawful relation of an abbot and lay-priests. The legal transformation did not immediately change attitudes and opinions on the part of ordinary priests and laymen; veneration of both the *honzan* and its abbot continued to make up two sides of the single coin.

After the Second World War, Japan's old civil code was revised. The conjugal family system gained legal support in the place of the traditional stem-family system. Among the impacts of the revised code was discouragement of primogeniture in cases of succession to the position of head priest of a temple. Yet the code is not powerful enough to disestablish the time-honored principle of hereditary succession; institutional identity of the temple with the stem family has been so vital that it has survived the sweep of the new code. On the other hand, the *honzan-matsuji* institution was given its death blow. It is true that the title of *"honzan"* is kept intact, but, since the title of *"matsuji"* was abolished, the nature of the *honzan* and *hon-matsu* relationships have been changed a great deal. Now the *honzan* is not the head temple but merely the largest temple where the center or headquarters of the sect is located. The *honzan* is no longer the sect itself but just one component, though remaining the core, of the sect, side by side with other ordinary temples. The step-by-step development was as follows: (1) in the Tokugawa period temples adhered as *matsuji* to their *honzan*, forming schools rather than sects; (2) in the post-Tokugawa but prewar period sectarian feeling grew, so that the *hon-matsu* relation was in the context of a sect affiliation; (3) in the postwar period, temples have come to belong to sects as individual entities, and any relation the temple may hold to a *honzan* is unofficial and irrelevant to sect adherence. Thus, the *hon-matsu* relation that was kept as a moral obligation on the part of subordinate temples has disappeared from the surface of the formal organization of the sect.

Conclusion

Let me conclude this discussion by reiterating a few points that seem most noteworthy:

1. The traditional pattern of Shin sect organization was strongly conditioned by the existing family system. The Shin sect is a clear example of the traditional *ie* system of Japan being extended to the sphere of religion.

2. Shin sect organization made its transition from traditional to modern style closely following the lead set by the polity of the nation, as illustrated at least twice, during the Meiji Restoration and the postwar reform.

3. The general direction of change has been from identity between two different institutions, familial and religious, to their structural and functional separation.

4. The coincidence of these two institutions has been one of the chief sources of the vitality of Shin temples, but at the same time one of the principal drawbacks of Shin Buddhism as a possible world religion.

5. The generalizations hold true, to a considerable extent, for all Buddhist sects in Japan and reveal the basic sociological patterns common to all of them.

6. THE CHANGING FAMILY AND BUDDHISM IN POSTWAR JAPAN

Introduction

The *ie*, or Japanese household, with varying degrees of institutionalization in different periods, has traditionally been the social unit of Buddhism in Japan. From the time of its early indigenization down to the postwar period, Buddhism was accepted and passed on to succeeding generations of Japanese as a household religion.

The close association of the *ie* with Buddhism was manifest on several levels. Not only was the social structure of Japanese Buddhism *ie*-based, as discussed in the previous chapter, but its functions were also *ie*-directed. Temples can be broadly classified into two categories, *bodai-ji* and *kitō-ji*. The former type was chiefly in charge of memorial services for ancestors and requiems for the dead. The deceased for whom these services were offered were typically the founder, successive heads and their wives, and the most recently deceased members of the household. Memorial services were held for the double purpose of pacifying the souls of the dead and soliciting ancestral protection for family life and business. At the *kitō-ji*, the second category of temples, prayers to invite good fortune and avoid evil in this world were offered for the *ie* itself or for an individual as a member of the family. Through the performance of religious ceremonies and rituals at these two kinds of temples, Japanese Buddhism fulfilled its functions vis-à-vis the needs of the *ie*. Compared with ritual or behavioral patterns, the teaching or ideological aspect of Buddhism was of minor importance. When sermons were given, however, they did not fail to emphasize the morals that sustained family life. It goes without saying that prayers and memorial services for ancestors gave strong implicit support to such domestic morals as filial piety.

Although the *ie* of the early modern period was not the same as that of feudal times, the practice of placing the greatest value on the succession of the household line did not change. Because Japanese Buddhism was structurally *ie*-based, and functionally *ie*-linked, its character remained consistent from pre-modern into modern times. However, the postwar shift in emphasis from family continuity to conjugal harmony was a revolutionary change from a vertical and lineal value orientation to a horizontal and individualistic one and involved too large a leap to be simply termed an evolution of the Japanese family. Obviously this change did not originate in the Buddhist concept of *ie*. Rather, Japanese Buddhism was influenced by changes in the family.[1] In the following sections, I wish to discuss the effects of family changes on Buddhism in

---

[1] I wish to define the model for family-religion relationships used in the present chapter. If F stands for family, R for religion, and Os for other social organizations or institutions, the total picture of family-religion relationships can be summarized in Fig. A.

Fig. A

(The arrows indicate directions of influence.)
From this overall model we can deduce the following three models:

Fig. B

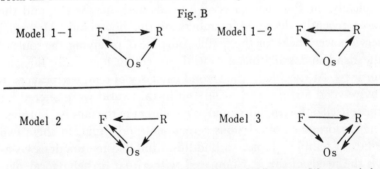

In Model 2 religion is an independent variable. While many Western scholars since Max Weber have regarded it as such, religion, in Japan, is a dependent variable rather than an independent one. I will, therefore, disregard Model 2.

In Model 3 the family is assumed to be an independent variable. Since the family's functions are concerned with the primary socialization of the child and the stabiliza-

postwar Japan, using as a model Shin Buddhism, which has always regarded priestly marriage as legitimate.[2]

Family Change and Buddhist Sects

If the *ie* is thought of as the Japanese stem family system, the postwar changes can be summarized as a shift to a type of conjugal family pattern. This change appeared first and most distinctly in its legal aspects, particularly in the revised civil code. From 1948 the essential points of the revised civil code including those dealing with the conjugal family system were propagated by means of instruction in schools (particularly social studies), social education, and the mass media so that the younger generation was exposed to the new concepts over and over again. The enormous amount of regional migration of labor and the sharp decline in the ratio of independent business owners, which accompanied an amazing economic growth from around 1955, together with the ideological change that had already occurred, contributed to an increase in the ratio of nuclear family households. Parallel to the changes in the dominant family forms, from group orientation to individual orientation and from husband-dominance to egalitarian sharing, noticeable changes occurred in intrafamily relations. These changes probably reflected the fact that an increasing number of women were becoming highly educated and gainfully

---

tion of the adult personality, however, it does not cause changes from within itself. At the most, it is affected by changes in, and transmits changes to, other social systems. Consequently, I will discard Model 3.

Model 1 represents a sequence of effects in which changes in economy, politics, law, ideology, and community cause changes in religion and changes in the family, which in turn influence religion (1-1), or changes in the family and changes in religion, which in turn effect the family (1-2). The present paper makes use of Model 1, particularly Model 1-1, but it does not imply that other models are not feasible (Naito 1941).

In Model 1, F stands for the Japanese family, R for Japanese Buddhism, particularly the Shin school, and Os for the postwar social changes.

[2] The Shin sect differs from other Buddhist sects in its centuries-old approval of priestly marriage and hereditary succession to the office of resident priest. In other sects, the abolition of celibacy for priests is a comparatively recent event. However, so far as social structure of the sect is concerned, there is little difference. Therefore, the Shin sect can be used to represent the general organizational principle of Japanese Buddhism.

employed. Responding to postwar legal reforms and to economic growth and cultural changes, the Japanese family changed considerably in its internal relations as well as in its institutional, ideological, and morphological aspects.

The amendment of the civil code, particularly the abolishment of the *ie* system, brought about first and foremost a modification of the rules governing the succession to the headship of a temple. Even in those sects which maintained the principle of succession by the most able senior disciple, the great majority of ordinary temples practiced, in fact, hereditary succession. Since they had not adopted any traditional familial terms, such as family head, in their statutes, however, they had no need to revise their rules to avoid possible contradictions with the new civil code.

This was not the case with the Shin sects, which had made hereditary succession legitimate. For example, articles of the statutes of the Shin Ōtani sect read: "In accordance with the principle of hereditary succession, the head of the family of Count Ōtani, having been ordained, shall assume the headship of the main temple" (Article 24, 1941), and "The headship of an ordinary temple shall be succeeded to by the head of the family resident in the temple" (Article 364, 1941). For the Shin sects, therefore, the need of revising these rules was pressing. Modifications were made accordingly, and articles of the new rules read as follows: "The headship of the main temple shall go to a male descendant of the founder in the following order: (1) the eldest son of the chief priest, (2) the eldest son of his eldest son . . . [rest omitted]" (Main Temple Statutes of the Ōtani Sect, Article 7, 1952), and "A priest bearing the family name N.N. shall be appointed resident priest (of the temple N.N.) by the chief priest of the sect" (Model of Statutes of Juridical Persons belonging to the Ōtani Sect, Article 6).

In the first rule concerning the main temple, explicit reference to the Ōtani family is eliminated, but it is quite obvious that the system of hereditary succession by the heads of the Ōtani family is kept intact. The change even furthers the systematization of hereditary succession by explicitly defining the time-honored order of priority (Morioka 1965b). The second rule, which is concerned with ordinary temples, makes no direct mention of hereditary succession. Nevertheless, the traditional pattern of succession by the eldest son has never been discarded by sect authority, and a device to prevent possible confusion has been instituted in connection with the application procedure for resident priesthood.

Limitation of space prevents me from referring to examples of other sects of Shin Buddhism, but the case of the Ōtani sect is representative of the general trend in all Shin sects. They have all rephrased their former rules concerning succession to temple headship in accordance with the amended civil code without any intention of abolishing hereditary succession in favor of inviting a qualified priest to take the chief office in the main temple or in ordinary temples. On the contrary, they have made every effort to maintain the vested interests in hereditary succession of the respective family lines that were shaken by the blow of the abolishment of the *ie* system.

Among parishioners, the *ie* survived the amendment of the civil code. However, adherence to primogeniture has declined and instances of succession by a daughter or son other than the eldest occur more frequently. (This holds true also with regard to priestly households.) In sectarian statutes, parishioners were defined as temple supporters who requested the resident priest to perform religious services for the ancestors of their family line (Article 476, 1941). The fact that this definition remained practically unchanged after the war reveals the continuation of the priestly concept of the parishioner as a household rather than as an individual. It cannot, therefore, be said that the legal abolition of the *ie* system dealt a fatal blow to the *ie*-based structure of Shin Buddhism. Damage from the blow was minimal.

The relation between the main temple and ordinary temples, another aspect of the *ie*-based structure of the sects, was not forced to change by the revised civil code but rather by the postwar surge of democratization. (The civil code does not contain any article pertaining to *ie* relationships.) During the Tokugawa period (1603–1867), the feudal government guaranteed the power of the head temple to control its subordinates. The Meiji government, however, deprived the main temple of this power and passed it to the chief abbot. Although the chief abbot was the same person as the resident priest of the main temple, the legal obligation of ordinary

temples to be subordinate to the main temple was gone. After
World War II even the term "subordinate temple" was dropped
from the sectarian statutes and any mention of the relations between
main and subordinate temples, which were already weakened,
disappeared from all formal documents. As the main temple lost
its power, emphasis was shifted to its place as the focal point of
veneration, the primary source of Buddhist propagation, and the
foremost training institute of the sect. From its place at the summit
of a pyramid, it has descended to the center of a circle. Among
other Buddhist sects that had not institutionalized hereditary succession to the position of chief priest of the main temple, many
have retained the term "subordinate temple" in official documents.
A phenomenon common to all sects, however, is the fact that in the
process of postwar democratization the main temple has changed
from being a center of power to becoming primarily an object of
faith.

Changes in the Local Community and Buddhist Sects

The erosion of the foundations of the Buddhist sects was caused
also by changes in economic factors in the local community. The
first of these was the land reform of 1948–1950. For those temples
that owned land but did not cultivate it the reform had serious
consequences. Even temples that did not have land to lose were
affected indirectly since landowners who had been prominent
supporters of the temple were forced to sell their land, often sus-
taining great economic losses. In addition, former tenants who
profited from the reform had little interest in accepting a greater
responsibility for the support of their temples. This change in class
structure combined with progressive inflation caused the destitu-
tion of many rural temples. Since most temples are situated in
rural or mountain regions (about 70% of all temples are located in
farming, lumbering, or fishing areas: 1959 Survey of Actual Conditions of the Shin Honganji Sect), the land reform dealt a terrific
blow directly or indirectly to local temples and hence to the Buddhist sects as well.

The postwar impoverishment of ordinary temples made priests and their families increasingly dependent on outside income, limiting the time and labor available for dedication to religious activities. One-third of all resident priests hold full-time outside jobs (1960 Survey of the Ōtani Sect). The institutional change of the family did not significantly affect relations between the resident priest and his parishioners, but the land reform and inflation took priests away from pastoral work and thus undermined the traditional ties of the parish.

In addition, during the years of rapid economic growth a large number of workers migrated from rural areas to urban centers. Although the families of origin of these migrants belonged to the temple parish in their home town, they themselves no longer had any relationship with the original parish. Only a few became members of a parish in the area of immigration. Metropolitan priests were not active in reaching out to these newcomers. Having lost all evangelical enthusiasm, the urban priests were fully employed with ceremonies for their parishioners. In this way, a large population, free from any parish ties, appeared in metropolitan areas.

Changes in Family Form and Buddhist Sects

A growing awareness of the concept of the conjugal family system and the demand for large-scale migration of labor promoted the formation of nuclear family households. Naturally, this trend was most pronounced in urban centers and among the younger generation. After 1960 the phenomenon of nuclearization of the family increased markedly and received wide attention. Nuclearization is not merely a simplification of family composition, but, in view of the prolongation of the average life span, it reflects a widespread acceptance of the conjugal family system. It also implies a change in family relations that accompany the ideological change. One piece of evidence confirming this trend is the low ratio of nuclear families maintaining household Buddhist altars. Of course the fact that a family has such an altar does not necessarily mean it retains traditional concepts regarding relationships among family members, and we must also bear in mind that the acquisition of a Buddhist altar is largely contingent on whether a death has occurred in the immediate family. Nevertheless, it cannot be denied that a household altar is an expression of family attitudes and behavior and that its presence also has a conditioning effect upon them.

A comparison of the ratio of Buddhist altars in nuclear family households and in extended family households shows a variation according to area and occupation of the residents. The difference is particularly marked in metropolitan residential areas where the inhabitants are almost exclusively white-collar workers: only about 30% of the nuclear families as against 90% of the extended families have altars in their homes. Those families that have Buddhist altars, irrespective of whether they are nuclear or extended families, tend to perform religious services for their ancestors and recently deceased members of the family who are enshrined in the altar. The observance of such traditionally Buddhist ceremonies tends to connect them to the Buddhist clergy and the Buddhist temple. Therefore, a household altar may be looked upon as the link between Buddhism and the household. The dense and widespread distribution of family Buddhist altars has guaranteed the economic stability of Japanese Buddhism, which, consequently, has survived as the religion of ceremonies for the dead. However, the ratio of Buddhist altars among nuclear families is quite low. The fact that the percentage of this type of family is rising suggests that the negative effects of the institutional reform of the family upon Buddhism have finally made themselves felt (Morioka 1970a).

In contemporary Japan, nuclear families are composed primarily of young or middle-aged couples, while the old people remain in extended family households. For this reason nuclear families only rarely observe memorial services for ancestors, and little attempt is made to train children to participate in traditional Buddhist events. The process of daily proselytization in the family has nearly disappeared. This is one more way in which the nuclear family presents a potential threat to the survival of Buddhist temples and sects.

Adjustment of Buddhist Sects to Family Change

Interest in performing memorial services for the ancestors of the family line diminished as a result of the decreasing importance given to lineal continuation of the family over generations. The funeral ceremony and a few subsequent memorial services maintained as minimum essentials are no longer necessarily in a Buddhist pattern, because traditional ways of observance are often modified by migrants to urban centers. The paucity of household Buddhist altars and the lack of intrafamily proselytization made the situation worse, and the demands addressed to Buddhism based on the requirements of the *ie* dwindled. At this conjuncture, Buddhism was forced to develop new policies to provide for its continued existence. The adjustments made by the Buddhist clergy can be summarized as follows:

1. Employment in outside jobs in order to secure additional income. In some cases temple facilities are kept in good shape thanks to this additional income, while in others their maintenance is virtually neglected. In both cases, religious services to parishioners have practically been abandoned except for the performance of burial and memorial rites.

2. The taking on of new money-raising projects that make use of temple facilities. A common project is the promotion of the temple as a place of interest to sightseers. In such cases temple facilities are necessarily improved, while religious activities are largely discarded.

3. Cultivation of new approaches and methods of propagation that attempt to reach people outside the existing parish network as well as dormant and marginal parishioners.

The first two items above should properly be called evasions of the problem rather than countermeasures to it. Such adjustments cannot help Buddhism to survive and meet the demands of people who are suffering from a sense of meaninglessness. On the other hand, the third item, though it has been taken up by only a minority of temples, can be expected to blaze the trail for the future of Japanese Buddhism.

Among the adjustments made by the Buddhist sects in response to changing family conditions, then, only item (3) is worthy of special attention. In this context, the "Brotherhood Movement" of the Shin Ōtani sect must be mentioned as a pioneering effort. It was the primary inspiration for subsequent efforts, such as the "Parishioners' Movement" of the Shin Honganji sect, the "Mobile Head Temple" of the Shin Kōshō sect, the "Service to Each Other Movement" of one Shingon sect, the "Seekers' Movement" of the Shin Bukkōji sect, and so on. Several of these movements have not developed any special programs, but concentrate instead on trying to revive the original functions of the sect. In such cases, there are few noteworthy innovations in approach or concepts and it is questionable to what extent the movements are accepted by ordinary priests and parishioners as something worthwhile following. However, the pioneering movement of the Ōtani sect suggests a possibility for the revival of the established Buddhist sects in Japan in an age when the *ie*, the smallest unit of their organization, is drastically changing. Therefore, in the following section, I will treat in a summarized fashion the nature of the movement and reactions to it as observed within the sect.

The Brotherhood Movement of the Ōtani Sect

This movement was initiated by the sect cabinet headed by Rev. Nobuo Kurube. He and his colleagues organized an association called Shinjin-sha (Association of Shin Buddhists) in 1948. For the first several years this body was simply a group of ardent seekers after the truth of Shin Buddhism as revealed to Shinran, the founder of the sect. Later it began to participate in elections and send representatives to the sect assembly. Finally in 1961, its delegates occupied a majority of the assembly seats, and a new cabinet empowered to carry on sect administration was made up exclusively of assemblymen belonging to the Shinjin-sha Association. After a year's preparation, President Kurube and his colleagues launched the Brotherhood Movement. President Kurube clarified the aim of the movement in the address he delivered before the 1962 regular session of the sect assembly which was convened to discuss a number of bills designed to spread the movement on a sect-wide scale. He declared:

> Even Shin Buddhism, based on the farming neighborhood, has been an *ie* religion. That is to say, the membership unit of the parish has been the *ie*. However, rural society has undergone great changes under the impact of industrialization and urbanization. Moreover, the *ie* is in danger of disintegration. At this turning point, we must restore the original form of Shin Buddhism and change the membership unit from the *ie* as a social entity to the individual as the recipient of the Grace of Amida. Cognizant of this fact, the Brotherhood Movement should reveal to the world the teachings of Buddha and Shinran, our founder, which can satisfy the ultimate yearnings of mankind. (Transcripts of the proceedings of the assembly.)

The regular sessions passed the bills submitted and the movement was launched with the enthusiastic approval of an absolute majority of the assemblymen. The movement was based on three main projects: (1) special mission work focused on selected districts; (2) training seminars at the main temple for those who had been exposed to the special mission work in their home towns; and (3) training of lay leaders who were to become the core members and promoters of the movement.

A strong objection to the proposal had already been registered, however, at a session of the assembly. After the session, a handbill entitled "The Brotherhood Movement as Land Reform of Our Sect" was distributed by assemblymen who opposed the movement. The promoters of the Brotherhood Movement maintained that it represented modernization of the sect by changing Shin Buddhism from an *ie* religion to a religion for individuals, making the membership unit of the parish the individual instead of the *ie*, and designating mission work as the primary function of the priest rather than the recitation of sutras and performance of rituals. The objections to this statement as described in the opposition's handbill can be summarized in the following four points: (1) People in this industrial age still hold the traditional family system in high esteem. The teachings of Shin Buddhism should be taught as a new family religion rather than as a religion for individuals;

(2) If the movement is carried out, the existing parish system will be disrupted and serious confusion will result in the organization of the sect. This is because the movement will lead to a reorganization of the parish by encouraging the faithful to be affiliated with nearby temples rather than the remote ones to which their families have belonged for centuries; (3) If priestly activities are missionary-centered to the neglect of funeral services and related rituals, the temples will eventually go bankrupt; (4) The new rules promoting the movement violate the sect constitution by establishing a new membership unit and fees that are not based on the constitution.

To counter these objections, the following arguments were advanced: (1) It is only proper to make use of family cohesion for training and mission work addressed to individuals, but the very nature of religion rejects the idea of a household religion; (2) In metropolitan areas where the number of residents per temple is large, local chapters of the Brotherhood Movement may be organized independent of any existing parishes. According to the rules of the movement, however, a local chapter shall be formed with a temple as its center wherever this arrangement is feasible. No confusion should result from the movement. The fear of possible confusion comes from the mistaken notion that parishioners are the private property of the priest. On the contrary, parishioners are the followers of Shinran, the founder of Shin Buddhism, and are entrusted by him to the priest, who is also his disciple. The priest is merely the caretaker and not the owner of his parishioners. He should not regard the souls saved by Buddha as his source of income; (3) If the temple becomes a center of fellowship and joy based on faith, the parishioners will spontaneously provide support for the resident priest and his family; (4) The membership fee is a kind of free contribution stipulated in the sect constitution. The above are official statements of the sect cabinet that were previously expressed during discussions in the assembly.

The Brotherhood Movement was motivated by the passionate desire for a revival of faith in the sect. When it came into being with a set of concrete programs, it exercised a deep influence on other Buddhist sects in Japan and was followed by similar movements, as mentioned in a preceding section. However, it fell short of its original goal in so far as membership recruitment can be used as an indication of the movement's level of achievement. (Only half of the number set as the goal were recruited.) The chief obstacles to the movement are three. First, the clergy's lack of recognition of the declining influence of Buddhism. Particularly those priests who reside in temples with a large or expanding parish appear oblivious to the impending crisis that the sect faces. Second, the clergy's desire to protect its vested interests. This is evident in their fears that the Brotherhood Movement may ruin the parish system, as mentioned earlier, and that the new office of lay leader instituted in connection with the movement may threaten the status of the priest as the exclusive dispenser of Buddhism. Third, opposition to the ethos of the Brotherhood Movement, which disapproves of the "traditional" precepts of Shin Buddhism.

Shin teaching, modified and elaborated during the feudal period, insists on the redemption of the sinner through the mediation of the chief priest who is the lineal descendant of Shinran and the head of the Ōtani family. Supporters of this traditional teaching naturally took a stand to preserve the privileges of the Ōtani family and made a strong emotional appeal to parishioners who held conservative notions of religion. The Ōtani family reacted very sensitively to the new trend, and, as a result, the gulf between the Ōtani family and the sect cabinet widened in proportion to the development of the Brotherhood Movement. This factor ultimately put the most effective brake on the progress of the movement.

The slogan "From a Household Religion to a Personal Religion" was liable to cause misunderstandings. It was probably due to the recognition of this possibility that the phrase "A Religion for All the Members of the Family" came to be emphasized instead. Although the two phrases meant essentially the same thing, the challenging effect of the former was almost missing in the latter since "A Religion for all the Members of the Family" did not sound very different from "A Family Religion" to many ears. The rephrasing constituted a compromise, but it failed to mitigate the fear on the part of the Ōtani family that it would be deprived of its vested interests. Finally in April 1969, immediately after the epoch-making Federation of Shin Sects was formed under the leadership of the cabinet of the Ōtani sect, the issue of the so-called *Kaishin* Problem was brought up by the chief priest himself. In a *kaishin*, or letter from the chief priest, he instructed the cabinet to effect immediately the succession of his eldest son to the office of chief priest. This instruction reflected the Ōtani family's determination to preserve their hold on sect administration and effectively put a sudden stop to the Brotherhood Movement (Maruyama 1971).

Modernization of Japanese Buddhism

Two ways are open for the modernization of Japanese Buddhism. One is to cultivate Buddhist teachings and create an entirely new organization truly in keeping with the times. The "new religions" of Buddhist extraction have followed this way. The other way, chosen by the established Buddhist sects, consists in modifying themselves in order to meet the demands of the times without destroying the best elements of their tradition. The primary task for those who follow the first way is to establish themselves as a religious organization independent of the mother body, which in itself often involves modernization. The main task for the followers of the second way is to liberate themselves from various additions made to the original message of their founders over time and set about reinstitutionalizing themselves.

Modernization of the established Buddhist sects has two aspects. The first is the organizational and institutional aspect and is concerned with external reforms in the sect corresponding to changes in the surrounding society. The other aspect is concerned with the ideological sphere. One method of modernization in regard to the latter is to innovate the teachings of the sect so as to meet present-day needs, while an alternative course is to rediscover the true message of the founder by discarding various impurities acquired over time.

The energy neccessary for sect modernization is not automatically generated by changes in societal organization and institutions. From where does this energy come? In some cases it springs from sources outside the sect, while in others it is generated internally. When it comes from outside forces, the organizational and institutional aspects of the sect are the first to undergo change, followed by new developments in ideology. When the energy comes from within, it is generated by efforts to restore the original message of the founder and stimulates organizational and institutional reforms. Buddhist sects, centerd on the main temple under the feudalistic system of the Tokugawa period and later on the chief priest under the modern system instituted at the time of the Meiji Restoration, owed their existence to political power. In other words, the political power of the age supplied Buddhist sects with the energy to carry out their reorganization. However, the present-day principle of division of politics and religion eliminates the possibility of any sect-reforming energies coming from political power. Such energies can emerge only from within the sect itself. The Brotherhood Movement of the Ōtani sect received the impetus for self-reorganization from the message of Shinran, founder of Shin Buddhism, as reinterpreted by Manshi Kiyozawa (1863–1903). It aimed at an extensive reform in response to rapid social change after World War II, change that involved the transformation of Japanese family life. The degree of success achieved by this movement will enable observers to predict whether present-day Japanese Buddhist sects still retain the capacity to reform themselves from within. In other words, the Brotherhood Movement constitutes a test case that will indicate the probable future of Buddhist sects in Japan, whether they are destined to a rapid decline in consequence of the changed quality of the *ie*, their basis for many centuries, or whether they will be able to absorb these changes and reform themselves, thereby gaining new life as religious bodies with the task of revealing their founders' message to mankind.

CHRISTIANITY

7. CHRISTIANITY IN THE JAPANESE RURAL COMMUNITY: ACCEPTANCE AND REJECTION

Introduction

Recent statistics (1972) indicate that Shintoists constitute 78.9% of the total population of Japan, Buddhists 77.9%, Christians 0.8%, and other religions 8.7%.[1] Of the Christians there are roughly 361,000 Catholics and 429,000 Protestants. They clearly form a minority group in the Japanese religious population.

Roman Catholic missions first came to Japan in the middle of the sixteenth century, and it is estimated that in 1614 there were approximately 300,000 Catholics.[2] However, from that year on, the Tokugawa Shogunate banned all missions and began a persecution of Christians, who were forced to either change their religion or go underground. The Shogunate pursued a "closed country" policy for two centuries; only after foreign trade agreements were made in 1858 was it possible for the missions to reopen. As soon as this happened, approximately 20,000 underground Catholics came under the protection of the Church once again, and its membership increased to the extent that in 1891 there were 41,000 Catholics, 85,000 in 1925, and 309,000 in 1963 (Spae 1964: 74). Protestant missions also started in 1859 with the arrival of missionaries from the American Episcopal Church. By 1891 Prot-

---

[1] It will be noticed that these percentages add up to about 166%. This total is reached by adding the numbers claimed by the religious bodies concerned, which often include what J. H. Fichter calls marginal and dormant parishioners, and even presumed adherents. Shrine Shintoists, who form the overwhelming majority of Shintoists, are usually Buddhists also. Christians, however, give more reliable figures than other religious groups. See Chapter 1.

[2] This figure corresponds to 1.5% of the then national population (Boxer 1951:321).

estant church membership totaled 31,000 and increased to more than 400,000 after the Second World War.

If we leave out of consideration the history of Catholicism before it was banned in the early seventeenth century, it is about a hundred years since Christian missions began to work in Japan. The number of converts who maintain church membership at present totals 885,000. Let us compare the achievement of other newly arisen religious groups. Tenrikyo, for example, a religion of Shinto color founded in 1838, now claims 2,061,000 adherents; Reiyūkai Kyōdan, a Buddhist religion founded in 1924, claims 2,268,000 believers; and Seichō no Ie, founded in 1929, which belongs neither to Shintoism nor to Buddhism, claims to have 2,189,000 adherents. Actual numbers are estimated to be less than half of what is claimed; even so, compared with Christianity, these groups have achieved outstanding results in a comparatively short space of time. What is more, they are religions that were created from almost nothing by charismatic leaders. Christianity, on the other hand, has gained its present footing with the help of many European and American churches that dispatched a great amount of money as well as a large number of missionaries. The three newly arisen Japanese religious groups mentioned above are, of course, exceptionally large; innumerable minor religious groups exist alongside them, and it may not be proper to compare Christianity only with these three larger entities. Even so, we are driven to conclude that the results achieved by Christianity during these hundred years are of little account when we remember what advantages Christianity possessed over other religions—the benefits of an organized theology, well-trained churchmen, substantial funds, and Western civilization.

At its inception, any religious group is in a minority and its activities can be classed as "deviant behavior"; but, as it acquires more and more adherents and sympathizers, it ceases to be a minority group and its activities come to be recognized as "modal behavior." Buddhism in Japan is a case in point. However, Christians are still very much in a minority and their practices still constitute "deviant behavior." The "tolerance limit of the community" toward this "deviant behavior" has been raised since the beginning of this century, and such behavior no longer attracts any degree of social pressure. It is, however, still "deviant behavior."

In this chapter, three questions concerning Christianity in Japan will be examined in detail. First, what was the social and individual character of those who embraced Christianity? Second, what was the source and the nature of the pressure on Christian converts? Third, were there not some elements intimately related with "modal behavior" in the activities of the Christians? The main object of the enquiry will be rural communities, where resistance to Christianity was stronger than in urban areas, and particular reference will be made to the Meiji period (1868–1912), when social pressures on Christianity were still strong. The main source materials are three sample studies of rural churches conducted by the author. As these churches differ in the date of foundation, scale, and affiliation, what emerges from a study of the three may be regarded as representing a general trend, the scope of which extends beyond the three samples.

The Character of Converts to Christianity

Annaka Church is Congregational and was founded in 1878. It is sited in Annaka, a country town that is one of the political, economic, and cultural centers of the western part of Gumma Prefecture. A large-scale rural church, it has a missionary area with a seven-mile radius. Of the first forty-four adherents of this church, thirty-seven were probably clansmen of the Annaka clan[3] and members of their families. These clansmen had a Bible-reading society even prior to the foundation of the church, so it seems that there was some sort of congeniality between them and Christianity.

There were two reasons for this congeniality. The first is that *samurai* were the largest literate class in Japan at the time and were able to gain a rough understanding of Christianity from reading a Chinese version of the Bible and such parts of a Japanese version as already existed. The second reason is that, deprived of their economic, political, and social privileges after the abolition of the

[3] The number of families connected with the Annaka clan in 1871 was 234 (Fukuchi 1956: Appendix).

clan system in 1871, they were looking for a new guiding principle to replace the old morality (Kataoka 1900); inflation had disorganized *samurai* domestic finances and, in addition, the disappearance of the feudal servant-master relationship had led to an internal crisis. These factors were applicable to the *samurai* class in general; in the case of Annaka, the first person to introduce Christianity was an Annaka clansman by the name of Joseph Niejima who had studied in America. Niejima's successor was also a *samurai*. Organizing a group of Christian converts was a new movement on the part of the Annaka clansmen in response to the days of suffering. However, as the economic situation of the *samurai* declined and inflation spiraled, more and more *samurai* left Annaka so that the church acquired fewer converts from among them.

Among the original forty-four adherents of Annaka Church there were five who were clearly not *samurai*. Among these five were the administrative head of a neighboring village, S. Uehara, and J. Yuasa, a manufacturer of bean-paste and soya sauce in Annaka, and his wife. Yuasa, typical of rising local businessmen, was quick to embrace the new ideas of the time, acquiring his knowledge from the then-famous magazine called *Meiroku Zasshi* and the writings of Yukichi Fukuzawa, a leading thinker of the early Meiji period. In 1892, Yuasa founded, at his own expense, an elementary library called Binransha, where people could read free of charge, and for a short period beginning in 1880 he ran a communal silkworm farm to help out the *samurai* believers. Yuasa contributed the mulberry trees and distributed the profits equally among the members. He was clearly a leader far ahead of his time and, to this extent, was "deviant." His deviation led him to a positive interest in new knowledge, techniques, and ways of thought. He became interested in Christianity and aligned himself with this progressive thinking precisely because it was a new, Western import (Yuasa 1932:133). Believing that religion is not so much something to be talked about as something to be practised, he became one of the pillars of the Annaka Church by putting the Christian concept of love into practice. The expansion of the Annaka Church was brought about by the proselytizing activities of its members assisted by their friends and relatives.

Since Yuasa was a businessman well-known and influential in the Annaka district, many of his friends and relatives were men of repute, up-and-coming businessmen, landowners, and rich farmers in villages within the missionary area. Proselytism spread from their friends and relatives to other friends and relatives and, as a result of this middle- and upper-class support, the church flourished. Among the 446 persons baptized between 1878 and 1887, there were few laborers or poor peasants. However, this is not to imply that the social character of Christianity had anything in common with the middle and upper classes in this community at the time; we must remember that only a small proportion of the middle and upper classes became converts. It is hard to believe that the staunchly conservative middle and upper classes would feel much affinity with the newly imported Christianity. It was only those among these classes interested in new ideas, impressed by the highly ethical lives led by Christians, and preoccupied with imitating this ethic themselves who were attracted to Christianity. Clearly, the middle and upper classes, with their greater resources, are more likely than the lower classes to adopt this attitude toward life; but in comparison with the attitudes held by the majority of the middle and upper classes, acceptance of Christianity must inevitably be regarded as "deviant behavior."

Why did Christianity fail to acquire more converts among the lower classes? The answer is comparatively easy. First, there was the view of the church as a kind of social club; once members of the middle and upper classes became the main body of a congregation, it was difficult for members of the lower classes to approach it and even those who had already joined were likely to fall away. In this aspect, the Christian church differs from the Buddhist parish in which one can maintain membership without active participation. In the second place, since for most members of the community the upper classes had a privileged position, the "tolerance limit" toward their deviant behavior was high. On the other hand, community pressure was sure to be exerted on the deviant behavior of members of the middle and especially the lower classes. Consequently, servants of upper-class Christians who joined the church found it difficult to retain their faith if they left their masters' employment (Morioka 1959).

Let us now consider the case of Shimamura Church, an American Methodist Episcopal institution founded in 1887 in Shimamura, Gumma Prefecture, a center of the silkworm-egg industry in the Kanto district. The church is small in scale, with a missionary area of two-mile radius. Between 1886 and 1900 this church acquired 111 converts. These first converts can be divided roughly into three groups: first, owners of silkworm-egg industry, particularly the powerful ones; second, their family members, servants, or branch households, and; third, other converts.

The social character of the first category is unique to Shimamura, and one can hardly find its counterpart among those who joined the Annaka Church, except perhaps for Yuasa. On the basis of wealth accumulated by the silkworm-egg industry, they were interested not only in learning and artistic activities as a refined hobby, but in a political movement against the despotic government. Admittedly, their attitudes, unfettered by tradition and very positive in introducing things new and advanced, helped them to accept Christianity. It should be remembered, however, that among about the 270 silkworm-egg industry owners then in Shimamura there were only 20 persons or less who confessed faith in God. Acceptance of Christianity was thus a sort of deviant behavior. Their contact with the European economic world through the channel of the silkworm-egg industry, with the attendant advantages of a broader outlook and increasing wealth, was undeniably one of the factors conducive to this deviant behavior. In the 1890's, however, the small-scale silkworm-egg industry of Shimamura suffered badly when overseas demand for silkworm-eggs ceased and big silk-reeling enterprises began to invade the silkworm-egg industry. As a result, the number of local industry owners fell to thirty or so, and the church ceased to make progress.

Converts of the second category conformed with the actions of the first. In other words, when the head of a family was baptized, the members of his family normally followed him *en bloc*, and his servants also tended to adopt their master's religion. If a branch household was dependent on the main household and the latter's head became a Christian, the head of the former was likely to follow suit. It seems that members of the second category became attached to the church indirectly through the first category converts and it is doubtful whether there were any real conversions among them deserving of the name (Morioka 1953).

Kusakabe Church is a Canadian Methodist foundation created in 1896, and situated in Kusakabe, a political center in the eastern part of Yamanashi Prefecture. The church is medium-sized, with a rural missionary area of a four-mile radius. Between 1896 and 1907, there were 145 baptisms. The character of the church members is typified by three early converts who did the greater part of the initial groundwork. They were Y. Koike, N. Iijima, and T. Nakazawa. Koike was baptized at Katsunuma Church (the mother church of Kusakabe Church) before he moved to the Kusakabe area; Iijima was baptized when he was in Tokyo and joined his local church when he came home; Nakazawa was baptized at Kusakabe Church.

Little is known of Koike beyond the fact that his father was in charge of Fukushima-ya, a pharmacy in Katsunuma. Iijima was an influential silk-reeling manufacturer, while Nakazawa was a typical silkworm and silkworm-egg raiser. All three were local industrial and commercial leaders. Most of the inhabitants of the missionary area gained their livelihood from agriculture or sericulture, and the Christian converts came from the industries connected with the mulberry tree—sericulture, the silkworm-egg industry, and silk-reeling manufacture. The number of such converts was ten or less, however, including Iijima and Nakazawa. When it is remembered that there were hundreds of owners of these industries in the area, one cannot, without going to extremes, find a causal relationship between mulberry tree-related industries and Christianity.

In comparison with rice culture, these industries are less controlled and limited by the regulations of a local community, and they demand, for market production, a broader outlook as well as a readiness for improvement in management. Such circumstances could have fostered, in the owners of those industries, a more or less open attitude toward Christianity. In addition to the social character unique to this class of people, we must also consider the personal characters of the leaders. Iijima and Nakazawa had positive interest in anything new and reasonable. They turned away from the outmoded ritual of Buddhism and the superstitions widely credited in the countryside. In contrast to these, Christianity was for them an ethical and reasonable faith essential to the new age (Nakazawa 1938:3). While such a characteristic led a few individuals to conversion, the great majority of industrialists held on to the traditional religions for the sake of convention, unattracted by Christianity. In this sense, the conversion of Iijima and others was deviant behavior (Morioka, 1965).

From the evidence left unrecorded as well as that presented above concerning these three local churches, the following conclusions emerge:

1. Conversion to Christianity occurred among the literate people of middle or upper classes in a community who, possibly due to the nature of their occupations, had a citydweller-like orientation. Influential industrialists and landlords, in particular, often became central figures in their church because of their financial contributions.

2. We can postulate an affinity between Christianity and the social character of those classes that produced a comparatively large number of converts, but it still appears that the attitude toward life of the individual convert played the decisive role. Since a great majority of people stuck to traditional Buddhism, conversion must be classed as deviant behavior.

Social Pressures on Deviant Behavior

Let us now discuss who exerted social pressure on Christian converts and what forms it took. I must first explain, however, why conversion to Christianity and subsequent acquisition of church membership is "deviant behavior." The inevitability of social pressure against it will then become obvious.

Religion in the Japanese rural community can be roughly divided into religion of the household and religion of the local community. The former centers on rituals for the dead officiated by a Buddhist priest. Religious observance involving the whole community is Shinto shrine-centered and is offered for the welfare and prosperity of the community (for an abundant harvest, for example). The villager almost invariably participates in both forms of religious observance. Since the Christian acknowledges no gods but Jehovah, he must stand outside such institutionalized behavior patterns.

While affiliation to a Buddhist temple is traditionally determined, there is a margin of choice between temples. Thus, a shift from Buddhism to Christianity will be met with disapproval, but the choice itself is possible. Affiliation to a Shinto shrine, however, is not a matter of choice but is determined by residence in a given community. This is because affiliation to a shrine is the religious manifestation of a sharing of community life. Hence, renunciation of one's shrine parish membership by withdrawal from Shinto religious observance tends to imply withdrawal from community life as well.

In order to demonstrate their decision to completely dissociate themselves from Buddhism and Shintoism, Christian converts disposed of their household altars—both Buddhist and Shinto —either by burning them or by storing them in some out-of-the-way place, such as the corner of the outhouse. Neighbors did not look favorably on such acts, for the Buddhist altar was believed to be the resting place of the ancestors' spirits, and to dispose of it was regarded as extremely unfilial. Conformity with community norms and filial piety were the two principal canons of rural life.

When Christianity was banned by the Tokugawa Shogunate, Christians were everywhere sought out and subjected to the most severe penalties. No opportunity was missed to depict Christianity as en evil religion. Even the Meiji government at first adopted an inhospitable attitude toward it so that, at the end of the nineteenth century, conversion to Christianity meant the jettisoning of traditional Japanese values and contamination by undesirable Western customs. Further, to become a Christian was considered to be working against the interests of Japan as a pawn of the West.

We have concluded that conversion to Christianity was deviant behavior, in that only a few persons were baptized and that the social character of the classes that produced a relatively large number of Christians was not a decisive factor in conversion. The cultural background just described supports the argument. We must now enquire into the source and the forms of social pressure brought to bear on this deviant behavior.

First, where the head of a family remained unconverted, it was difficult for any member of that family to change his religion. Even when a member was converted to Christianity, it remained difficult for him to exercise an influence on other members of his family. A Christian wife in her husband's parental home, where neither husband nor parents-in-law were Christians, tended soon to withdraw from the church and eventually lose her faith. Where the household religion was Buddhism, pressure to apostatize was exerted on any Christian member within the family. There were examples of such intrahousehold pressure in both the Annaka and the Kusakabe Churches.

In the second place, there was community pressure against Christians, which was often informally exercised. Non-Christians insulted Christians with such phrases as, "*Yaso, Miso, Inu no Kuso*" (Jesus, bean-paste, dog-muck), taunted them with fanatical songs, such as "*Yasokyō Taiji*" (Down with Christianity), and stoned their houses at night. The children of Christians were shunned as playmates by other children. There are examples of this kind of community disapproval in each of the three churches under discussion.

In Haraichi, for instance, which is in the missionary area of Annaka Church, Christians refused to contribute money to religious festivals at the Shinto shrine. Enraged non-Christians in the area decided, after discussion, to leave Christians out of the social life of the community and to boycott all shops run by Christians.

Organized antagonism on the part of Buddhists was led either by priests or by influential laymen.[4] Opposition often took the form of Buddhist lecture meetings, which were designed to denounce Christianity by oratory. It is reported that this sort of opposition occurred in Annaka and Shimamura in the late 1880's and in Kusakabe in the 1890's. When Annaka Christians also held lecture meetings in response, both sides claimed with equal confi-

---

[4] In Shimamura, Buddhist opposition was led by silkworm-egg industrialists. For this reason, it is maintained that the silkworm-egg industry and Christianity did not necessarily go together.

dence to have won the day. These controversies between Buddhism and Christianity, like those carried on between Catholic missionaries and Buddhist academics in the middle of the sixteenth century (Okada 1956:41–53), exemplified the debate between the widely divergent ideological worlds of East and West, where successful persuasion of the opposite side was almost impossible. For the audience, common-sense lectures by Buddhist priests were more understandable, and Buddhist lecture meetings were effective to some extent in turning public opinion against Christianity.

Persecution of Christians by individual Buddhist priests focused on the problem of graves. Before conversion Christians were affiliated to a Buddhist temple, and the graves of their families were situated in many cases in a corner of the temple precincts. After conversion, when death occurred to their families, they found it almost impossible to secure new cemetery plots elsewhere and attempted to retain the original sites. But the Buddhist priests who had control of the temple properties, either refused to allow Christian converts to continue to use their plots or insisted that, if they wanted to use the original family plot, they should apply to the priests for a Buddhist-style funeral service. Such instances occurred both in Annaka and Kusakabe.

How did the Christians manage to bear up under such social pressure and persecution? They apparently exercised remarkable patience and endurance. On the other hand, persecution generally did not mount beyond the bounds of what was bearable for them. That this was so was largely attributable to two factors. First, the central Christian figures were often men of local repute, and it was their fame and authority that took the edge off the severity of the persecution of Christianity. Second, even within the deviant patterns of life that Christianity involved, there were some elements of "modal behavior" shared by ordinary people.

"Modal Behavior" in Christian Converts

We might hypothesize that, the social cohesion of the community and the readiness of Buddhists for mobilization being constant, if the deviation had been greater and the tolerance limit of the community to the deviation lower, then the social persecution would likely have become more severe. However, the inadequacy of documents in the Meiji period does not enable us to make a comparative study of the three model churches to verify this particular hypothesis. Instead, I now wish to show that "deviant behavior" was in fact interwoven with "modal behavior."

Both in Annaka and in Shimamura, Christians dissociated themselves from the Buddhist parish once and for all by contracting an arrangement whereby the Christians paid for the use of their plots in the temple cemetery. In Kusakabe, however, Christians did not renounce parish membership, and accordingly many of them continued to perform some of the essential duties of parishioners, making presents to the priest at the Bon (Buddhist All Souls' Day) Festival and at the year-end. In the matter of the funeral service, not a few Christians arranged to be buried according to both Christian and Buddhist rites, although the one ritual was usually much simpler than the other.

There were places where Christians refused to share the festival expenses of the Shinto shrine dedicated to the community guardian deities, as happened in Annaka; but in Shimamura and Kusakabe, Christians shared such expenses, even though they did not visit the shrine on festival days. The intention behind such donations was not so much to give financial aid for the maintenance of the Shinto shrine as to keep good relations with neighbors who were non-Christians.

Shinto and Buddhist household altars and small shrines for house-site guardian deities were sometimes thrown away or burnt by Christians during the early period immediately following the foundation of a church. But in later years when the spirit of youthful proselytizing zest was almost gone, such household altars were left as they stood, simply ceasing to be objects of worship, though care was taken not to handle them roughly. As the Christians' faith became weaker, some of these household altars came back into use. Their appearance, at least, became similar to that in the non-Christian households. A survey conducted in 1935 in a part of the missionary area of Kusakabe Church identified the traditional religious facilities and practices listed in Table 23 in eleven Christian households. The survey has some shortcomings; it failed to distinguish between families where all members were converted to Christianity *en bloc* and families where only certain members were Christians, and between objects actually used for worship and those not so used. Nor is it clear how their involvement in folk religious practices were discerned. Nevertheless, information in Table 23 makes clear that a surprisingly large number of folk religious practices remained even in Christian households.

Even though there was no longer a Buddhist altar in the house, Christians held memorial services for their ancestors on the days dedicated to ancestor veneration, such as Bon and the equinoxes. Since there were non-Christians among the relatives and neighbors attending such services, the altar was arranged in such a way as not to discomfort Buddhists. Again, in the case of funeral services, the basic pattern of arrangements followed was Buddhist, since the neighbors of a bereaved family were customarily in charge of all preparations, and most of them remained Buddhist.

As the foregoing discussions have clearly shown, there were many elements of modal behavior interwoven with the deviant behavior of Christians; the modal formed a basis for the deviant, and the gulf between them was bridged as far as possible. It was due to this syncretism that a local Christian church could be established and maintained as an institution surviving social pressures.

Reconciliation between deviant behavior and modal behavior can be achieved not only when the deviant is accommodated in part to the modal but also when the deviant behavior becomes modal through an increase in its influence and the number of its supporters.

The Christian moral reform movement chose this second course with success. The movement focused on abstinence from alcohol and tobacco and strict observance of monogamy. Any convert who did not terminate relations with his concubine, divorced his wife without proper grounds, associated with prostitutes, or acted in any other way contrary to the dictates of Christian sexual morality was excluded from church membership or deprived of the privilege of taking holy communion. This sort of instance occurred both in Annaka and Shimamura. In Annaka, two Christians who had been running brothels changed their trade due to the influ-

Table 23

Traditional Religious Facilities and Practices in Christian Households
(Kanoiwa Town, Yamanashi Prefecture, 1935)

Ref. number of family household	Shinto Altar	Buddhist Altar	Ancestor Rites	Grave Visits	Observance of Folk Religious Practices
1	Yes	Yes	Bon, Equinoxes and Anniversaries of Death	Yes	Tenrikyo, Ontake-san, the Sun, *Tenjin* (the Deified Spirit of *Michizane*), *Suijin* (the God of Water), House-site guardian deity
2	Yes	Yes	Bon, Equinoxes and Anniversaries of Death	Yes	House-site guardian deity
3	Yes	Yes	Bon and Equinoxes	Bon and Equinoxes	The Sun, *Tenjin, Suijin,* House-site guardian deity, *Dōsoshin* (the Village-boundary Guardian Deity), the Moon, *Toshigami* (the God of a Good Crop and Happiness for the Year), *Jizō* (Guardian Boddhisattva of children)
4	Yes	Yes	Bon, Equinoxes and Anniversaries of Death	Bon, Equinoxes and Anniversaries of Death	The Sun

5	Yes	Yes	Bon and Equinoxes	Monthly	The Sun, *Sujin*, *Dōsoshin*, the Moon, *Toshigami*
6	Yes	Yes	Bon, Equinoxes and Anniversaries of Death	Bon, Equinoxes and Anniversaries of Death	The Sun, *Dōsoshin*, the Moon, *Toshigami*
7	Yes	Yes	Bon, Equinoxes and Anniversaries of Death	Bon, Equinoxes and Anniversaries of Death	*Dōsoshin*, *Ubusunagami* (the Tutelary Deity of One's Birthplace)
8	Yes	Yes	Bon	Monthly	House-site guardian deity
9	No	No	Bon, Equinoxes and Anniversaries of Death	Bon, Equinoxes and Anniversaries of Death	House-site guardian deity, *Dōsoshin*, the Moon, Stars
10	No	No	No	No	The Sun
11	Yes	Yes	No	No	*Sujin*, *Dōsoshin*, *Toshigami*, *Yakushi* (the Boddhisattva of Medical Care)

SOURCE: Yamanashi Women's Normal School (ed.), *Bisai Kyōdo Kenkyū* (An Intensive Study of Kanōiwa Town), 1937, p. 251.

ence of the church; one became a news agent and the other a silk cocoon broker.

The Annaka Church conducted a forceful campaign against adultery and, in cooperation with other churches in Gumma Prefecture, vigorously promoted a movement to make prostitution illegal. In 1893 this movement gained a triumphant success by crushing the tenacious opposition of those who had vested interests in the continuation of the brothels. Among the leaders of this movement were J. Yuasa, Speaker of the Gumma Prefecture Assembly, and J. Miyaguchi, Deputy Speaker, both of whom were members of the Annaka Church. Z. Tajima, a member of the Shimamura Church, also played a part in this successful crusade, as a member of the Assembly. It was not until after World War II that anti-prostitution legislation was passed on a nation-wide scale, but its origin can be traced to the Annaka Church.

As regards abstinence from alcohol and tobacco, there are anecdotes in Annaka and Shimamura that a brewer became a soya sauce manufacturer after conversion and that men who resolved to give up smoking either locked their pipes in a wooden box or threw them into the rapids of the Tone River. Lecture meetings were held repeatedly advocating abstinence from smoking and drinking. The campaign against alcohol in Kusakabe was particularly energetic: it was the cornerstone of the evangelical activities of the Kusakabe Church since total abstinence was considered to be the gateway to Christianity. Around 1896, the Higashiyamanashi Temperance Association was formed in the church; the core of its membership was Christian but there were also many non-Christian members. Temperance associations were formed in several places within the missionary area, some of them even achieving a membership that included all the young people of a village. As this movement attracted more and more non-Christians, it increasingly lost its Christian character. The advocacy of temperance was thus able to stand outside the sphere of deviant Christian practice.

In rivalry with the anti-alcohol movement of the Christian churches, Buddhist priests advocated a sort of semi-temperance during the period of funeral services and anniversaries of death only. The term for this was *butsuji-kinshu* (temperance on the occasion of a Buddhist service), and in parts of the Kusakabe district Buddhist priests were successful to the point of organizing temperance associations. *Butsuji-kinshu* was a half-measure and, though it appeared an easy alternative, it failed to exert as strong a social influence as the total abstinence of Christians and amounted to no more than a passive countermeasure on the part of the Buddhists. In rather the same way, it may be remembered, Buddhists merely held lecture meetings in an attempt to counter the active missionary work of the Christians.

There were many other institutional works that originated with Christianity and later became modal behavior; among them, in Annaka and Kusakabe, were high schools for girls, Sunday schools, use of such Western musical instruments as the organ, private English schools, cooking classes, and so on. These institutions and practices made the Christian church the cultural center of its district during the Meiji period (1868–1912). However, as the Buddhist temple and secular agents adopted items that had been under Christian monopoly, the appeal of the churches inevitably diminished. In other words, the Christians' deviant behavior, which had been subject to social pressure, lost prominence as it was syncretized, whereas their deviant behavior provoking social respect or envy became widely accepted and absorbed into modal behavior. Through these processes, the unique characteristics of Christianity in the early Meiji period were eventually lost.

8. THE IMPACT OF DEMOGRAPHIC CHANGES ON CHRISTIAN CHURCHES*

Introduction

Clarification of the geographic distribution of contemporary religious practices and its explanation by means of historical, economic, and social factors appear to be a dominant approach among the sociological studies of religion in Europe, particularly in France (Boulard 1960; Anzai 1962). This approach is, precisely speaking, in the field of ecology of religion, rather than in that of sociology of religion. The ecology of religion inquires into the geographic distribution of religious groups, group members, and religious practices, and delineates its conditions and religious consequences. Therefore, the ecology of religion ought to include, in addition to the problems covered by European scholars, research on the influences that an increase or a decrease, or an influx or outflow, of population and changes in transportation facilities have on religious groups (Moberg 1962:44–47). This chapter attempts to analyze one of the most crucial problems facing contemporary religions in Japan, namely, the influences exerted on local religious bodies by demographic changes resulting from the recent rapid growth of Japan's economy.

I chose member churches of the United Church of Christ in Japan as the object of this study for three reasons. First, since the individual rather than the household was made the basic unit for compilation of church statistics, our conception was applicable to their materials. Second, their materials were found on the whole

* The author is greatly indebted to Dr. Yoshiya Abe, a section chief at the Japan Society for the Promotion of Science, who made the translation of the original draft.

to be so precise and reliable as to permit a scientific analysis. Finally, their materials were accessible.

Materials and Methods of Research

The present study will examine the effects of demographic changes on Christian churches in a limited area, postponing a large-scale or nation-wide survey to another occasion. The following three criteria were set up and applied in selecting my field of research:

1. Districts where demographic changes show marked contrast. This criterion will facilitate discovering the relations between church membership and population size in a given district.

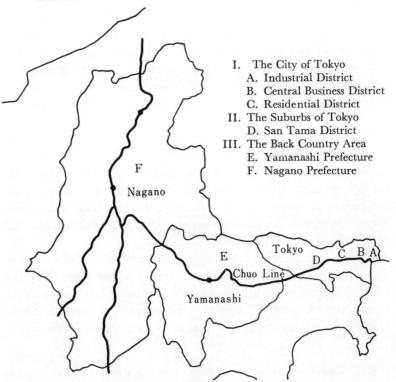

I.   The City of Tokyo
   A. Industrial District
   B. Central Business District
   C. Residential District
II. The Suburbs of Tokyo
   D. San Tama District
III. The Back Country Area
   E. Yamanashi Prefecture
   F. Nagano Prefecture

Map 2   Areas along the Chuo Line

2. Districts adjoining one another, rather than those scattered over a wide area. Adjacent districts are desirable because they are expected to have some common background as well as differences in their type of population mobility.
3. Districts in and around Tokyo. Field surveys to supplement the quantitative observations can be conducted more easily than in any other area because the principal investigator and his assistant are living in Tokyo.

Five districts meeting the above criteria were selected along the Chuo Line, a major commuter railway that runs through downtown Tokyo, its western suburbs, and the back country areas. To them, I added the eastern section of Tokyo, so that an industrial district would be represented. The field was thus composed of six districts, which are indicated by letters of the alphabet, as shown below.

1. The City of Tokyo
    A. Industrial District
       Koto-ku, Sumida-ku, Katsushika-ku, Edogawa-ku
    B. Central Business District
       Chiyoda-ku, Shinjuku-ku

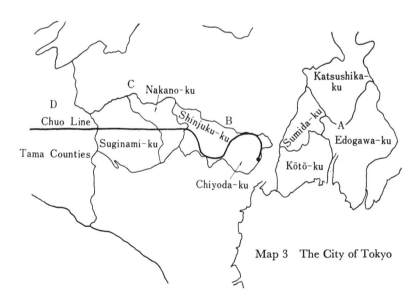

Map 3   The City of Tokyo

    C. Residential District
       Nakano-ku, Suginami-ku
  2. The Suburbs of Tokyo
    D. San Tama District
  3. Back Country
    E. Yamanashi District
       Yamanashi Prefecture
    F. Nagano District
       Nagano Prefecture

These six adjoining districts differ markedly in terms of their trends in population mobility. As of 1966, there were 172 churches and preaching centers within this area affiliated with the United Church of Christ in Japan.

The indices of measuring the growth of a Christian church vary widely in accordance with one's interest and viewpoint. The opinion that the growth of a church is subject to the decision of God, transcending human knowledge, or that religion is a matter of the individual's inner spiritual life and is not to be measured by external manifestations, are quite valuable from certain points of view. The present study, however, places these opinions aside and deals with the growth of a church only in terms of human and external indices. Among external indicators are the sum of offerings, the number of newly baptized members, the number of catechumens, the frequency and kinds of meetings held and the number of participants therein, the number of church school students, the number of communicant members, and so on. Of all these, the last-named is the most basic, because the sum of offerings depends largely upon it, and newly baptized members and catechumens either immediately or eventually become communicant members. The present study, therefore, makes use of the number of communicant members in order to represent the growth of a church.

An annual report of a definite form is submitted to the headquarters of the United Church of Christ in Japan from each member church and preaching center. This report provides information relevant to this study, including the number of communicant members. Part A of the report gives the number of various kinds of members and of participants by types of activities, and Part B is a financial report. Part A, then, concerns us here.

Table 24
Distribution of Churches by Submission of Annual Reports

District \ Annual Report	Total	Annual Reports 5 years	Annual Reports less than 4 years	No Annual Reports
A Industrial				
District	26(8)	14(2)	11(6)	1
Sumida-ku	5	4	1	
Kōtō-ku	7(3)	1	6(3)	
Katsushika-ku	8(4)	5(2)	2(2)	1
Edogawa-ku	6(1)	4	2(1)	
B Central				
Business District	19(1)	18(1)	1	
Chiyoda-ku	4	4		
Shinjuku-ku	15(1)	14(1)	1	
C Residential				
District	40(3)	35(1)	3(2)	2
Nakano-ku	14(1)	11	1(1)	2
Suginami-ku	26(3)	24(1)	2(1)	
D Suburban				
District	39(8)	25(2)	12(6)	2
E Back Country (Yamanashi)	15(1)	12	3(1)	
F Back Country (Nagano)	33(5)	28(2)	5(3)	
Total	172(26)	132(8)	35(18)*	5

The figures in parentheses indicate preaching centers.
* Seven of 18 preaching centers were founded after 1961.

Of 172 churches and preaching centers in the area, the 132 (76.7%) that submitted reports for all five consecutive years between 1960 and 1964[1] were selected as the objects of analyses in order to maintain comparability of the data (Table 24). Thereupon, I tried to determine the qualitative trend of the districts rather than that of each local church. The ratio of the selected

[1] The annual reports between 1960 and 1964 were made available to me thanks to the good offices of the Reverend Ryōzō Hara of the Research Institute on the Mission of the Church, the United Church of Christ in Japan.

Table 25

Distribution of Churches by Founding Date

District	Until 1885	1886–1895	1896–1905	1906–1915	1916–1925	1926–1935	1936–1945	1946–1955	1956–1965	Unknown	Total
All the churches in the area											
A Industrial District	2	1	1		2	3	1	14(7)	2(1)		26(8)
B Central Business District		2	1	4	3	1	1	7(1)			19(1)
C Residential District	4	1	1	1	4	8	6	13(1)	2(2)		40(3)
D Suburban District		1	1		2	3	2(1)	21(3)	9(4)		39(8)
E Back Country (Yamanashi)	1	2	4		2	1		2	3(1)		15(1)
F Back Country (Nagano)	3	7	2	4	2(1)	4	1	6(2)	3(2)	1	33(5)
Total	10	14	10	9	15(1)	20	11(1)	63(14)	19(10)	1	172(26)
Percentage	5.8	8.1	5.8	5.2	8.7	11.6	6.4	36.6	11.0	0.6	100.0
Churches studied											
A Industrial District	2	1	1			2		8(2)			14(2)
B Central Business District		2	1	3	3	1	1	7(1)			18(1)
C Residential District	4			1	5	8	6	11(1)			35(1)
D Suburban District			1		1	2	2(1)	15(1)	4		25(2)
E Back Country (Yamanashi)	1	2	3		2	1		2	1		12
F Back Country (Nagano)	3	7	2	3	2(1)	4	1	4(1)	1	1	28(2)
Total	10	12	8	7	13(1)	18	10(1)	47(6)	6	1	132(8)
Percentage	7.6	9.1	6.1	5.3	9.8	13.6	7.6	35.6	4.5	0.8	100.0

The figures in parentheses indicate preaching centers.

churches against the total was 53.9% in district A, 94.7% in district B, 87.5% in district C, 64.1% in district D, 80.0% in district E, and 84.8% in district F. Since the figures for districts A and D are relatively low, special care should be taken in interpreting their data. However, an examination of the founding dates by ten-year periods (Table 25) proves that the sample well represents the distribution of the total, except those local bodies founded later than 1956.[2] Thus, it should be possible to observe the general trend by means of the data at our disposal.

Analysis

The present chapter attempts to determine the growth of Christian churches using the number of communicant members as an index. The increase or decrease of members is represented by the balance of the number of members of the year N and that of the year N plus 1, and this balance is attributable to the activities of the members in the year N rather than in the year N plus 1. Therefore, the ratio of the increase or decrease is designated by the percentage of the actual number of the increase or the decrease against the number of the members in the year N. If we compare 1960 and 1964 and identify the growth rate for each district, the actual number of increase or decrease shall be contrasted against the total of communicant members in the district for the four consecutive years between 1960 and 1963. The totals are shown in the far left column of Table 26. On the basis of this number, I calculated the district average of communicant members per year, the average membership of a local body, and then the average of growth or decrease of a local body for the four years. The central three columns of Table 26 show these figures.

First, the average number of communicant members indicates that the size of a church varies remarkably according to districts. The churches in the central business district are the biggest (170

[2] I eliminated all those churches and preaching centers founded later than 1961 from the sample since the analysis was confined to those that submitted complete reports from 1960 to 1964. It is an unavoidable limitation of the present study, therefore, that the bodies founded later than 1956 were not well represented.

Table 26

Changes in Church Membership, 1960–1964

(△ indicates decrease)

District	1960–1963 Cumulative	1960–1963 Average per year		1960–1964	
	Total communicants		Communicants per church	Increase per church	Increase per 100 members
A Industrial District	5,022	1,255.5	89.7	△0.7	△0.8
B Central Business District	12,210	3,052.5	169.6	△5.1	△3.0
C Residential District	12,838	3,209.5	91.7	10.5	11.5
D Suburban District	6,394	1,598.5	63.9	14.2	22.2
E Back Country (Yamanashi)	2,606	651.5	54.3	△3.2	△5.9
F Back Country (Nagano)	5,600	1,400.0	50.0	△2.0	△4.0

members on the average), and are followed at a considerable interval by the churches in the residential and the industrial districts (90 members on the average). The average size of churches in the suburbs is even smaller (64 members), and finally, churches in the back country areas are the smallest (54–50 members). Thus, the size of churches shows a gradient with the peak in the central business district, which lowers toward the peripheral agrarian area. In explaining this gradient, we should take into account such factors as the different developmental stage of each district, the difference in the founding date of the churches, and the size and population density of the territory of the churches.

Second, in terms of the cumulative changes in the size of a church over the four years, the suburbs record the largest increase (14 members per church), which is followed by the residential district (11 members), whereas the industrial district shows a slight decrease. The central business district records a decrease of 5 members per church, and the back country areas a decrease of 2–3 members. When we calculate the increase or decrease per 100 members in each district, this point becomes more apparent: the increase in the suburbs and the decrease in the back country areas are quite remarkable (see the far right column in Table 26). If we were to take the Chuo Line from Tokyo Station, we would successively pass by the big downtown churches with a definitely decreasing membership, the relatively well built churches of the residential district in which membership has markedly increased until recent times, the smaller but rapidly developing churches of the suburban area, and the smallest churches of the back country areas which have suffered a considerable loss of membership.

Such is a comparison of the churches in the six districts seen through the increase and the decrease of membership during the five consecutive years. The annual increase or decrease of membership is, of course, the balance of the increase and the decrease that occur each year. I next classified the increases and decreases according to their causes and compared the cumulative numbers for five years by districts and causes. Among the causes of increase, namely baptism, moving-in, confirmation, and revival of inactive members, the first two were much more numerous than others. Among the causes of decrease were death, moving-out, and dropping-out, which were all important quantitatively. Moving-out and dropping-out are both the removal of living persons from membership in a church, but the former is accompanied by a formal procedure of transference to another Christian church, while the latter is not. A dropout was defined as one who has neglected his duties as a church member for three years or longer. In most cases the dropping-out is not only from a particular church but also from Christianity as such. A main cause for it is one's departure from the community where one's church is located.

Increase or decrease of population is usually classified as natural or social. Natural increase or decrease is the balance of births and deaths, and social increase or decrease that of influx and outflow. When this classification is applied to growth and decline of church membership, natural increase or decrease corresponds to the balance of baptisms and deaths, and social increase or decrease to that of moving-in and moving-out by church members, or that of moving-in and moving-out plus dropping-out. By classifying the causes of increase or decrease into these two kinds, we can study the changing size of the churches in each district with more precision. In order to facilitate observation, I prepared Table 27, where

Table 27
Changes in Church Membership Analyzed by Causes,
1960–1964

	Increase or De-crease($\triangle$)	Baptism	Moving-in	Others	Death	Moving-out	Dropping-out and others
Actual numbers							
A	$\triangle$10	270	71	9	32	57	113
B	$\triangle$92	503	254	48	87	220	30
C	369	608	437	59	93	275	101
D	356	423	409	22	65	131	26
E	$\triangle$39	161	45	14	35	73	50
F	$\triangle$55	376	125	18	49	208	53
Percentage against 4 years accumulation							
A	$\triangle$0.2	5.4	1.4	0.2	0.6	1.1	2.3
B	$\triangle$0.8	4.1	2.1	0.4	0.7	1.8	0.2
C	2.9	4.7	3.4	0.5	0.7	2.1	0.8
D	5.6	6.6	6.4	0.3	1.0	2.0	1.2
E	$\triangle$1.5	6.2	1.7	0.5	1.3	2.8	1.9
F	$\triangle$1.0	6.7	2.2	0.3	0.9	3.7	0.9

cumulative numbers for five years by causes of increase and decrease are noted, coupled with their percentages against the total
membership of the four consecutive years from 1960 to 1963.
Table 28 was compiled on the basis of Table 27 so that the contrast of the two kinds of increase becomes clearer.

Table 28
Natural Increase and Social Increase in Church Membership,
1960–1964
($\triangle$ indicates decrease)

District	Natural Increase	Social Increase			Balance	
	(a) baptism —death	(b) moving-in —moving-out	(c) mov.-in —(mov.-out +drop.-out)		(a)+(c)	a+b
A Industrial District	4.8%	0.3%	$\triangle$2.0%		2.8	(5.1)%
B Central Business District	3.4	0.3	0.1		3.5	(3.7)
C Residential District	4.0	1.3	0.6		4.6	(5.3)
D Suburban District	5.6	4.4	3.2		8.8	(10.0)
E Back Country (Yamanashi)	4.9	$\triangle$1.1	$\triangle$3.0		1.9	(3.8)
F Back Country (Nagano)	5.8	$\triangle$1.5	$\triangle$2.4		3.4	(4.3)

As Table 28 shows, the central business district (3.4%) and the
residential district (4.0%) had lower rates of natural increase than
the suburbs (5.6%), the back country areas (4.9–5.8%) and the
industrial district (4.8%). The central business district and the
suburbs are at opposite extremes in this regard. Referring to Table
27, we may well assume that the different rates of natural increase
depend largely on the number of the baptized, as the death rate
does not vary greatly anywhere. The number of the baptized per
100 church members is the smallest in the central business district
(4.1), the highest in the suburban (6.6) and the back country
(6.2–6.7) areas, and in between in the residential (4.7) and the
industrial (5.4) districts. The aforementioned loss of membership
in the back country areas, which took place in spite of the high

rate of baptisms, may be explainable only in terms of a greater social decrease.

The greatest social decrease is revealed, as anticipated, in the back country areas, in contrast to the greatest social increase in the suburbs. As is obvious in Table 27, the influx is quite conspicuous in the suburbs (6.4%), while the ratio is much lower in the industrial district (1.4%), the central business district (2.1%), and the back country areas (1.7–2.2%). On the other hand, the largest outflow is recorded in the back country areas (2.8–3.7%), and the smallest in the industrial district (1.1%). While dropping-out is most conspicuous in the industrial district (2.3%), it is much less in the central business district (0.2%). To sum up, the suburban areas have the greatest social increase due to the high rate of influx, and, contrastingly, the back country areas have a radical social decrease caused by a marked outflow. The decrease in the industrial district must primarily be ascribed to the high ratio of dropping-out. In the central business district, influx and outflow plus dropping-out are in equilibrium, so that there is neither increase nor decrease worthy of note. In the residential district, however, the influx exceeds the outflow and dropping-out, so that there is a social increase.

The balance of natural increase and social increase must be equal to the total increase. However, the figures in the far left column of Table 27, which show the total increase, and those in the far right column of Table 28, which indicate the crude balance, are far from being identical. This is because a significant difference between the two kinds of figures was noticeable in the annual reports from individual churches and preaching centers. The difference is assumed to be derived from the tendency of ministers to report the increase accurately and the decrease inadequately. Hence, the left column of Table 27 is more reliable than the column on the far right of Table 28. Consequently we shall make little reference to the latter in the following summary.

The decrease in the back country areas, to begin with, is not because of a low rate of baptism. It is rather high there, and yet the baptized move into the metropolitan areas, thus causing a large number of cases of outflow and dropout. On the other hand, the decrease in the central business district is due to a lower rate of baptism, together with a relatively high rate of outflow. In the suburban areas, where the numbers of baptism and moving-in are both large, total church membership is growing steadily. In the residential district, the tendency is the same as in the suburbs, but the growth rate is lower. In the industrial district, though baptisms are not few in number, dropouts are more numerous, and consequently the total membership is on the decrease.

Relationship to Demographic Change of the Community

The growth of Christian churches observed in terms of increase or decrease of the communicants has, it is assumed from the foregoing analyses, a close relationship to population mobility of the respective communities. The relationship is such that population mobility of the communities is the independent variable and the growth of Christian churches indicated by the number of communicants is the dependent variable. There may, of course, be several intermediary variables, but it is unlikely that the causality between the two variables is reversed or that these two are dependent variables of any other basic factor. We must examine, therefore, how close a relationship exists between the two.

The local community corresponding to a particular Christian church is the area where its members are numerous and for which it is evangelically responsible. But it is difficult to delineate such an area for each of the 132 churches and preaching centers. Moreover, such an area cuts across the boundaries of local municipalities, which are government statistical units, and hence it is virtually impossible to compile statistical data on population mobility for each missionary area. Thus, for convenience' sake, I regard the local municipality in which a church exists as the local community representing the missionary area of the church.

How great, then, is the discrepancy between the local municipality and the evangelic area of a church? A clue to determining the gap between them is provided by the geographic distribution of the officers of a church, which we can secure from the annual reports. Table 29 shows the distribution of the churches by percentages of the officers who live within the boundary of the munic-

Table 29
Ratio of In-Community Resident Officers of Churches to
Total Number of Officers (Relationship between Christian
Churches and Corresponding Municipalities)

District / Percentage	A	B	C	D	E	F	Total
under 25%		9	7	3		1	20
under 50%	3	7	12	3	1	1	27
under 75%	6	2	10	8	4	1	31
over 75%	5		6	11	7	25	54
Total	14	18	35	25	12	28	132

ipality in which the church is located. (They are classified into
four groups: less than 25%, 25% or more but less than 50%, 50%
or more but less than 75%, and 75% or more.) In the back
country areas, the officers reside mainly within the local municipalities of the churches. This suggests that members' residences are
concentrated in the missionary area of a church. In the suburbs and
in the industrial district, the officers' concentration in the local
community is relatively marked. But, in the residential district,
the ratio is about 50%, and in the central business district it is
definitively lower. In Table 30 I compared church membership
with the total population of all the local municipalities concerned
in each district. If we define the local community in this broad
sense, the ratio of the in-community residence of officers must be
higher than shown on Table 29. Therefore, the discrepancy between the evangelic area and the local municipality may be considered smaller. Nonetheless, the low correspondence between the
location of the officers' residence and the municipality in the
central business district demands a special prudence in examining
the growth or decline of churches there in terms of population
mobility.

Table 30 shows the growth rates of the Christian churches by
years and districts, contrasted with those of the total population of
the municipalities in which the churches are located. The growth
rates of both the Christian churches and the total population are
the highest in the suburbs, with the latter even greater than the
former. This implies that further development of the Christian
churches in the suburban area may well be expected, beyond the

Comparison of Growth Rates of Church Membership and District Population
(△ indicates decrease)

	Year	Membership	Increase	Inc. rate	Population	Increase	Inc. rate
A	1960	1,178	74	6.2	1,376,213	37,167	2.7
	1961	1,252	24	1.9	1,413,380	35,597	2.5
Industrial	1962	1,276	40	3.1	1,449,927	35,702	2.5
District	1963	1,316	△148	△11.2	1,485,629	26,886	1.8
	1964	1,168			1,512,517		
B	1960	2,883	228	7.9	530,634	2,854	0.5
	1961	3,111	△1	△0.0	533,488	△3,556	△0.7
Central	1962	3,110	△4	△0.1	529,932	△2,423	△0.5
Business	1963	3,106	△315	△10.1	527,509	△9,110	△1.7
District	1964	2,791			518,399		
C	1960	2,977	156	5.2	838,570	20,212	2.4
	1961	3,133	112	3.6	858,782	13,148	1.5
Residential	1962	3,245	238	7.3	871,930	10,445	1.2
District	1963	3,483	△137	△3.9	882,385	△5,119	△0.6
	1964	3,346			877,266		
D	1960	1,464	50	3.4	914,788	65,128	7.1
	1961	1,514	118	7.7	979,916	83,530	8.5
Suburban	1962	1,632	152	9.3	1,063,446	92,893	8.7
District	1963	1,784	36	2.0	1,156,339	147,113	12.7
	1964	1,820			1,303,472		
E	1960	679	△7	△1.0	375,850	2,337	0.6
	1961	672	△37	△5.5	378,187	2,636	0.7
Back Country	1962	635	△15	△2.3	380,823	2,771	0.7
(Yamanashi)	1963	620	20	3.2	383,594	2,553	0.7
	1964	640			386,147		
F	1960	1,408	△7	△0.5	977,127	1,687	0.2
	1961	1,401	6	0.4	978,814	2,069	0.2
Back Country	1962	1,407	△23	△1.6	980,883	4,615	0.5
(Nagano)	1963	1,384	△31	△2.2	985,498	8,323	0.8
	1964	1,353			993,821		

considerable progress that has already been achieved. In the residential district, where the growth rate of church membership is
next highest after the suburban area, the increase rate is larger
than that of the total population. This suggest an affinity to
Christianity among white-collar workers who constitute the majority of the population moving into the residential district. In
the back country areas, where the ratio of decrease in church
membership is the highest, the total population remains almost
the same with no sign of decrease. But if we observe the age composition of the population of these areas, we are reminded of the
salient fact that outflow occurs mostly among the younger generation. It is the outflow of the younger generation that is linked to
the moving-out and dropping-out of Christians and leads to a
decrease in church membership in these areas.[3] In the central
business district, both church membership and the total population are decreasing, but the former's ratio of decrease is not as high
as that of the latter. This coincides with the fact that a majority of
the downtown church members are assumed to be living outside
of the municipalities (wards) where their churches are located.
Finally, the growth rate of the population in the industrial district
has slowed down but is still higher than that in the residential
district; yet the rate of increase in church membership is by far
lower than that in the residential district, the size of a church in
the industrial district remaining almost unchanged. This is indicative of the tendency for the population moving into this district to
be less congenial to Christianity, in contrast to those who move
into the residential district.

Conclusions

We have found that a causal relationship exists between the
demographic changes in a local municipality and the growth of
Christian church membership, although the extent of this rela-

[3] Speaking in terms of age composition of members, Christian churches in Japan
are supported primarily by the youth and young adults and characterized by the fact
that the average age of members is much lower than that of other religious bodies
(Mombushō Shūmuka 1962:46–47).

tionship depends upon a number of intermediary variables, such as the degree of geographic concentration of church members and the social class and age composition of the moving-in and moving-out population. This investigation is in a sense a development of a case study of a Christian church in Yamanashi Prefecture that I reported on at the 1964 Annual Convention of the Japanese Association for Religious Studies (Morioka 1965c). Using the conclusion of the case study as a hypothesis, I expanded the object of investigation to all the churches along the Chuo Line area, applying quantitative analyses to the materials. I am in the process of pursuing similar examinations of the number of participants at Sunday services and Sunday schools, in order to establish the aforesaid conclusion more firmly. I plan also to observe the data for a longer period since 1955 for the same purpose. Finally, I would hope that appropriate materials will be provided by other groups so that similar studies will be possible.

CONCLUSION

9. THE IMPACT OF THE PHYSICAL MOVEMENT OF POPULATION ON JAPANESE RELIGIONS AFTER WORLD WAR II*

Social Foundations of Religions in Japan

In terms of their underlying social foundations, the Japanese religions that have survived in the past century can be classified into three categories:

a. those based on the local group, such as a community or a hamlet, the subunit of the community;

b. those based on the *ie*, or the Japanese household;

c. those based on the individual (Morioka 1968e).

Indeed, none of the Japanese religions stands strictly on only one basis. A particular religion may take a dominant stand based on one of these categories but may also relate, with varying degrees of significance, to one or both of the other two. Thus, this classification merely emphasizes the dominant social foundations of the various religions in Japan today.

Religions based on the local group are a form of what may be termed "diffused religion": all members of the local group are at least presumably bound together by shared sacred beliefs and religious rituals (Young 1961: chapter 12). Institutionalized Shinto (or Shrine Shinto) is one such example. In most cases, all residents in the locality—such as a community or hamlet—have maintained their own shrines. The Meiji Government, established in 1868, encouraged this trend. Around the year 1910, the then governing authority deliberately reorganized the parish of each shrine in such a way that the parish became equivalent to an administrative unit—such as city, town, or village. The parish-

* The author wishes to express his sincere appreciation to Professor Mitsuru Shimpo, St. Jerome's College, Canada, co-author of the original draft, for his generous permission to publish it in the present form.

ioners in each locality adopted gods as their guarding deities (or patrons). Most of these gods appeared in two of the classics that were written during the eighth century—*Kojiki* and *Nihon-shoki*. Prayers were offered to the chosen gods for protection, prosperity, and a fruitful harvest. If their prayers were considered to be answered, additional prayers of thanks were offered to their gods. Shinto has developed a variety of rituals based on this form of prayer and thanksgiving, and its dogma remains fluid. Identity of the locality and the parish appears to be perfect in those places where the traditional life pattern is maintained or where an extensive network of assistance and cooperation remains indispensable for the residents. Annual festivals are held to strengthen the social cohesion of the local group.

In this form of religion, prayer is also offered for protection and prosperity of the household and the individual as a component of the household. Prayer for the local group is, in a sense, a communal prayer for the household, which is the unit of local life.

Religions based on the household are another form of diffused religion. In this type, rituals for ancestors are emphasized. Buddhism is an example. This religion originally stressed the enlightenment of the individual, but, in Japan, it has become a religion devoted to rituals for ancestors. The Japanese people believe that their deceased ancestors will protect them and their children in return for these tributes.

Shinto shrine membership is determined by residence in a particular locality; membership in a Buddhist temple is a matter of household choice. The household has been the basic social unit in the structure of Japanese society. Buddhism, which has long been the religion of the household, has been adopted to its needs, becoming an integral part of household life and thus exercising a strong influence over the traditional beliefs and customs of the people in Japan.

Unlike Shinto, Buddhism has a formalized set of dogmas. An individual may have an active faith in Buddha—in which sense it is a religion based on individual needs. Then again, in localities where only one Buddhist temple exists, the residents treat the temple in the same way that they would treat a Shinto shrine, and in this sense Buddhism is a religion based on the local group. It is rare, however, for all the residents in a locality to belong to the same temple. As a rule, a local group is composed of members of different Buddhist temples.

Religions based on the individual usually have a unique set of dogmas and are positively oriented toward converting non-believers. Christianity, which was reintroduced into Japan in the latter half of the nineteenth century, Tenrikyo and Konkōkyo, which appeared in the same period, and some newer religions that

Figure 1 Social Foundations
         of Religions

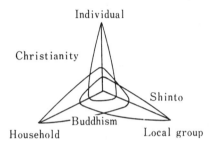

emerged after World War II, all fall into this category. Some of these religions, on making a convert, may attempt to persuade his household members to follow the same course or, at least, to accept their rituals as part of the household rituals.

In summary, surveying the major Japanese religious forms, it is apparent that the household occupies a significantly strategic position in the religious life of Japan.

Population Movement in Japan after World War II

Before discussing the impact of the physical movement of the population on Japanese religions after World War II, it is necessary to have some understanding of the magnitude of this movement. Figure 2 depicts changes in the migration-ratio (that is, the ratio of migrants to the total population in a given year) during the period from 1956 to 1967. In the latter half of the 1950's, the migration-ratio reached the level of 5%. From the beginning of the 1960's, however, it accelerated considerably, reaching a high of 7% in only a few years. This level of migration was maintained throughout the 1960's. The Japanese economy was able to sustain its rapid growth rate partly because of the enormity of this migration.

Figure 2   Shift of Migration Ratio (1956–1967)

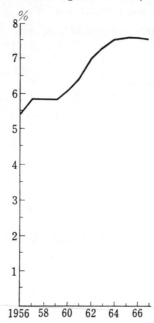

SOURCE: Y. Okazaki and T. Suda, "Recent Trends of Migration in Japan," *Journal of Population Problems*, No. 109 (Jan. 1969), p. 54.

The rural population in the Tōhoku District (northeastern part of the mainland), the Chūbu District (central part of the mainland), the Chūgoku District (western part of the mainland), Shikoku Island, and Kyūshū Island emigrated directly or indirectly into such metropolitan areas as Tokyo, Osaka, and Nagoya. Thus, some areas constantly lost emigrants while others continually absorbed immigrants. Table 31 summarizes the annual changes of population density in selected areas of emigration as well as some areas of immigration during the period between 1950 and 1970. In metropolitan areas, migrants from rural communities and small towns contributed to the development of disharmony between the growing population and the limited environmental facilities—commonly referred to as an "overpopulated" situation. In the emigrating rural communities, on the other hand, population losses began to undermine the traditional social organization—a phenomenon called the "underpopulated" situation. Hence, this population movement has had unprecedented impact upon various aspects of Japanese society, including its religion.

Table 31
Population Density by Prefectures, 1950–1970 (per 1 km²)

Prefecture	(District)	1970	1965	1960	1955	1950
Tokyo	(Tokyo)	5,324	5,357	4,778	3,973	3,091
Kanagawa	(Tokyo)	2,295	1,866	1,458	1,236	1,054
Saitama	(Tokyo)	1,018	793	640	595	564
Aichi	(Nagoya)	1,060	948	832	745	672
Osaka	(Osaka)	4,110	3,618	3,006	2,552	2,126
Akita	(Tōhoku)	107	110	115	116	113
Fukui	(Chūbu)	178	179	180	177	177
Shimane	(Chūgoku)	117	124	134	140	138
Kōchi	(Shikoku)	111	114	120	124	123
Kagoshima	(Kyūshū)	189	203	215	224	231
All Japan		280	266	253	242	226

SOURCE: *Selected Population Statistics in Recent Years*, No. 20, Institute of Population Problems, Ministry of Health and Welfare, 1970.

Population Movement and Shinto Shrines

A great number of young men emigrated into metropolitan areas while older people remained in the rural communities. Consequently, the local population of the underpopulated areas has become older. At the annual festival of the Shinto shrine, attendant parishioners used to experience the presence of the supernatural through such lively rituals as the carrying of *mikoshi* by vigorous youths and through the subsequent elevation of group feelings. Because of the emigration of youths from rural areas such vivacious rituals were dropped out of these festivals, thereby reducing the attractiveness of the shrine. In some of the local groups, the decreasing size of population even began to make it difficult to support the shrines.

A certain amount of the labor force remained in less underpopulated areas. But the differentiation of income resources in these localities undermined the sense of social solidarity that the resident-farmers once had, consequently weakening the residents' interest in their shrine.

In overpopulated areas, the indigenous population could not recruit the bulk of new settlers into the traditional parish organization. Rather, they were affected by the apathetic attitudes of the immigrants, so that the parishioners' faith in the Shinto shrine subsided. According to a study I conducted in a suburban community in the Tokyo Metropolitan area, the shorter the period of settlement of immigrants in the locale, the lower the proportion of those who identified themselves with the parish organization and attended the local shrine during celebrations like New Year's Day or the annual festival. Let us call those residents who have a clear awareness of parish membership and who behave in the prescribed manner, as *nuclear parishioners*, and those who lack both the membership consciousness and the appropriate ritual behavior as *dormant parishioners*. One finds more nuclear parishioners among old immigrants and more dormant parishioners among the newer immigrants. It is apparent that in overpopulated areas where the number of new immigrants is large, only a handful of "old-timers" (indigenous population and old immigrants) support the local shrine, and that the great majority of the residents will have nothing to do with it (Chapter 3). If affiliation to a local shrine provides a measure of social prestige to the supporters, shrine maintenance will become a privilege of the old-timers and even some of the new immigrants may then wish to obtain parish membership. Actually, however, membership in small shrines in suburban communities is no longer a source of social prestige for either group.

In summary, both in areas of emigration and in areas of immigration, Shinto is decaying. In the former, the decay is due to a steadily declining population, while in the latter it is due to rapid population growth. As Shinto is based on the local group, such drastic changes in population have upset the parish organization. However, a new trend has emerged. Some Shinto leaders are making an effort to reorient the religion from one based on the local group to one based on the individual. Apparently, the idea has come from nationally prestigious shrines that are not bound so closely to the locality and are attracting followers from wide areas (Kishimoto 1964).

Population Movement and Buddhist Temples

The impact of the population movement on Buddhist temples has two aspects: a direct one similar to the case of Shinto shrines and an indirect one. Let us first survey the direct impact of the population movement.

In areas of emigration, one can notice a decrease in the member-households of Buddhist temples and a subsequent serious decline in the temples' economic foundations. In areas of immigration, the number of member-households of temples has increased, and the temples are enjoying economic security or even prosperity (Fujii 1970). The increase in membership, however, is not so remarkable as one might expect. Most of the migrants moving into the metropolitan areas are young people who do not obtain definite membership in any temple because they have no need for rituals for the deceased, such as funerals. In other words, these young immigrants are in a state of religious suspense until the first deaths occur in their families.

The population movement indirectly affected temples because of the weakening of household ties. A brief mention should be made about this institution of the Japanese household. Until the end of World War II, a household was normally formed by, or around, the nucleus of a conjugal family and might include relatives and non-relatives other than immediate family members; it was the basic unit of production. The economic basis of the household was household property. Occupations with this unit of production were usually handed down from the father to the eldest son (the heir). The household was an entity continuing through time, changing in its members but unchanging in identity. Individual positions with different degrees of authority and responsibility formed a hierarchical order in the household, with the househead holding the highest social status and exercising authority over the other members. The househead's authority had at least two sources of legitimization. The first was the ancestors: they entrusted to the contemporary household members the responsibility for handing down the inherited property to the next generation. The household head was also the mediator between the deceased and the living. Second, the Meiji Civil Code legally institutionalized the household head's authority and primogeniture. In the household, therefore, every one of the members was aware of the expected behavior and, in addition, the household provided guidelines for the lives of its individual members.

After World War II, a few social factors brought about changes in the household. First, the revision of the Civil Code abolished the authority of the household and primogeniture, giving more freedom and rights to the rest of the household members. Second, the government, leading academics, and journalists propagated the ideology of the beauty of conjugal families. Third, the unprecedented rural exodus described earlier removed younger members from the household, including the heir. Consequently, the traditional institution of the household has been seriously weakened and a vast number of new conjugal families formed.

In contemporary Japan, conjugal families include few aged members: the older folks still cling to the old-style households. There has also been a drastic decline in infant mortality. Thus, many conjugal families still have nothing to do with temples as they do not require rituals for the deceased. An extremely small proportion of conjugal families are equipped with altars, the instrument for Buddhist rituals, as compared with stem families, most of which have one. Even when conjugal families have altars, the family members tend to neglect the rituals that were once performed by the elders. Very few parents in the modern conjugal families socialize their children under the influence of the Buddhist faith. Physical movement of population reduced the frequency of interaction between the migrants and the temple of their native households, and interaction was further reduced by the absence of old people in conjugal families. Thus, the population movement tended to promote the decline of Buddhism indirectly through weakening the institutional household and encouraging the subsequent formation of conjugal families.

In the past decade, to ameliorate such an unfavorable situation, some leading Buddhist sects, such as the Ōtani sect of Shin Buddhism, have been trying to reorient Buddhism. This sect is reorganizing Buddhism from a religion based on the household into one based on the individual. It places more emphasis on the propagation of religious principles among the living rather than the observance of rituals for the deceased. It is also aiming at the formation of Buddhist families in which all the members have an individual faith in Buddha (Chapter 6).

Population Movement and the Christian Churches

About 81,000 Shinto shrines claim more than 70% of the Japanese people as their parishioners while about 76,000 Buddhist temples have an almost equal number of members. One can clearly see the impact of the population movement on these religious institutions, since their followers include the majority of the nation. On the other hand, the members of about 4,000 Christian churches comprise less than 1% of the total population. Hence, it is difficult to measure the degree of the impact of these population movements on the churches effectively.

Chapter 8 dealt with the impact of population movements on Christian churches. In the Tokyo Metropolitan area, churches in the city center, where the population is decreasing, are losing their members to the emerging suburban areas. In those residential zones immediately outside the city center, where the population is growing, church membership is also increasing. In suburban areas outside the residential zones, the population is mushrooming and one can readily see a tendency for the churches to increase in number as well as in size of membership. In the hinterland outside the suburban areas, the population remains relatively stationary, and the churches in these areas are losing members. At least one explanation lies in the fact that majority of the migrants are young people from the back country areas. Also, they include young Christians converted and disciplined at local churches. Hence, in the areas of emigration, churches loose their members, while in areas of immigration churches are recruiting new members. Despite the effects of certain variables, such as the migrants' socioeconomic background or the density of church members in a given area, one can see a high correlation between population movement and fluctuations in church membership.

These population movements threatened the social basis of institutionalized Shinto. They also affected the Buddhist temples directly and indirectly through changes in the household as well as by the formation of new conjugal families. The destructive impact of the population movement on the Christian churches ought to be minimal, because this religion is based on the individual. Some of the younger members who were disciplined in the local churches may emigrate into the metropolitan areas and drop out of this religious institution. But other young Christians may join urban churches, enlarging the size of the church membership. Both shrines and temples are more densely distributed in the rural communities while Christian churches are concentrated in the metropolitan areas. Hence, the population movement ought to operate in favor of churches. Despite these favorable variables, however, the churches have so far not demonstrated an impressive growth.

Population Movement and the New Religions

The population movement directly and indirectly threatened the social foundations of Shinto and Buddhist temples, compelling them in one way or another to reorient themselves as religions based on the individual. New religions basically favor this trend; hence, contemporary Japan may be favorable to their religious activities.

Generally speaking, migrants moving into the metropolitan areas have much less frequent interaction with religious institutions than they did in their native communities. In addition, both Shinto and Buddhism basically provide services for their own congregations rather than attempting to appeal to the public. Christianity is more evangelical, but it tends to attract only a small proportion of the intellectuals. The majority of migrants are thus alienated from the established religions. It is the newer religions that appeal to the lonely among them.

Immediately after World War II, a number of new religions emerged from the political, economic, and sociocultural confusion. They largely attracted those people who were suffering from anxiety, disease, or shortages of material goods. From around 1955, when the Japanese economy began its high rate of growth, new religions offered the people guidelines for living, rather than for resolving material problems. Some new religions, such as Sōka Gakkai or Risshō Kōsei Kai, achieved impressive success. They reconfirmed traditional cultural values rather than refuting them and emphasized layman evangelism instead of making a sharp distinction between the sacred and the profane. These strategies attracted those people who had found little satisfaction in the established religions. Subsequently, many people from both the migrant and indigenous populations in the metropolitan areas became supporters of these new religions.

In the metropolitan areas, "instrumental" values are emphasized in the sphere of occupational activities and related life sectors. People seek elsewhere for a way to realize "expressive" values. The family is by far the most effective means of achieving this desirable end, and, consequently, most Japanese place a great deal of emphasis on establishing a comfortable and congenial home. Unlike the traditional households, however, conjugal families in contemporary Japan offer few guidelines for living. Thus, it is religion that enhances expressive values and offers the needed guidelines for living. The new religions are also able to meet this "felt need" of the public.

Both the dramatic decline in the birth rate and the extension of life expectancy that took place after World War II enabled women in their middle or later years to engage in non-domestic activities. Some women began to work in business firms, while others participated in social and/or religious activities. Through their organizations, the new religions also provided an outlet for women to discharge their potential energies. These social factors, joined with the swelling population movement, contributed to the success achieved by the new religions in satisfying the emergent needs of the Japanese people.

Concluding Remarks

In Japan, there is no elaborate and rigid network cutting across the different social groups in the way the Hindu caste network in India cuts across the various village groups. In addition, the religious beliefs of the Japanese people are syncretic, that is, an individual can adhere to more than one religion without suffering any inner conflicts. Indeed, most of the Japanese people belong to at least two religious institutions—a Shinto shrine and a Buddhist temple. As suggested in the previous discussion, in terms of their underlying social foundations Japanese religions can be classified into three categories: those based on the local group, those based on the institutional household, and those based on the individual. In addition, any particular religion may take a dominant stand based on one of these three categories. Consequently, any changes that occur in the underlying foundations of a religion will, in fact, cause changes in the religion itself. On the basis of the above, we may formulate a more general proposition. When there is an absence of a social network cutting across the different groups and when syncretic religious beliefs are present, the magnitude of the physical movements of the population (an independent variable) will cause changes in the underlying social foundations (the intervening variable) that will, in turn, effect changes in religious institutions (the dependent variable).

In summarizing the findings of this concluding chapter in light of the above proposition, it must be remembered that religions in Japan have never openly stimulated population movement. Rather, they tended to inhibit the migration of heirs from rural households. Heirs were considered to possess future responsibility for the succession of the family line and continuation of rituals for their ancestors, both of which are fundamental to most Japanese religions. Around 1955, the development of industrialization in the metropolitan areas drew young labor from the rural areas, exerting a noticeable influence on prevailing religious beliefs. This and other kinds of population movements have affected Japanese religions in many unanticipated ways. The severest blow was sustained by those religions based on the local group, followed by those based on the household. Religions based on the individual actually benefited from the migrational trends. The shifting population thus functioned as a factor to promote a reorientation of Japanese religions, a reorientation that moved away from the long-standing, traditional group and household religions toward emergent cultural values based on the individual.

Further application of this proposition may be explored. In societies in which there is no constricting social network cutting across the diverse social groupings and in which syncretic religious beliefs prevail, changes in the devotional aspects of the local groups and the households will very significantly affect religions based on these foundations. On the other hand, religions based on individual values are not adversely affected by this new form of social change.

The above argument is based on the assumption that the inception of this dynamic process of social change emanated from a relatively stable social system in which both the local groups and the households promoted a state of equilibrium. The argument further assumes that an enormous migrational movement is taking place in the social system. Hence, the above argument will apply in those developing countries that are departing from traditional patterns and aiming at rapid industrialization. When such societies satisfy the two conditions specified above, the movement of the population from the rural areas into industrial centers will undoubtedly undermine the well-established traditional religions and will stimulate the emergence of new religions based on individual values.

APPENDICES

IO. DEVELOPMENT OF THE
SOCIOLOGY OF RELIGION IN
JAPAN, 1900-1967*

I

The term "sociology of religion" was first used in Japan by Masaharu Anezaki (1900). In his book, *Shūkyōgaku Gairon* (Outlines of Comparative Religion), one chapter is headed "Sociology of Religion," in which he defines it as a field of study dealing with religion as a social force, focusing attention on the relationship between society and religion. In 1898, only two years prior to the appearance of Anezaki's book, the term was coined for the first time in the writings of E. Durkheim in France and of G. Simmel in Germany, both of whom attempted to make a rough sketch of this emerging branch of social science. On the basis of this coincidence it may be said that the history of sociology of religion in Japan is as old as it is in France and Germany. Although in Japan, once the initial start was made, subsequent development of this field of study was not so vigorous as in France or Germany, there have been many significant contributions to it which deserve mention.

The development of sociology of religion in Japan has two important characteristics. One is the great interest in, and the enthusiastic introduction of, outstanding writings and publications from the West, which have given an international flavor to Japanese sociology of religion. On the other hand, this tendency to import is an indication of the backwardness of Japanese studies in this field.

* In making a summary of this chapter for presentation at the sociology of religion session of the Seventh World Congress of Sociology, Varna, Bulgaria, September 1970, the author was kindly assisted by Professor Robert M. Marsh of Brown University, U.S.A.

The other characteristic is that studies in this field have been advanced by the contributions not only of scholars trained in religious studies or sociology but also of historians, ethnologists, and folklore experts. We might even say that in its early development Japanese sociology of religion owed more to scholars in the latter than in the former group. This is a reflection of the fact that phenomena which come within the sphere of sociology of religion in Japan are deeply rooted in history and folklore. At the same time, however, this has made the boundaries of the field extremely vague.

The scope of sociology of religion will be tentatively confined here to studies of religion as a social institution (in the sense of Malinowski's use of the term). It includes all studies and research on religious groups; religious ideas, practices, and rituals as group phenomena; and the relationship of religious institutions to other social institutions or to the larger society. The aim of this chapter is to survey the development of the sociology of religion within this framework.

II

The major part of this survey will be devoted to presenting a general view of the range and depth of studies in the sociology of religion in Japan. Before proceeding, however, a brief outline will be given on how Western works and theories have been introduced.

E. Durkheim was the first Western scholar in the sociology of religion to be introduced to Japan. The initial work of introducing him was undertaken by Chijō Akamatsu (1916), continued by Hisatoshi Tanabe (1926 and 1928), and completed by Kiyoto Furuno (1930–1933, 1933, 1935, and 1938). Furuno not only translated the major works of Durkheim but also went on to introduce the theories of the sociology of religion of Marcel Mauss and other scholars of the new French School. He also conducted some research himself under the influence of Durkheim and his followers, making use of documents about primitive societies.

Georg Simmel was introduced about ten years after Durkheim

by Megumi Hayashi (1928a and 1928b). Max Weber was introduced next by Yuzuru Okada (1931). While the influence of Durkheim disappeared almost totally after 1940, the interest in Weber came to the forefront about that time. For example, Tōgo Mori (1937) discussed the typology of the charismatic ruler on the basis of Weber's theory; Iichi Oguchi (1935 and 1955a) wrote an introduction to Weber and under his influence did research on religion in Asian societies; Hisao Ōtsuka (1948) studied and developed Weber's theories from the viewpoint of an economic historian; parts of Weber's major works were translated into Japanese (Hosoya 1940 and Kajiyama 1946). The study of his theories has continued to the present (Numa 1953, Uno 1957, Kubota 1962, Sugiura 1946 and 1953, Uchida 1962–1964).

Other Western scholars who have attracted the attention of the Japanese since prewar days are R. Bastide (Itō 1939), B. Malinowski (Furuno 1938, Kokubu 1941, and Abe 1959), and, J. Wach (Oguchi 1935, Tanase 1951, and Hirai 1955). Like Durkheim, Simmel, and Weber, these three were also Europeans; only after World War II did the theories and research findings of American sociology of religion come into the Japanese scene. Some of the main figures to be introduced were J. H. Fichter (Morioka 1958), T. F. Hoult (Yamaguchi 1960), T. Parsons (Yanagawa 1960–1961), and R. N. Bellah (Hori and Ikeda 1962). At the same time, contact with European achievements was maintained with the introduction of the French sociology of religion of Le Bras and his followers, who approached this field more from an ecological angle (Anzai 1960 and 1962), and with a continued interest in German sociology of religion (Toyoshima 1964).

Although a few more names of Western sociologists of religion who were introduced into Japan could be mentioned, the above list includes the more significant scholars. Particularly important among them are Durkheim, Weber, and Bellah. It appears, however, that strenuous efforts devoted to studying their theories have not necessarily been followed by effective application of them to analyses of religious institutions in Japan. Kanji Naito's study (1941), conspicuously in the Weber fashion, which treats the relationship between the teachings of Shin Buddhism and the ethical attitude toward business on the part of the Ōmi merchants, is probably the only exception. There is a tendency for theories developed in the West to be studied merely as theories. That they have not been digested and applied to the investigation of Japanese institutions seems to be due largely to the wide gap between the West and Japan in the social background of religion. Although the influence of Western theories did not bring about works of a similar nature in Japan, they have made a great impact on the frame of reference of Japanese scholars, and, especially since World War II, with the increasing emphasis on empirical studies, have provided useful clues to theory-building.

III

The following sections will review the empirical research done in Japan in the sphere of sociology of religion. Serious interest and effort in undertaking empirical studies began only after 1935. As has already been mentioned, till then Japanese sociology of religion was almost totally dominated by the tasks of importing and introducing foreign theories. There were, however, some exceptions to this trend that marked the beginning of empirical studies (Yanagita 1914, Nakayama 1924, Fukuba 1925 and 1930).

The significant shift of emphasis to empiricism in the sociology of religion first occurred in the field dealing with indigenous religious practices in rural villages, which became the melting pot of interests for sociologists, ethnologists, and those studying folklore and religion. Some salient examples are studies of the rituals connected with rice planting by Kizaemon Aruga (1935 and 1938), the research done by Eitarō Suzuki on house-site gods and Shinto shrine worshipping groups (1935 and 1938), Ken'ichi Sugiura's studies of mountain gods (1935a and 1935b), the work of Kazuo Higo on the *miyaza*[1] system (1938 and 1941), Toshimi Takeuchi's research on the local organization of Shinto shrine worshippers and on the religious group called *kōshin-kō* (1941 and 1943), a study by Hiroshi Oikawa on the local religious belief in *mairi no hotoke* (1941), and Anshō Togawa's work on the Haguro mountain

---

[1] The Shinto parish organization performing the *za* ritual on the festival day of its guardian deities.

priests (1943). The collaborative research on rituals connected with agricultural production in Japan by Enkū Uno (1946), Toshiaki Harada (1943), and Kiyoto Furuno set an important example in fieldwork for the postwar studies of religion.

There was little foreign influence in these early studies, which aimed at the scientific understanding of Japanese religious life through observing daily events and rituals on special occasions. Rather they were, to a greater or lesser extent, under the strong influence of Kunio Yanagita who was about to establish the groundwork for Japanese folklore studies. Undoubtedly these empirical studies before and during the war provided the basis for the postwar development of a sociology of religion.

One of the most distinct features in the development of this field of study after World War II has been the enthusiastic undertaking of empirical research. This tendency has been fostered by the influence of fieldwork done in American sociology and cultural anthropology. The preoccupation with foreign theories has ceased to be the dominant feature in academic pursuits. Moreover, in undertaking fieldwork, postwar researchers have been inclined toward intensive study of a particular religious group or local community, rather than toward extensive observation of a particular subject as was the case with many prewar researchers. This means that efforts have been made to investigate religious phenomena against the total context of the social and cultural structure of the community concerned. This inclination was brought about by the influence of the functional approach in American and British anthropology. Finally, the scope of interest has widened to cover not only the established area of study dealing with folk belief and Shinto but also phenomena related to Buddhism, Christianity, and the so-called newly arisen religions. Interest in each area has produced a considerable output. The result of the growing interest in the three new areas mentioned above is that attention is being paid to interaction and relationships among the three as well as between them and Shinto.

IV

It may be said that phenomena related to Shinto and folk beliefs display sociological characteristics different from those seen in other religions, in that the former are neighborhood- or community-based. Studies in these areas have made steady advances following in the footsteps of prewar accomplishments. On the basis of a large amount of data and materials collected before the war, Toshiaki Harada (1949, 1961, and 1963) published a series of articles in *Shakai to Denshō* (Society and Folklore), first published in 1956 under his editorship, which focused attention on the worship of village gods and relevant customs. Study of the *miyaza* system, which was one of the major topics in the prewar period, developed a new perspective so that attempts were made to see it in its relationship to the social structure of the neighborhood or community where the shrine is located; the traditional approach emphasized more the understanding of the inner organization and functioning of the system per se. Studies made by Chōshū Takeda (1954), Kiyomi Morioka (1954b), Akira Ikeda (1958, 1959, 1962, and 1965), Tatsuo Hagiwara (1962), Shōji Yonemura (1962 and 1963), Mikiharu Itō (1958 and 1961), Kazuhiko Sumiya (1963), and Minoru Sonoda (1967) all followed the new approach. Another area of interest has been the way in which political power works on Shinto shrines from outside, as it has an important bearing on the relationship of the local Shinto organization to the political-economic structure of the village (Kurosaki 1958, Aruga 1962, and Morioka 1966b). There are also studies tracing the process of formation of the Shinto shrine in a new frontier settlement to determine what functions the Shinto rites perform in village life (Ojima 1954, Okada 1955, and Morioka 1957). A number of studies have confined their scope of interest largely to the inner organization of local groups which conduct Shinto rituals (Wakamori 1952, Sakurai 1960 and 1966b, Miyaji 1959, 1960, 1962, and 1963). Thus, the study of Shinto phenomena has enriched itself, not only by mere accumulation but also by ramification of interest.

There are some local beliefs among the people that cannot be readily classified as Shinto or that are not at all Shintoistic. Attention is drawn first to rituals related to ancestors and *dōzoku* gods. Contributions by Toshimi Takeuchi (1958–1959) and others (Andō 1960, Aruga and Naka 1962) are examples. By far the most energetic and thorough in exploring this area of study were Ichirō Hori and Chōshū Takeda. Hori (1951) systematized the folkloristic materials concerning the worship of *dōzoku* deities and ancestral spirits in rural society. Takeda (1951, 1955, 1957a, 1957b, 1959b, 1960, and 1964) elucidated, theoretically and empirically, the structural relationship between ancestral cult and the Japanese *ie* and *dōzoku*; further he probed various forms of rites for ancestors that appeared in Japanese history and studied them in terms of "Japanization" of Buddhist thought and rituals. Second, there are studies on mountain worship and group organization for its rites; Anshō Togawa (1949 and 1964), Yoshihiko Umeda (1951), Keiichi Yanagawa (1955, 1958, and 1959), Hiromasa Ikegami (1958a, 1958b, and 1960), Hitoshi Miyake (1962 and 1964), and Noboru Miyata (1961 and 1965) have published their research findings on this subject. Ichirō Hori (1953a) studied the role that communication played in the spread of mountain worship. Third, there are a number of studies concerned with local religious practices called *kō* and the social organization for *kō* activities. Kanji Naito (1943 and 1954) conducted research in the field of Buddhist *kō* groups on the basis of his earlier documentary work during the war. Giyū Ikeda (1957) presented a theoretical framework for studies of *kō* groups. Naofusa Hirai (1960) and others (Yamaguchi 1961, Miyata 1963, and Yoneji 1963) discussed the structure and function of *kō* groups in the village on the basis of their own field research. In addition to surveying documents available in this area, Tokutarō Sakurai (1958b and 1962a) conducted an extensive field investigation, thus synthetizing existing information concerning the structure and function of *kō* groups as well as their historical process of formation. Fourth, there are studies on shamanism. Already before the war a laborious study was made by Chijō Akamatsu and Takashi Akiba (1937–1938) on Korean oneiromancy. During the postwar period, fieldwork in the islands south of Kyūshū was resumed and findings on the necro-

mancers (*noro* and *yuta*) of the Amami Oshima Island were
reported by Mikiharu Itō (1958) and others in a series of publications (Takagi 1957, Oguchi 1959, Sumiya 1963, and Kleiner
1963). Studies were also made on mediums in northern Japan
(Togawa 1954 and Satō 1958) and on diviners in the Oki Islands
(Oguchi 1960). Tokutarō Sakurai (1966d) organized the stock of
knowledge concerning mediums and shamans and suggested problem areas for future studies. Fifth, there are studies dealing with
the social aspects of belief in possession. Examples are those by
Ichirō Hori (1953b) and Takatoshi Ishizuka (1959).

V

Let us now turn to studies treating Buddhist phenomena. Originally Buddhism had its basis in the individual's faith, but in Japan
it developed a connection with the *ie* (household), that is to say, an
affiliation with Buddhism is determined in terms of the *ie* to which
one belongs. Quite a number of historical studies on Buddhist
phenomena have been made, beginning with the prewar period,
but it was only after the war that a sociological approach appeared
also in this field.

Studies on the temple or smaller Buddhist groups called *kō* as
the primary unit of Buddhist sects were carried out by Kiyomi
Morioka (1954a and 1955), Shunshō Terakawa (1954), Hikojirō
Shimamoto (1957), Chōshū Takeda (1958a, 1958b, and 1959a),
Eshō Kawasaki (1959–1962), Tokutarō Sakurai (1964 and 1966c),
and others. With the one exception of Kawasaki's statistical survey
of Buddhist temples in urban areas, all were case studies dealing
with temples and Buddhist groups in the country. Shin Buddhist
sects were most frequently studied. On the other hand, few
attempts were made to analyze the Buddhist sect per se, probably
due to the complexity and immensity of the task involved. Sociological analysis of the relationship between the main temple and
its subordinate temples and that between a priest and his parishioner households is a key to understanding the unique character of
the Japanese Buddhist organization, as these two relationships
constitute the backbone of the whole structure. Marking this

point, Shūken Suzuki (1959) and Kiyomi Morioka (1962) investigated the structure of Buddhist organizations, with special attention to the Shin sects. Morioka in particular went into a thorough analysis of the organization of Shin sects and found out that it was patterned after the *ie* system and that it had gone through a change corresponding to changes in the latter. Yoshio Toda (1952 and 1955) studied the spread of Shin Buddhism in the Tsushima and Noto regions. Shunshō Terakawa (1957) and Tsuneya Wakimoto (1967) traced the emergence of Manshi Kiyozawa's "spiritualism," which had a great impact on modern Shin sects. All the above are studies dealing with Shin sects. Besides them nothing much has been done except for a few studies made on the organization of the Nichiren sect (Numa 1954 and Kubota 1962) and of the Jōdo sect (Takahashi 1962).

When a local group of Buddhist converts was formed as the result of missionary work, the boundary of the group was determined by various social conditions, such as kinship network, class structure, factionalism, and neighborhood relations in the area. Studies with this theme by Toshiaki Harada (1947, 1957a, and 1957b) were based on his observation of contemporary Buddhist groups. Through intensive field research at a number of places, Tokutarō Sakurai (1955, 1962a, 1962b, 1962c, 1963a, 1963b, and 1966e) dealt with the question of how Buddhist beliefs and rituals modified, and were modified by, the local folkways of the regions into which they had been introduced. Kiyomi Morioka (1962), Toshio Iwasaki (1963), and Ichirō Hori (1963) demonstrated through field research that Shin Buddhist customs tended to maintain their identity even after having been in contact with customs of other faiths.

VI

Christianity has its foundation in the faith of individuals, and therefore it is the individual who decides whether to belong to a church or not. This characteristic feature of Christianity is absent in established Buddhism or Shinto.

When Protestantism was introduced into Japan and local

churches were established in many places, which social stratum
of people accepted it most readily? What kinds of resistance were
there on the part of indigenous religious believers and organizations? What were the reactions of Christians to this resistance?
These were some of the questions raised and pursued in case
studies by Kiyomi Morioka (1953, 1959, and 1966a), Fumio Iwai
(1957–1959 and 1963), Eiichi Kudō (1959), Masao Takenaka
(1959), Mitsuru Shimpo (1962), Tetsuya Ōhama (1963 and
1965), among others. Morioka, particularly, took an interest in
the interaction of Christianity and indigenous customs, that is,
how the former changed the latter and vice versa. He found that
the Japanese belief in *ie no kami* (household gods) had a vitality
that sustained itself unaffected by the coming of Christianity and
indeed caused some changes in Christianity itself. He argued that
Japanese indigenous belief in household gods might be the focus
of Japanese culture. In another instance, Morioka (1965) and
Ōhama (1966) analyzed the process of how a financially weak
church grew into a self-sufficient, independent entity. Studying
the class background of Christian converts from a more statistical
point of view, Fujio Ikado (1954) found that the former *samurai*
and leaders of local industries who took the lead in the Christian
church during the early period of Meiji have been replaced by
well-educated white collar workers since the latter part of the
Meiji period.

Studies of Japanese Catholicism include one by Kenkichi Numa
(1961) on the role Catholics of the early Meiji period played in
the movement for the emancipation of outcasts, others by Nobukiyo Nomura (1962) and Masataka Hayashi (1965) on Catholic
settlements, and the work of Shin Anzai (1965 and 1966b) and
Ichirō Hori (unpublished), which analyze the social background
of postwar cases of group conversion. Another series of studies, by
such scholars as Kiyoto Furuno (1951, 1957a, 1957b, and 1959),
Minoru Shibata (1951), Kōya Tagita (1953, 1954a, 1954b, 1956,
and 1958), and Washio Kurata (1958, 1959, and 1964), deal with
the *kakure kirishitan* (hidden Christians) who went underground
when Catholicism was prohibited during the 250 years of the
Tokugawa Shogunate. Today this group still remains isolated
without identifying itself with the Catholic Church. Furuno con-

cluded that the religion as held by *kakure kirishitan* is a syncretism of medieval Catholicism and Buddhism, Shinto, and other folk beliefs; it would be more proper, he argued, to call it "Kirishitanism." There is also a study concerning the Orthodox Church by Kenkichi Numa (1965).

VII

During the period of great social upheaval in Japan following the end of World War II, many new religions came into existence. The basic social unit of these new religions is neither the individual nor the *ie* but the nuclear family household. Sociologically speaking, this, along with other considerations, calls for their separate treatment from the three religions that have been dealt with in the foregoing sections.

It was Iichi Oguchi (1951, 1955b, 1956a, 1957a, and 1957b) who played the leading role in cultivating this new field of study. For one thing he tried to analyze the role of the leader and his relationship to the group of followers in the new religions. He also studied the dynamics of the organizational structure of shamanistic religions. Analyzing Sōka Gakkai as a mass movement was yet another task he undertook. Hiroo Takagi (1954, 1956, 1958, and 1959a) studied Tenrikyo during the late Tokugawa and Meiji periods to analyze the process of formation of a new religious organization. In his attempt to locate major new religions emerging before and after the war in the broader framework of a mass movement, he tried to show why the new religions could so successfully attract support from huge masses of people in spite of the vulgarity of their teachings and their reactionary attitude toward political issues. Shūken Suzuki (1956) defined "Seichō no Ie" (House of Growth) as a religion of the middle class, and Hiroshi Suzuki (1963-64) demonstrated with his sampling survey that Sōka Gakkai is a religion accepted mostly by the urban lower class, in particular people on the border of poverty. Ichirō Hori (1962) contended in a theoretical discussion on the social role of new religions that their emergence and spread, just as in the case of the adoption of foreign religions or a new course of development in traditional religions, could be understood as a response to the *anomie* created by social upheaval.

VIII

When Keiichi Yanagawa made a survey in 1960 of postwar empirical studies of religion based on field research, he found a significant proportion of structural-functional analyses, that is, studies concerned with locating religion in a static setting. In his 1966 review, however, he drew attention to the fact that an increasing number of studies tend to carry the theme of social change and religion. This recent trend can be explained by the fact that the base of religion in Japan has been shaken radically in the process of rapid social change, which has accompanied the high rate of economic growth beginning in the late 1950's. Fujio Ikado (1961, 1964a, 1964b, and 1965b) was the first to take up this problem directly. He argued that religious organizations go through certain transformations along with the modernization of society, that is, from the clergyman-centered church type to the denomination type where members' active participation in missionary activities is stressed. Later he expanded this argument further, showing concretely the direction toward which the administrative set-up of religious organizations is being, or should be, modified in an industrial society. In this connection, his approach to new religions was based on the premise that they are religions in urban society.

Besides the general treatment of the subject by Ikado, there are a number of studies related to Shinto. In a study of the impact of urbanization on Shinto, Hideo Kishimoto (1964) pointed out that, on the one hand, the traditional *ujiko* (Shinto parishioner) organization was dying out in the turmoil of population migration and that, on the other hand, there was a high degree of concentration of worshippers at a few famous shrines. He also tried to construct a model of a Shinto shrine that would be viable in an urban environment. Kiyomi Morioka (1964b) made a case study showing how the traditional identity of a Shinto shrine with a particular geographical parish was becoming meaningless in suburban areas where population influx was at an extremely high rate. Two case studies were carried out by Mikiharu Itō (1965a and 1965b) demonstrating that the form of Shinto rites in a mountain village remained more or less unchanged so long as there was no change in traditional social organization, even if some ecological change might have been brought about by urbanization. Masazaburō Hanashima wrote a monograph (1967) on the process of dissolution and reconstruction of a village Shinto organization when a dam was built and the whole village had to be moved to a new area.

It appears that the extent of technological and ecological change due to industrialization and urbanization determines the degree of change in social organization, which in turn determines the rate of change in village Shinto organization. Although there may be various instances of time lag in particular situations, it can generally be concluded that, the more radical the change at the ecological level, the more greatly is the village-based Shinto organization affected. This hypothesis was tested by Morioka in the above-mentioned study (1964b), paying special attention to the factor of migration among other factors accounting for ecological change. Further, Morioka and Kumagai (1966) applied the same hypothesis with some modification to the Christian church and found that in Tokyo and two other neighboring prefectures the increase or decrease in church membership was closely related to the rate of population mobility in the area. Masao Fujii (1967) examined the increase in number of parishioners of a metropolitan Buddhist temple in relation to the general trend toward rapid increase in the number of households moving into that part of the city where the temple was located.

IX

This review of the sociology of religion in Japan is incomplete. For instance, studies of the distribution of religions (Ikegami et al. 1963 and 1964) or of the style of the religious life of ordinary people (Takagi 1955) have not been included. Nevertheless, it may suffice to provide a general idea of the development of the sociology of religion in Japan up to 1967. As has been shown, the range of study today covers almost all areas that fall within the scope of the sociology of religion. Not only the range of study but also the amount of study done in each area has expanded considerably; the studies mentioned here constitute only the most important part of the total. They have made contributions to the field by cultivating a new problem area or helping to raise the standard of research. On the whole, most of the remaining studies contain only descriptive information without a clearly formulated frame of study, a logical argument to support a certain thesis, or any coherent conclusion.

In developing a new subject area, efforts are concentrated first on collecting data and materials. This is followed by a stage where attention is drawn to describing the structure of the phenomena concerned. The third stage may be characterized as analytical, where a certain hypothesis about the relationship of two or more variables is tested. Today the sociology of religion in Japan is about to move into this third stage. In order to promote this shift, it is necessary to do the preparatory work of coordinating research findings, interdefining relevant terms, and identifying a set of propositions according to the problem area. The fact that such work has begun to be undertaken (Miyake 1966, Sakurai 1966d, Spae 1966, Yanagawa 1966, and *Shūkyō Kenkyū* No. 191) suggests that a new era is now dawning in the sociology of religion in Japan.

11. AN INTEGRATED BIBLIOGAPHY

This bibliography, compiled in alphabetical order by authors' names, is derived from two sources; (1) References cited in the foregoing chapters of this book; (2) Titles of publication in the field of the sociology of religion that appeared in Japan during the period 1900–1973.

ABE, Shigeo
1959   Malinowski no Jujutsu to Shūkyō no Kinō-setsu ni tsuite (Malinowski's Functional Theory of Magic and Religion). *Shūkyō Kenkyū*, 158, 34–63.
AKAIKE, Noriaki
1971   Matsuri to Chōkai (Functional Relations between Shinto Festivals and Community Organization). *Bungakubu Kiyō*, Aichi Gakuin University, 1, 1–16.
1972   Shūkyō Shūdan to Community (Functional Relations between Religious Groups and Community). Ibid., 2, 77–87.
AKAMATSU, Chijō
1916   Saikin no Shūkyō Shinrigaku to Shūkyō Shakaigaku (Recent Status of Psychology of Religion and Sociology of Religion). *Shūkyō Kenkyū*, 1: 1, 1–42.
AKAMATSU, Chijō, and AKIBA, Takashi
1937–38 *Chōsen Fuzoku no Kenkyū* (A Study of Korean Oneiromancy), 2 vols. Seoul: Akazaki Sansuke.
AKIBA, Takashi
1950   *Chōsen Fuzoku no Genchi Kenkyū* (A Field Study of Korean Oneiromancy). Tenri: Yōtokusha.
ANDŌ, Keiichirō
1960   Dōzoku Ketsugō no Bunkai to Yashikigami Saishi (Dissolution of *Dōzoku* Groups and Rituals of House-Site Gods). *Shakaigaku Hyōron*, 37, 57–76.
ANEZAKI, Masaharu
1900   *Shūkyōgaku Gairon* (Outlines of Comparative Religion). Tokyo: Tokyo School of Special Studies Press.
1961   (Rev. by KISHIMOTO, H.) *Religious Life of the Japanese People*. Tokyo: Kokusai Bunka Shinkōkai.
ANZAI, Shin
1960   Oubei ni okeru Shūkyō Shakaigaku—Sengo ni okeru Tenkai to sono Kadai (Sociology of Religion in the West—Its Development after World War II and Major Issues). *Shakaigaku Hyōron*, 41, 109–120.
1962   Shūkyō Jissen to Shakai-Keizai-teki Kankyō (Religious Practices and Their Socioeconomic Environment). *Shūkyō Kenkyū*, 173, 73–93.

1964a   *Gendai Nihon Shakai to Kirisutokyōto* (Modern Japanese Society and the Christians). Tokyo: Chūōshuppan.
1964b   Kōkaigi to Nihon no Fukyō (Conciliation and Propagation in Japan). In *Kōkaigi to Kyōkai Icchi* (Conciliation and Ecumenism). Tokyo: Risōsha.
1965   Hekichi Shakai to Catholic no Juyō (Acceptance of Catholicism in a Remote Village). In *Nihon no Fūdo to Kirisutokyō* (Japan's Natural Features and Christianity), ed., OKADA, Jun'ichi, pp. 191–208. Tokyo: Risōsha.
1966a   *Shūkyō to Shakai* (Religion and Society). Tokyo: Nihon Shūkyō Shakaigaku Kenkyūjo.
1966b   Dentō-teki Shinkō to Inyū Shinkō no Kongō to Henyō (Contact of Traditional Faith with Imported Religion and Subsequent Changes). *Jinrui Kagaku*, 18, 76–90.
1968   Catholicism in an Isolated Village. *Journal of Asian and African Studies*, 3: 1–2, 44–53.
1970a   The Religious Attitudes of University Students. *Social Compass*, 17: 1, 119–135.
1970b   Le catholicisme dans un village isolé. *Social Compass*, 17: 1, 153–156.
1971a   Shinkō-Sha no Shūkyō Taido no Sho-sō (Aspects of Religious Attitudes of Believers). *Shūmu Jihō*, 26, 17–31.
1971b   Toshi Sho-Daigaku Gakusei no Shūkyō-Kan Chōsa ni okeru Hitei-teki Kenkai no Sho-Sō (Negative Responses of University Students as Revealed by a Survey of Views about Religion). Ibid., 27, 16–31.
1973   Miyako-Jima no Kisō Shinkō to Inyū Shūkyō (Indigenous Beliefs and Imported Religion on Miyako Island). *Jinrui Kagaku*, 25, 27–30.

ARUGA, Kizaemon
1935   Taue to Mura no Seikatsu Soshiki—Tokuni Yoshuku Gyōji ni tsuite (Rice Planting and the Pattern of Village Life—A Study of Festive Events). *Minzokugaku Kenkyū*, 1: 3, 31–50.
1938   Sanaburi—Taue to Mura no Seikatsu Soshiki (The *Sanaburi* Rituals —Rice Planting and the Pattern of Village Life). *Minzokugaku Kenkyū*, 4: 1, 23–48, and 4: 2, 1–34.
1962   Sonraku ni okeru Ujigami Saishi Soshiki to Seiji-Keizai Kōzō tono Kanren (The Relation between the Organization for Shinto Rituals and the Political and Economic Structure of the Village). *Shakaigaku Kenkyūka Kiyō*, Keiō University, 1, 38–43.
1967   Senzo to Ujigami (Ancestor and *Uji-gami*). *Minzokugaku Kenkyū*, 32, 175–184.

ARUGA, Kizaemon, and NAKA, Yasushi
1962   Maki to Iwaijin-Kō (Lineage Groups and Their Religious Festivals). *Shakaigaku Kenkyūka Kiyō*, Keiō University, 1, 105–115.

BEARDSLEY, Richard K., HALL, John W., and WARD, Robert
1959   *Village Japan*. Chicago: University of Chicago Press.

BEST, Ernest E.
1966   *Christian Faith and Cultural Crisis: The Japanese Case*. Leiden: E. J. Brill.

BOULARD, F.
1960   *An Introduction to Religious Sociology*. Trans. by JACKSON, M. J.
        London: Darton, Longman and Todd.
BOXER, C. R.
1951   *The Christian Century in Japan*. Berkeley: University of California
        Press.
BUKKYŌ DAIGAKU MINKAN NEMBUTSU KENKYŪKAI
1966   (ed.) *Minkan Nembutsu Shinkō no Kenkyū* (A Study of Folk Buddhist
        Beliefs). Tokyo: Ryūbunkaku.
BUNKACHŌ SHŪMUKA
1973   (eds.) *1972 Shūkyō Nenkan* (1972 Yearbook of Religion). Tokyo:
        Agency for Cultural Affairs.
1974   (eds.) *1973 Shūkyō Nenkan* (1973 Yearbook of Religion). Tokyo:
        Agency for Cultural Affairs.
CHIBA, Jōryū
1969   Aru Sanson no Shakai to Shūkyō (Society and Religion in a
        Mountain Community). *Ryūkoku Shidan*, Ryūkoku University, 61,
        1–35.
CHIBA, Masaji
1970   *Matsuri no Hō-Shakaigaku* (Shinto Festivals: An Approach from the
        Sociology of Law). Tokyo: Kōbundō.
CHOI, Kil-Sung
1973   Kankoku Shamanism ni okeru Nyūfu Katei (Initiation in Korean
        Shamanism). *Minzokugaku Kenkyū*, 38: 2, 108–119.
DAHSIAR, S.
1973   Indonesia no Shomin-teki Shinkō—Shisha-Gami ni tsuite (Dead-
        God—An Indonesian Popular Belief). *Bunka*, Tōhoku University,
        37: 3–4, 110–332.
DALE, Kenneth
1973   Bunka Ruikei to Shūkyō—Sono Ichi-Rei (Culture Pattern and
        Religion—A Japanese Case). *Shingaku Zasshi*, Japan Lutheran
        Theological College and Seminary, 8, 44–52.
DEGUCHI, Eiji
1970   *Ōmoto-Kyō Jiken* (The Ōmoto Affairs). Kyoto: San'ichi-shobō.
DUMERMUTH, Fritz
1968   Religion in Sociological Perspective. *Contemporary Religions in Japan*,
        9, 1–29.
EMBREE, John F.
1941   Some Social Functions of Religion in Rural Japan. *American
        Journal of Sociology*, 47, 184–189.
FICHTER, Joseph H.
1954   *Social Relations in the Urban Parish*. Chicago: University of Chicago
        Press.
FUJII, Masao
1967   Ichi Toshi Jiin no Kōzō Henka (Structural Change in a Metro-
        politan Temple). *Shūkyōgaku Nempō*, Taishō University, 17, 15–26.
1968   Shinsōsai-ka no Yōin to Shimbutsu Kankei (Factors Conducive
        to the Change in the Patterns of Funeral Service and Relations
        between Buddhism and Shinto). *Shintō Shūkyō*, 51, 13–45.

188 RELIGION IN CHANGING JAPANESE SOCIETY

1970a   Toshika to Shūkyō (Urbanization and Religion). *Shūmu Jihō*, 24, 2–14.
1970b   Ichi Toshi Jiin to Shūkyō Fudō Jinkō (An Urban Buddhist Temple and the Religiously Unaffiliated Population). *Shūkyō Kenkyū*, 201, 93–122.
1970c   Un temple de grande ville et la population religieuse flottante. *Social Compass*, 17: 1, 67–96.
1970d   Otetsugi-Undō to Kyōdan-Saihensei no Mondai-Ten (The *Otetsugi* Movement and the Task of Sect Reorganization). *Bukkyō Ronsō*, Jōdoshū, 14, 57–64.
1972   Kotsu-Botoke to Datsu-Shūkyō Fudōjinkō-Ka (Human Bones as Buddha and Defection from Religion). *Taishō Daigaku Kenkyū Kiyō*, Taishō University, 57, 125–142.
1973   Okinawa ni okeru Bukkyō no Dempan to Juyō (Diffusion and Acceptance of Buddhism in Okinawa). *Jinrui Kagaku*, 25, 31–34.

FUJIOKA, Mitsuko
1968   Kyōkai no Kyōsei to Chiiki Shakai no Jinkō Dōtai (Impact of Population Mobility on Christian Churches). *Senkyō Kenkyū*, United Church of Christ in Japan, 2, 11–50.

FUKUBA, Hoshū
1925   Shūkyō to Hanzai no Kankei ni tsuite (On the Relation between Religion and Crime). *Shakaigaku Zasshi*, 11, 26–52.
1930   Kōsha Kō (On the *Kō* Group). *Shakaigaku Zasshi*, 69, 1–27.

FUKUCHI, Shigetaka
1956   *Shizoku to Samurai Ishiki* (The Samurai Class and Samurai Consciousness). Tokyo: Shunjūsha.

FUKUI, Genchō
1942   Jinkō no Shakai Keitaigaku-teki Sayō to Tohi Kyōdan (The Social-Morphological Effect of Population on Religious Organizations in Town and Country). *Otani Daigaku Kenkyū Nempō*, Otani University, 1, 237–281.

FURUNO, Kiyoto
1930–33 *Shūkyō Seikatsu no Gensho Keitai* (trans. of DURKHEIM, É, *Les formes élémentaires de la vie religieuse*). 2 vols. Tokyo: Tōkō-shoin.
1933   Gendai Shūkyō Shakaigaku no Dōkō (Recent Trends in Sociology of Religion). *Shūkyō Kenkyū* (New Edition), 10: 2, 144–162.
1935   France no Shūkyō-Shakaigakukai (Sociology of Religion in France). Ibid., 12: 1, 165–166.
1938   *Shūkyō Shakaigaku Gakusetsu Kenkyū* (Sociology of Religion—Theoretical and Empirical Studies). Tokyo: Kawade-shobō.
1952   Bunka Nenkan ni okeru Amakusa no Kirishitan (Kirishitans in the Amakusa Island during the Early Nineteenth Century). *Kyūshū Bunkashi Kenkyūjo Kiyō*, Kyūshū University, 2, 19–69.
1957a   Ikezuki no Kirishitan Buraku—Tokuni Saishi Soshiki ni tsuite (Kirishitan Villages in the Ikezuki Island: Their Organization for Rites). Ibid., 5, 1–44.
1957b   Kirishitan Kazoku ni okeru Girei-teki Shinzoku Kankei—Padrinazgo no Hikaku Kenkyū (Ritual Kinship in Kirishitan Families

—A Comparative Study of Padrinazgo). *Minzokugaku Kenkyū*, 21: 4, 79–88.
1959 *Kakure Kirishitan* (Hidden Christians). Tokyo: Shibundō.
1969 France Shūkyō Shakaigaku-Setsu ni tsuite (A Review of the Sociology of Religion in France). *Shūkyōgaku Ronshū*, Komazawa University, 3, 1–16.
1970 *Nōkō Girei no Kenkyū* (A Study of Agricultural Rites). Tokyo: Tōkai University Press.
1971a *Shūkyō Seikatsu no Kiso-Kōzō* (The Basic Structure of Religious Life). Tokyo: Shakai-Shisōsha.
1971b *Genshi-Shūkyō no Kōzō to Kinō* (Structure and Functions of Primitive Religion). Tokyo: Yūrindō-shuppan.
1972-3 *Furuno Kiyoto Chosaku-Shū* (Collected Works of K. Furuno). 7 vols. Kyoto: San'ichi-shobō.
1973 *Genshi Shūkyō* (Primitive Religion). Kyoto: San'ichi-shobō.

FUSE, Toyomasa
1970 Religion and Socio-Economic Development: The Case of Japan. A Study in the Sociology of Development. *Social Compass*, 17:1, 157–170.

HAGIWARA, Tatsuo
1962 Tenkei-teki na Miyaza (A Typical *Miyaza*). In *Chūsei Saishi Soshiki no Kenkyū* (A Study of Medieval Organization for Shinto Rituals), pp. 743–767. Tokyo: Yoshikawa Kōbunkan.

HANASHIMA, Masazaburō
1964 Buraku no Tōgō to Miyaza (*Miyaza* and Social Integration of a Village). *Shakai to Denshō*, 8:2, 22–41.
1967 Suibotsu ni yoru Buraku no Kaitai, Saihensei to Miyaza (The *Miyaza* System in Dissolution and Reorganization of a Village Community due to Dam Construction). *Nihon Bunka Kenkyūjo Kiyō*, Kokugakuin University, 20, 190–257.

HARADA, Toshiaki
1943 Buraku Saishi ni okeru Seiji no Kankei (The Role of Politics in Village Shinto Rituals). *Shūkyō Kenkyū*, 5:1, 23–48.
1947 Dendō to Kaikyū (Proselytization and Class Structure). *Minzokugaku Kenkyū*, 12:1, 52–54.
1949 Buraku Saishi ni okeru Shamanism no Keikō (Shamanistic Tendencies in Village Rites). *Minzokugaku Kenkyū*, 14:1, 7–13.
1957a Jōdoshū no Dempan (The Spread of Jōdo Buddhism). *Shakai to Denshō*, 1:3, 5–21.
1957b Buraku to Shūkyō no Dempan (The Village and the Spread of Religion). *Shakai to Denshō*, 1:5, 9–18.
1961 *Jinja* (The Shinto Shrine). Tokyo: Shibundō.
1963 Miya no Za to Kabu—Miyaza no Iroiro (Various Types of *Miyaza*). *Shūkyō Kenkyū*, 175, 1–12.
1970a *Shūkyō to Minzoku* (Religion and Folkways). Tokyo: Tokai University Press.
1970b Nenrei Kaitei-Sei no Za (Age Class System in the *Za*). *Shakai to Denshō*, 12:1–2, 8–24.

1971   Jinja no Seikaku (Nature of the Shinto Shrine). *Shakai to Denshō*, 13:1, 1–20.
1972   *Shūkyō to Shakai* (Religion and Society). Tokyo: Tokai University Press.
1973   Buraku Saishi no Kigen (Origin of Hamlet Communal Shinto Ceremonies). *Shintō Shūkyō*, 70–71, 1–10.

HAYASHI, Inae
1972   Daisan-Kō no Henbō (Changes in *Daisan-Kō*, an Index of Rural Community Disorganization). *Gifu Joshi Daigaku Kiyō*, Gifu Women's University, 1, 21–28.

HAYASHI, Masataka
1965   Shūkyō to Sonraku—Catholic to Chikugo Imamura (Religion and the Village—Catholicism in Imamura, Chikugo Province). *Shakai no Kagaku*, Yamaguchi University, 155–171.

HAYASHI, Megumi
1928a   Simmel no Shūkyō Shakaigaku (Sociology of Religion by Simmel). *Shūkyō Kenkyū* (New Edition), 5:1, 56–86.
1928b   Simmel Shakaigaku no Kompon-Mondai toshiteno Shūkyō Nin-shikiron (Religious Epistemology as the Basic Problem of Simmel's Sociology of Religion). *Shakaigaku Zasshi*, 48, 1–20.

HAYASHI, Takeshi
1973   Futatsu no Islam Shakai (trans. of GEERTZ, Clifford, *Islam Observed: Religious Development in Morocco and Indonesia*, 1968). Tokyo: Iwanami-shoten.

HAZAMA, Hiroshi
1964   *Nihon Rōmu Kanrishi Kenkyū* (A Study of the History of Labor Management in Japan). Tokyo: Daiamondosha.

HIGO, Kazuo
1938   Omi ni okeru Miyaza no Kenkyū (A Study of the *Miyaza* System in the Omi Province). *Bunka Kiyō*, Tokyo University of Literature and Science, 16.
1941   *Miyaza no Kenkyū* (A Study of the *Miyaza* System). Tokyo: Kō-bundō.

HIRAI, Naofusa
1955   Joachim Wach Kyōju no Gyōseki (Works of Professor Joachim Wach). *Shūkyō Kenkyū*, 145, 68–73.
1960   Oki no Sho-Kō (*Kō* Groups in the Oki Islands). *Kokugakuin Zasshi*, Kokugakuin University, 61:2–3, 44–53.

HIRAYAMA, Binjirō
1955   Minkan Shūzoku (Folk Custom). In *Noto: Shizen, Bunka, Shakai* (Noto: Its Nature, Culture, and Society). Tokyo: Heibonsha.

HIRAYAMA, Binjirō, and TAKEDA, Chōshū
1958   Nenchū Gyōji (Annual Functions). In *Kyōdo Kenkyū Kōza*, ed. OTA, T., et al., vol. 5, pp. 211–331. Tokyo: Kadokawa-shoten.

HORI, Ichirō
1951   *Minkan Shinkō* (Folk Beliefs). Tokyo: Iwanami-shoten.
1953a   Nihon Shūkyō-shi ni okeru Kōtsū no Mondai (The Problems of Communication in Japanese History of Religion). *Jinrui Kagaku*, 5, 38–50.

1953b   Sonraku ni okeru Shūkyō-teki Kinchō (Religious Tension in the
         Countryside). In *Shakai-teki Kinchō no Kenkyū* (Study of Social
         Tension), pp. 195–208. Tokyo: Yūkikaku.
1953c   *Wagakuni Minkan Shinkō-Shi no Kenkyū* (Historical Study of Japanese
         Folk Beliefs). 2 vols. Tokyo: Sōgensha.
1962   *Nihon Shūkyō no Shakai-teki Yakuwari* (The Social Role of Religion
         in Japan). Tokyo: Miraisha.
1963   *Shūkyō-Shūzoku no Seikatsu Kisei* (Religious Customs as a Normative
         Factor of Life). Tokyo: Miraisha.
1971a   *Minkan Shinkō-Shi no Sho-Mondai* (Problems in the History of Folk
         Religion). Tokyo: Miraisha.
1971b   *Nihon no Shamanism* (Shamanism in Japan). Tokyo: Kōdansha.

HORI, Ichirō, and IKEDA, Akira
1962   *Nihon no Kindaika to Shūkyō-Rinri* (trans. of BELLAH, R. N., *Toku-
         gawa Religion*). Tokyo: Miraisha.

HOSOYA, Tokusaburō
1940   Jukyō to Dōkyō (trans. of WEBER, M., *Konfuzianismus und Tao-
         ismus*). Tokyo: Kōbundō.

HOZUMI, Nobushige
1912   *Ancestor-Worship and Japanese Law*. Tokyo: Maruzen.

HYUN, Yong-Joon
1972a   Family and Religion in South Korea—Chiefly Based on Cheju
         (Quelart) Island. *East Asian Cultural Studies*, 11:1–4, 113–124.
1972b   Saishū-To no Fuzoku (Shamanism on Cheju Island). *Minzokugaku
         Kenkyū*, 36:4, 269–279.

IDE, Magoroku
1973   Chichibu Jiken no nakano Misogikyō (Misogikyō in the Chichibu
         Affair). *Nihon no Shūkyō*, 1:1, 92–101.

IETSUKA, Takashi
1971   Gendai Sei-Shōnen no Shūkyō-Ishiki ni tsuite (Religious Con-
         sciousness among Contemporary Japanese Youth). *Kokusai Shūkyō
         News*, 12:4, 8–15.
1972   Shūkyō-Ishiki no Inshi-Bunseki-teki Kenkyū (A Factor Analysis of
         Religious Consciousness). *Shūkyō Kenkyū*, 212, 25–52.

IKADO, Fujio
1954   Wagakuni Protestant ni okeru Shinto Kōzō no Hensen—Kirisuto-
         kyō Shugi Kyōiku o tsūjite mita Ichi Shiron (Shift of Class Back-
         ground of Protestants in Japan: An Approach to the Subject
         through Christian Education). *Shūkyō Kenkyū*, 139, 1–35.
1960   Kindai Shakai ni okeru Kirisutosha no Taido (Social Attitudes of
         Christians in Modern Society). *Kirisutokyō Shigaku*, 10, 29–75.
1961   Shūkyō-Shi ni okeru Kindaika no Mondai—Kindaika to Denomi-
         nation (The Problem of Modernization in the History of Religion:
         Modernization and Denomination). *Shūkyō Kenkyū*, 139, 1–24.
1963   Eikoku Kokkyōkai ni okeru Sho-Seido Kaisei Mondai ni tsuite
         (Some Problems of Amendments of Systems in the Church of Eng-
         land). In *Gaikoku ni okeru Shūkyō Gyōsei no Jitsujō* (The Actual
         Circumstances of Religious Administration in Foreign Countries),

pp. 55–116. Tokyo: Ministry of Education, Section for Religious Affairs.

1964a   Kyōdan Soshiki-Ron Josetsu—Sangyō Shakai ni okeru Kyōdan Taisei no Henyō (Introduction to the Theory of Religious Organization: Change in Religious Organization in Industrial Society). *Tōyō Bunka Kenkyūjo Kiyō*, University of Tokyo, 34, 109–225.

1964b   Shinkō Shūkyō no Dōkō to Kadai (The Trend and Problems of New Religions). *Jiyū*, 7, 128–139.

1964c   Tōkei—Shūkyō Tōkei o Yomuhito ni (Statistics—for Those Who Read Religious Statistics). In *1964 Shūkyō Nenkan* (1964 Yearbook of Religion). Tokyo: Ministry of Education, 244–254.

1965a   Seikyō Bunri ni kansuru Seisaku Shiryō (Collected Materials for the History of Religious Education, 1868–1947: Church and State in Japan). *Tōyō Bunka Kenkyūjo Kiyō*, University of Tokyo, 37, 219–319.

1965b   Toshi Shakai ni okeru Shūkyō-teki Tenkai (Development of Religion in Urban Society). *Tōkai Bukkyō*, 11, 1–12.

1966a   Sangiin Senkyo Zenkokuku Chihōku Tōha-betsu Sōtokuhyō Kaisetsu (Comments on the Total Number of Votes Obtained in Upper House Election by the Different Parties). *Showa 41 Nen Fukyō Kenkyūkai Shiryō* (Materials, 1966 Seminar for Mission Work). Kyoto: Nishi Honganji.

1966b   Toshi Dendō no Hōkō (Urbanism and Religion). In *Gendai no Kyōkai* (Christian Church Today), pp. 187–213. Tokyo: United Church of Christ in Japan Press.

1968a   Trend and Problems of New Religions: Religion in Urban Society. *Journal of Asian and African Studies*, 3:1–2, 101–117.

1968b   Sangyō Shakai ni okeru Kyōdan Taisei (Organization of the Religious Body in Industrial Society). *Senkyō Kenkyū*, United Church of Christ in Japan, 1, 14–28.

1972a   *Sezoku-Shakai no Shūkyō* (Religion in Secular Society). Tokyo: United Church of Christ in Japan Press.

1972b   Genze-Riyaku—Sono Ronri to Shinri (This-Worldly Benefits—Theoretical and Psychological Background). *Nihon Bukkyō*, 34, 1–23.

IKADO, Fujio, and YOSHIDA, Mitsukuni
1970   (eds.) *Nihon-Jin no Shūkyō* (Religion of the Japanese). Kyoto: Tankōsha.

IKEDA, Akira
1958   Kabuza no Kaitai Katei (Dissolution of the *Kabuza* System). *Shakai to Denshō*, 2:2, 11–17.

1959   Sonraku ni okeru Ken'i Shinkō (Worship of Authority in the Village). *Nihon Shūkyō-Shi Kōza*, III, 245–278. Kyoto: San'ichi-Shobō.

1962   Miyaza to Sonraku Kōzō (The *Miyaza* System and Village Social Structure). *Shakai to Denshō*, 6:3, 14–22.

1965   Miyaza no Hembō Katei (Transformation of the *Miyaza* System). *Shakai to Denshō*, 9:1, 36–54, and 9:2, 13–20.

1968   Sonraku ni mirareru Shūkyō Kōdō (Religious Behavior in a Village). *Shakai to Denshō*, 11:1, 10–20.

1970 Max Weber ni okeru Asia Shūkyō Bunseki no Kihon-teki Waku-
gumi (Max Weber's Basic Framework for Analyzing Religions in
Asia). *Shakaigaku Hyōron*, 20:3, 2–17.
1972 *Sect—Sono Shūkyō-Shakaigaku* (trans. of WILSON, B., *Religious Sects*,
1970). Tokyo: Heibonsha.
1973a Max Weber ni okeru Sei to Zoku no Benshōhō (Dialectics of the
Sacred and the Profane in Max Weber). *Shisō*, 586, 24–43.
1973b Max Weber ni okeru Shi to Teikō no Ronri (Max Weber's Theoretical Grounds for Death and Resistance). *Risō*, 480, 13–27.
IKEDA, Genta
1968 Yama no Shinkō (Japanese Beliefs Surrounding Mountains). *Minzokugaku Kenkyū*, 32, 279–292.
IKEDA, Giyū
1957 Kō Shūdan no Shakai-teki Seikaku (The Social Character of the
Kō Group). *Tetsugaku Kenkyū*, Kyoto University, 453, 15–35.
IKEGAMI, Hiromasa
1955 Minkan Shinkō (Folk Religions). In *Gendai Shūkyō Kōza*, vol. 4,
pp. 148–155. Tokyo: Sōbunsha.
1958a Nagano-ken Kiso no Ontake Kō (The Mt. Ontake Worshipping
Kō in Kiso, Nagano). *Shakai to Denshō*, 2:1, 10–17.
1958b Dewa Sanzan no Shinkō (Worship of the Three Mountains in
Dewa Province). *Shakai to Denshō*, 2:3, 1–6.
1960 Sangaku Shinkō no Sho-Keitai (Various Forms of Mountain
Worship). *Jinrui Kagaku*, 12, 163–173.
IKEGAMI, Hiromasa, et al.
1933 Sho-Shūkyō no Zenkoku Bumpu—Tōkei Shiryō ni yoru (Distribu-
tion of Various Religions in Japan: A Statistical Analysis). *Jinrui
Kagaku*, 15, 41–78.
1964 Shūkyō Bumpu no Shosō—Okayama-kenka ni okeru Baai (The
Patterns of Distribution of Religions in Okayama Prefecture).
Jinrui Kagaku, 16, 71–87.
INABA, Masamaru
1948 (ed.) *Rennyo Shōnin Gyōjitsu* (The Life and Work of Saint Rennyo).
Kyoto: Hōzōkan.
INOUE, Aiko
1969 Tokyo ni okeru Toshin Kyōkai no Kenkyū (A Study of Christian
Churches in the Central Business District of Tokyo). *Senkyō Kenkyū*,
United Church of Christ in Japan, 3, 102–124.
1970 Les effets de la mobilité spatiale sur les communautés chrétiennes
du centre du Tokyo. *Social Compass*, 17:1, 97–118.
INOUE, Egyō
1969 *Shūkyō Hojin-Hō no Kiso-teki Kenkyū* (A Basic Study of the Religious
Juridical Person Law). Tokyo: Daiichi-shobō.
ISHII, Yoneo
1973a Thai-Koku ni okeru Kokumin Tōgō to Bukkyō Sanga no Yakuwari
(Buddhism and the National Integration of Thailand). *Tōnan Asia
Kenkyū*, Kyoto University, 11:3, 338–359.
1973b Thai no Sennen-Okoku-Undō (Millenary Movements in Thailand). *Asia Review*, 4:4, 157–162.

ISHINO, Iwao
1953   The *Oyabun-Kobun*: A Japanese Ritual Kinship Institution. *American Anthropologist*, 55, 695–707.

ISHIZU, Teruji
1969a   Tōhoku no Fuzoku Saihō Oboe-gaki (1) (Notes on Shamanistic Practices in the Tōhoku District, No. 1). *Shakaigaku Kenkyū-ka Kiyō*, Keio University, 9, 1–20.
1969b   Shamanism no Tokushitsu to Hankei (Characteristics and Patterns of Shamanism in Tohoku District). *Tōyō Bunka* (Oriental Culture), 46–47, 1–53.
1970   Tōhoku no Fuzoku Saihō Oboe-Gaki (2) (Notes on Shamanistic Practices in the Tōhoku District, No. 2). *Shakaigaku Kenkyū-ka Kiyō*, Keio University, 10, 1–16.
1971   Tōhoku no Fuzoku Saihō Oboe-Gaki (3) (Notes on Shamanistic Practices in the Tōhoku District, No. 3). Ibid., 11, 1–16.

ISHIZUKA, Takatoshi
1959   *Nihon no Tsukimono* (Phenomena of Possession in Japan). Tokyo: Miraisha.

ISOZAKI, Sadamoto
1972   Islam no Junrei Gyōji (The Pilgrimage in Islam). *Kokusai Shūkyō News*, 13:4, 8–17.

ITŌ, Dōgaku
1939   Shūkyō, Seiji oyobi Keizai—Bastide Shūkyō-Shakaigaku no Kōsō ni yorite (Religion, Politics, and Economy—From the Viewpoint of Bastide's Sociology of Religion). *Shūkyō Kenkyū*, 1:3, 169–192.

ITŌ, Mikiharu
1958   Amami no Kami-Matsuri (*Noro* Worship in the Amami Islands). *Nihon Bunka Kenkyūjo Kiyō*, Kokugakuin University, 3, 53–139.
1961   Takara-Jima no Shakai to Shūkyō no Kōzō-teki Rikai (Structural Interpretation of Society and Religion in the Takara Island). Ibid., 8, 58–95.
1965a   Toshika to "Mura" no Seikatsu Kōzō Josetsu (Some Thoughts on Urbanization and the Pattern of Life in the Village). Ibid., 16, 181–220.
1965b   Kuro-Shima no Shakai to Shūkyō no Kōzō to Henka (The Structure and Change of Society and Religion in the Kuro Island). Ibid., 17, 78–108.
1970   Ujiko no Shakai-Jinruigaku Josetsu (A Social Anthropological Study of the *Ujiko*, or Shinto Parishioner). Ibid., 25: 1–29.

IWAI, Fumio
1957–59 Tamba ni okeru Kirisutokyō no Juyō (Acceptance of Christianity in the Tamba Region). *Kirisutokyō Kenkyū*, Dōshisha University, 30:3, 55–74, and 31:1, 53–75.
1963   Tamba-Chihō ni okeru Kirisutokyō no Juyō (Acceptance of Christianity in the Tamba Region). In *Nihon ni okeru Kirisutokyō to Shakai-Mondai* (Christianity and Social Problems in Japan), ed. SUMIYA, Etsuji, pp. 310–376. Tokyo: Misuzu-shobō.

IWASAKI, Toshio
1963   *Hompō Shōshi no Kenkyū* (A Study of Minor Shrines in Japan). Sōma: Shuppan Kōenkai.
IZUMI, Ryūji
1972   Sanson ni okeru Kirisutokyō no Juyō (1) (Acceptance of Christianity in a Mountain Community, No. 1). *Machikaneyama Ronsō*, Osaka University, 5, 101–123.
JAPANESE SOCIETY OF ETHNOLOGY
1973   (eds.) *Okinawa no Minzokugaku-teki Kenkyū* (An Ethnological Study of Okinawa). Tokyo: Minzokugaku Shinkōkai.
KAGAMISHIMA, Genryū
1969   Zenshū ni okeru Keizai-Seikatsu (The Economic Life of Zen Buddhists). *Bukkyō Keizai Kenkyū*, Komazawa University, 3, 27–51.
KAJIYAMA, Tsutomu
1946   *Protestantism no Rinri to Shihon-shugi no Seishin* (trans. of WEBER, M., *Die protestantische Ethik und der Geist des Kapitalismus*). Tokyo: Yūhikaku.
KAMADA, Onko
1973   Matsuri ni mirareru Wakashū no Kinō (The Role of Young Men in Shinto Festivals). *Shakai Denshō Kenkyū*, 1, 18–23.
KANEKO, Keisuke, HAYASAKA, Masaaki, and ITŌ, Fusakazu
1970   Yamato ni okeru Jinja to Ujiko (Shinto Shrines and Parishioners in the Yamato Province). *Gakuhō*, Tenri University, 65, 20–63.
KASAHARA, Kazuo
1960   *Seiji to Shūkyō* (Politics and Religion). Tokyo: Asoka-shuppan.
1970   *Sōka Gakkai to Honganji Kyōdan* (Sōka Gakkai and the Honganji Sect). Tokyo: Shin-Jimbutsu Ōraisha.
KASAHARA, Kazuo, and MURAKAMI, Shigeyoshi
1971   (eds.) *Gendai Nihon no Shūkyō to Seiji* (Religion and Politics in Contemporary Japan). Tokyo: Shin-Jimbutsu Ōraisha.
KATAKOZAWA, Chiyomatsu
1956   Meiji Shoki Protestant no Shinto Kōzō—Kaigan Kyōkai o Chūshin to shita Danjo-betsu Nenrei-betsu (Sex and Age Composition of Members of a Protestant Church in Early Meiji: The Case of Kaigan Church). *Kirisutokyō Shigaku*, 7, 43–60.
KATAKURA, Motoko
1968   Kōran ni Arawareru Kazoku Kyōdōtai (The Arabic Family as Reflected in the Qur'an). *Shūkyō Kenkyū*, 197, 1–24.
KATAOKA, Kenkichi
1900   Bushidō to Kirisutokyō (Bushido and Christianity). *Jōmō Kyōkai Geppō*, Annaka Christian Church, 18.
KATAOKA, Yakichi
1967   *Kakure Kirishitan: Rekishi to Minzoku* (Hidden Christians: Their History and Folklore). Tokyo: Nihon Hōsō Shuppan Kyōkai.
KATAYAMA, Ichiryō
1973   Ceylon ni okeru Bukkyō to Jujutsu-teki Animism (Buddhism and Magical Animism in Ceylon). *Shūkyōgaku Ronshū*, Komazawa University, 6, 71–92.

196   RELIGION IN CHANGING JAPANESE SOCIETY

KATŌ, Kumaichirō
1925   *Minkan-Shinkō Shi* (History of Folk Beliefs). Tokyo: Heigo-shuppan.
KATŌ, Kunio
1966   Tōkei-jō kara mita Sengo ni okeru Kiristokyōkai no Ugoki (A
       Statistical Survey on Postwar Trends in the Christian World).
       Shūmu Jihō, 12, 1–22.
KATŌ, Takahisa
1968   Sorei-sha no Ichi Kōsatsu (A Study of a Communal Ancestral
       Shrine in Tsuwano District). *Nihon Bunka Kenkyūjo Kiyō*, Kokuga-
       kuin University, 22, 213–243.
KAWAI, Hidekazu
1973   Shakai Henkaku to Shūkyō Rinri (trans. of BELLAH, R. N.,
       Beyond Belief, 1970, parts I and II). Tokyo: Miraisha.
KAWASAKI, Eshō, et al.
1959–62 *Toshi Jiin no Shakai-teki Kinō* (The Social Functions of Buddhist
         Temples in Urban Areas). 2 vols. Tokyo: Bukkyōto Kōryū Kyōkai.
KAWASAKI, Eshō, et al.
1970   *Kayakabe, Kakure Numbutsu* (Kayakabe, Hidden Buddhists). Kyoto:
       Hōzōkan.
KAWASHIMA, Takeyoshi
1957   *Ideorogi to shiteno Kazoku Seido* (Family Institution as an Ideology).
       Tokyo: Iwanami-shoten.
KEYES, Charles F.
1971   Kindai Thai-Koku ni okeru Bukkyō to Kokka (Buddhism and
       National Integration in Thailand). *Kokusai Shūkyō News*, 12:5,
       21–36.
KISHIMOTO, Hideo
1954   (ed.) *Meiji Bunkashi Shūkyō Hen* (Cultural History of the Meiji
       Period. VI: Religion). Tokyo: Yoyosha. (Trans. by HOWES, J.,
       Japanese Religion in the Meiji Era, Century Cultural Council Series,
       III. Tokyo: Ōbunsha, 1958).
1961   *Shūkyōgaku* (Science of Religion). Tokyo: Taimeidō.
1964   Shinto no Toshika (Urbanization of Shinto). *Nihon Bunka Ken-
       kyūjo Kiyō*, Kokugakuin University, 14, 58–72.
KITAGAWA, Joseph M.
1971   J. Wach ni okeru "Rikai" to "Kyūsai" no Gainen ni tsuite (Vers-
       tehen and Erlösung: Some Remarks on Joachim Wach's Work).
       Kokusai Shūkyō News, 12:3, 8–27.
KLEINER, Joseph
1963   Amami Oshima no Sonraku Kōzō to Saishi Soshiki (The Village
       Structure and the Organization for Shinto Rituals in the Amami
       Oshima Island). *Shakai to Denshō*, 7:1, 43–63.
KOBAYASHI, Masayoshi
1972   Robert Bellah ni okeru Shūkyō Riron no Tenkai (Development
       in Robert Bellah's Theory on Religion). *Shukyō Kenkyū*, 212, 53–71.
KOBAYASHI, Sakae
1971   Osore-Zan Sampaisha Shūkyō Chōsa (Data from a Religious
       Survey of Pilgrims to Mt. Osorezan). *Shingaku Kenkyū*, Kansei
       Gakuin University, 19, 43–84.

KOKUBU, Keiji
1941   *Shinwa to Shakai* (trans. of MALINOWSKI, B., *Myth in Primitive Psychology*). Tokyo: Sōgensha.
KOKUBU, Naoichi
1971   Taiwan ni okeru Shamanism no Sekai (Shamanism in Taiwan). *Minzokugaku Hyōron*, Otsuka Folklore Society, 6, 1–22.
KŌMOTO, Mitsugi
1973   Jinja Gōshi (Shrine Mergers). In *Kindai to no Kaigō* (Confrontation with the Modern Age), ed. TAMARU, Noriyoshi, et al., pp. 67–112. Tokyo: Kosei-shuppan.
KUBO, Noritada
1956   *Kōshin Shinkō* (*Kōshin* Beliefs and Practices). Tokyo: Yamakawa-shuppan.
1971a   *Okinawa no Shūzoku to Shinkō* (Folkways and Beliefs in Okinawa). Tokyo: Tōyō Bunka Kenkyūjo, University of Tokyo.
1971b   Taiwan no Tochi Gami Shinkō (The Earth-Deity in Taiwan). *Shūkyō Kenkyū*, 207, 81–102.
1973a   Okinawa ni okeru Chūgoku no Shinkō to Shūzoku (Okinawan Beliefs and Folkways Brought from China). *Jinrui Kagaku*, 25, 44–47.
1973b   Okinawa no Minzoku Shūkyō to Chūgoku (Okinawan Folk Religion and Its Relationship to China). In *Okinawa no Minzokugaku-teki Kenkyū* (An Ethnological Study of Okinawa), ed. Japanese Society of Ethnology, pp. 421–456. Tokyo: Minzokugaku Shinkōkai.
KUBOTA, Shōbun
1962   *Bukkyō Shakaigaku* (Sociology of Buddhism). Tokyo: Nisshin-shuppan.
KUCHIBA, Masuo
1972   Kedah ni okeru Malay Nōmin no Minzoku Shūkyō (Folk Religion of the Malay Peasants in Kedah). *Minzokugaku Kenkyū*, 37:2, 81–94.
1973   Indonesia no Shūkyō Undō (Religious Movements in Indonesia). *Asia Review*, 4:4, 180–186.
KUDŌ, Eiichi
1959   *Nihon Shakai to Protestant Dendō* (Japanese Society and Mission Work of Protestant Churches). Tokyo: United Church of Christ in Japan Press.
KURATA, Washio
1958   Kakure Kirishitan no Soshiki to Sonraku Kōzō (Organization of Hidden Christians and Village Structure). *Shakaigaku*, Kansei Gakuin University, 4, 48–51.
1959   Kakure Kirishitan no Fukkatsu to Sonraku Kōzō—Kirishitan Fukkatsu no Amakusa-Gata (Revival of Underground Christians and Village Structure: The Amakusa Type of Revival). Ibid., 5, 39–67.
1964   Shinkō Soshiki to Buraku Kōzō (Religious Organization and Village Structure). *Shakaigakubu Kiyō*, Kansei Gakuin University, 8, 15–30.
KUROKAWA, Minako
1968   Durkheim to Weber no Shūkyōron (On Sociology of Religion of

Durkheim and Weber). *Shakaigaku Hyōron*, 72, 58–67.

KUROSAKI, Yasujirō
1958   Oyagō to Edagō (A Parent Village and Its Branch Villages).
        Shakaigaku Hyōron, 34, 85–96.
1973   Shugoshin no Saishi ni tsuite (Rites for Worshiping Guardian
        Deities). *Atarashii Dōshi*, Hokkaido Prefectural Government, 10:7,
        1–12.

KUSUNOKI, Masahiro
1973   Java-Tō no Shūkyō (Folk Religions in Java). *Bunka*, Tohoku Uni-
        versity, 36:4, 1–44.

KUYAMA, Yasushi
1956   (ed.) *Kindai Nihon to Kirisutokyō* (Modern Japan and Christianity).
        2 vols. Tokyo: Sōbunsha.

LEBRA, Takie S.
1971   Shūkyō-teki Eshin to Bunka Henyō (Religious Conversion as a
        Breakthrough for Transculturation: A Japanese Sect in Hawaii).
        Kokusai Shūkyō News, 12:4, 16–34.

LINTON, Ralph
1945   *The Cultural Background of Personality.* New York: D. Appleton Cen-
        tury Crofts.

MAEDA, Takashi
1965   *Sosen Sūhai no Kenkyū* (A Study of Ancestor Worship). Tokyo: Ao-
        yama-shoin.
1971   *Junrei no Shakaigaku* (A Sociological Study of Pilgrimage). Kyoto:
        Minerva-shobō.

MAEYAMA, Takashi
1968   Brazil no Nikkei Minority Shakai ni okeru Shūkyō Kōdō no Ichi
        Kōsatsu (A Study of Religious Behavior in the Minority Society of
        Brazilians of Japanese Ancestry). *Kenkyū Report*, Human Science
        Research Institute of São Paulo, 3, 109–133.

MAKI, Masami
1971   Kirishitan Catholic Sonraku Kurosaki no Shakai Kōzō (Social
        Structure of Kurosaki, a Kirishitan Catholic Village in Nagasaki
        Prefecture). *Shakaigaku Hyōron*, 21:4, 51–71.
1972   Kirishitan Sonraku Neshiko no Shūkyō to Shakai Kōzō (Religion
        and Social Structure of Neshiko, a Kirishitan Village). *Tetsugaku
        Nempō*, Kyushu University, 31, 115–147.

MARUYAMA, Teruo
1971   Shinran eno Kaiki—Shinjinsha Undō kara Dōbō-no-Kai Undō e
        (Return to Shinran, the Founder). In *Honganji Kyōdan* (Honganji
        Sect), ed. UEHARA, Senroku, et al., pp. 266–293. Tokyo: Gaku-
        gei-Shorin.
1972   *Kyōdan towa nanika?* (What is the Church?) Tokyo: Dentō to
        Gendaisha.

MATSUMOTO, Masaaki
1967   Minami-Jima ni okeru Sonraku no Sairei to Sosen no Saishi
        (Neighborhood Festival and Ancestor Worship in the Southern
        Islands). *Shakai to Denshō*, 10:4, 10–28.

MATSUSHIMA, Shizuo
1962   Rōmu Kanri no Nihon-teki Tokushitsu to Hensen (Japanese Labor
        Management: Characteristics and Changes). Tokyo: Daiamondo-
        sha.

MINAKAWA, Kōgi, et al.
1972   Sōsai ni taisuru Hitobito no Ishiki (People's Attitudes toward Funerals
        and Subsequent Services). Sōtōshū Kyōka Kenshūjo, Komazawa
        University (mimeo.).

MIYAJI, Harukuni
1959   Shimane Hantō ni okeru Jinja Saishi no Kenkyū (A Study of
        Shinto Rituals in the Shimane Peninsula). Nihon Bunka Kenkyūjo
        Kiyō, Kokugakuin University, 5, 97–219.
1960   Oki ni okeru Buraku no Saishi ni tsuite (Village Shinto Rituals in
        the Oki Islands). Kokugakuin Zasshi, Kokugakuin University, 61:2–
        3, 54–66.
1962   Oro-Jima ni okeru Buraku Saishi (Village Shinto Rituals in the
        Oro Island). Shūkyō Kenkyū, 171, 85–106.
1963   Jinja Saishi no Soshiki—Fukuoka-Kenka no 2,3 no Jirei ni tsuite
        (The Organization for Shinto Rituals—Some Cases Observed in
        Fukuoka Prefecture). Nihon Bunka Kenkyūjo Kiyō, Kokugakuin Uni-
        versity, 13, 29–65.

MIYAKE, Hitoshi
1962   Gendai Shugen-Kyōdan Kenkyū Josetsu (Introduction to Studies
        of Mountain Priests). Shūkyōgaku Zasshi (Journal of Comparative
        Religion), 1, 18–26.
1964   Shugendō to Shomin Seikatsu (The Role of Mountain Priests in
        People's Lives). Ibid., 4, 1–15.
1966   Shūkyō no Shakaigaku (Sociology of Religion). In Gendai Shakai no
        Shakaigaku (Contemporary Sociology), ed. YONEYAMA, Keizo,
        pp. 261–287. Tokyo: Sekaishoin.
1969   Shugendō ni okeru Shūkyō Girei no Kōzō (Pattern of Religious
        Rituals of Mountain Priests). Tetsugaku, Keio University, 54, 235–
        245.
1971   Shugendō Girei no Kenkyū (A Study of Rites in the Religion of Moun-
        tain Priests). Tokyo: Shunjūsha.
1972a   Okinawa no Jinja Shinkō: Sono Dempan to Juyō (Beliefs about
        the Shinto Shrine in Okinawa: Their Diffusion and Acceptance).
        Hōgaku Kenkyū, Keio University, 45:3, 299–322.
1972b   Nihonjin no Shūkyō Seikatsu to Genze Riyaku (Religious Life of
        the Japanese and Worldly Benefits). Nihon Bukkyō, 34, 24–37.
1973a   Yamabushi—Sono Kōdō to Soshiki (Mountain Priests: Their Practices
        and Organizations). Tokyo: Hyōronsha.
1973b   Okinawa ni okeru Gongen Shinkō no Juyō (Acceptance of the
        Religious Ideology Called Gongen in Okinawa). Jinrui Kagaku, 25,
        40–43.

MIYARA, Takahiro
1966   Saishi Keishō kara mita Sonraku Kyōdōtai no Kōzō (Transmission
        of Religious Rites and the Social Structure of a Village Com-

200 RELIGION IN CHANGING JAPANESE SOCIETY

munity). *Kyōdōtai no Hikaku Kenkyū*, Society for the Comparative Study of the Community, 4, 53–70.
1973   Okinawa Sonraku no Shakai Soshiki to Saishi Seikatsu (Social Organization and Religious Life of an Okinawan Village). *Jinrui Kagaku*, 25, 49–55.

MIYATA, Makio
1973   Kyōdan Tōrisha Senshutsu no Hensen (A Change in the Procedure for Electing the President of the Konkō Sect). *Konkō Kyōgaku*, Konkō Research Institute, 13, 33–69.

MIYATA, Mitsuo
1970   Shūkyō to Seitō (Religion and Political Party—A Case of West Germany). *Shisō*, 548, 156–173.
1973   Sezoku-ka to Shūkyō Rinri (Secularization and Religious Ethics). *Shisō*, 586, 1–23, and 589, 62–87.

MIYATA, Noboru
1961   Sangaku Shinkō to Kō Shūdan (Mountain Worship and *Kō* Groups). *Nihon Minzokugaku Kaihō*, 21, 5–14.
1963   Buraku to Shinkō Shūdan (Neighborhoods and Religious Groups). In *Mimasaka no Minzoku* (Folklore in the Mimasaka Province), ed. WAKAMORI, Tarō, pp. 249–265. Tokyo: Yoshikawa Kōbunkan.
1965   Asama Shinkō (Worship of Mt. Asama). In *Shima no Minzoku* (Folklore in the Shima Province), ed. WAKAMORI, Tarō, pp. 308–321. Tokyo: Yoshikawa Kōbunkan.
1968   Yonaoshi to Miroku Shinkō (The Renewal Concept and *Miroku* Belief). *Minzokugaku Kenkyū*, 33, 32–44.
1969a   Kinkazan Shinkō to Miroku (Beliefs in Mt. Kinka and *Miroku*). In *Rikuzen Hokubu no Minzoku* (Folklore in the Northern Rikuzen Province), ed. WAKAMORI, Tarō, pp. 261–274. Tokyo: Yoshikawa Kōbunkan.
1969b   Daishi Shinkō to Miroku (Beliefs in *Daishi* and *Miroku*). *Shigaku Kenkyū*, Tokyo University of Education, 71, 1–25.
1970a   *Miroku Shinkō no Kenkyū* (A Study of *Miroku*, the Japanese Traditional View of Messiah). Tokyo: Miraisha.
1970b   *Ikigami Shinkō* (Man-God Belief, Custom of Worshiping Men as Gods). Tokyo: Hanawa-shobō.
1971   Okinawa no Miroku Gami (*Miroku* Belief in Okinawa). *Minzokugaku Kenkyū*, 36:3, 253–259.
1972   *Kinsei no Hayari Gami* (Popular Beliefs in the Edo Period). Tokyo: Hyōronsha.

MIYAZAKI, Noriya
1971   Danjo-betsu Jidan Kankei to Jidan Ronsō (Sex Differential Buddhist Parish Affiliation and Disputes). *Shakai to Denshō*, 12:4, 1–24.

MIZOBUCHI, Hiromi
1972   *America no Kokujin Kyōkai* (trans. of FRAZIER, E. Franklin, *The Negro Church in America*, 1964). Tokyo: Miraisha.

MOBERG, David O.
1962   *The Church as a Social Institution: The Sociology of American Religion*. New York: Prentice-Hall.

MOCHIZUKI, Tetsuya
1970   Max Weber no Shūkyō Rinri-Ron (Max Weber's Religious Ethics).
        Shohō, Nichiren-shū Gendai Shūkyō Kenkyūjo, 4, 77–94.
MOMBUSHŌ, Shumuka
1962   (eds.) *Shūkyō Dantai Ruikei Chōsa no Kaisetsu* (Findings of Study of
        the Patterns of Religious Groups). Tokyo: Ministry of Education.
MORI, Mikio
1973   Minami Vietnam no "Kiki no Shūkyō" (Religion in Crisis—A
        Case in South Vietnam). *Asia Review,* 4:4, 163–168.
MORI, Tōgo
1937   Charisma-teki Shihaisha no Ruikei—Shūkyō Shakaigaku no Ichi
        Mondai (Types of the Charismatic Ruler: A Problem of Sociology
        of Religion). *Shakaigaku,* 5, 78–91.
MORIOKA, Kiyomi
1953   Nihon Nōson ni okeru Kirisutokyō no Juyō (Acceptance of Chris-
        tianity in a Japanese Rural Community). *Minzokugaku Kenkyū,* 17:
        2, 1–14.
1954a   Machino-machi Kawanishi ni okeru Shinshū Monto no Kyōdan
        Naikon (Religious Endogamy and Shin Buddhist Parishioners in
        Machino-machi, Ishikawa Prefecture). *Jinrui Kagaku,* 6, 219–232.
1954b   Sonraku no Kaikyū Kōzō to Miyaza (Class Structure and the
        Miyaza System in a Village). *Shakai Kagaku Ronshū,* Tokyo Uni-
        versity of Education, 1, 110–161.
1955   Shukyō Seikatsu (Religious Life). In *Noto—Shizen, Shakai, Bunka*
        (Noto: Its Nature, Society, and Culture), pp. 209–244. Tokyo:
        Heibonsha.
1957   Hokkaidō Shinotsu Heison no Tenkai to Sonraku Kōzō—Saishi
        Soshiki o Chūjiku o shite (Social Structure of Shinotsu, a Hokkaido
        Village Founded by the Colonial Troops). *Shakai Kagaku Ronshū,*
        Tokyo University of Education, 4, 1–97.
1958   Review of FICHTER, J. H., *Social Relations in the Urban Parish.*
        Soshioroji, 20, 66–75.
1959   (ed.) *Chihō Shō-Toshi ni okeru Kirisuto-Kyōkai no Keisei* (The Estab-
        lishment of a Christian Church in a Small Local City). Tokyo:
        Research Institute on the Mission of the Church, United Church
        of Christ in Japan.
1962   *Shinshū Kyōdan to "Ie" Seido* (The Shin Buddhist Orders and the *Ie*
        System). Tokyo: Sōbunsha.
1964a   Budō-Saku Nōson ni okeru Rōjin to Shinkō (Old People and Their
        Religious Beliefs in a Grape-Farming Village). *Nihon Rōnen Igakukai
        Zasshi* (Japanese Journal of Geriatrics), I, Supplement, 136–138.
1964b   Kinkōka ni yoru Chiiki Kōzō no Henka (Change in Neighborhood
        Structure due to Suburbanization). In *Kinkō Toshi no Hembō Katei*
        (Process of Change in a Suburban City). Tokyo: International
        Christian University.
1965a   Nihon Nōson ni okeru Kirisutokyō no Dochaku-ka (Indigenization
        of Christianity in the Japanese Rural Society). *Shakai Kagaku Ron-
        shū,* Tokyo University of Education, 12, 1–82.
1965b   Honganji no Kaken to "Ie" Seido (The Constitution of the Hon-

ganji and the Japanese Family System). *Toyō Bunka Kenkyūjo Kiyō*, University of Tokyo, 35, 77–92.

1965c   Ichi Shō-Toshi Kirisuto-Kyōkai no Bokkai-Keitai to sono Henka (Pastoral Form and Its Changes in a Protestant Church in a Small City). *Shūkyō Kenkyū*, 181, 161–162.

1966a   Christianity in the Japanese Rural Community: Acceptance and Rejection. *The Sociological Review Monograph*, 10, 183–197.

1966b   Meiji-Makki ni okeru Shūraku Jinja no Seiri (Local Shrine Mergers in the Closing Years of Meiji). *Tōyō Bunka* (Oriental Culture), 40, 1–50.

1966c   Aru Tsujimoto no Kiroku (Family Record of the Patron of a Buddhist Temple). In *Shinshū-Shi no Kenkyū* (A Study of the History of Shin Buddhism), pp. 761–790. Kyoto: Nagata Bunshōdo.

1967a   Eidai Dōjōyaku no Buppandaka Shihaiken (The Right of a Hereditary Director of a Local Buddhist Group over Its Property). *Sōbun*, 46, 6–8.

1967b   Les religions contemporaines du Japon: Coexistence et conflit. *Revue française de sociologie*, 8, 348–354.

1968a   Kinsei Bukkōji ni okeru Honmatsu Kankei no Tokushoku (Characteristics of Relationships between Central and Subordinate Temples in the Bukkōji Sect of Shin Buddhism in Tokugawa Period). In *Hoken, Kindai ni okeru Kamakura Bukkyō no Tenkai* (Development of Kamakura Buddhism in Feudal and Modern Ages of Japan), ed. KASAHARA, Kazuo, pp. 314–345. Kyoto: Hōzōkan.

1968b   Development of the Sociology of Religion in Japan. *Journal of Asian and African Studies*, 3: 1–2, 3–12.

1968c   Religious Behaviour and the Actor's Position in his Household. *Journal of Asian and African Studies*, 3: 1–2, 25–43.

1968d   Industrialization and Shinto. In *Continuity and Change* (Proceedings of the Second International Conference for Shinto Studies), pp. 141–146. Tokyo: Institute for Japanese Culture and Classics, Kokugakuin University.

1968e   Toshika Genshō to Shūkyō (Urbanization and Religion). *Shūkyō Kyōkagaku Kenkyūkai Kiyō*, Otani University, 2, 31–49.

1969a   Shinshū Jōkōji-Ha no Seiritsu (Establishment of the Jōkōji Sect of Shin Buddhism). In *Nihon Jōdokyō-Shi no Kenkyū* (Historical Studies of Pure-Land Buddhism in Japan), pp. 593–606. Kyoto: Heirakuji-shoten.

1969b   Meiji-Makki ni okeru Shūraku Jinja no Seiri (2) (Local Shrine Mergers in the Closing Years of Meiji, No. 2). *Shakai Kagaku Ronshū*, Tokyo University of Education, 16, 1–118.

1969–70 Meiji Tennō Yōhaiden Mondai Shimatsu-Ki (The Dispute Concerning a Hall for Worshiping Late Emperor Meiji from a Distance). *Sōbun*, 73, 10–13; 74, 25–28; 80, 29–32; 81, 25–28.

1970a   *Nihon no Kindai Shakai to Kirisutokyō* (The Development of the Christian Church in the Modern Society of Japan). Tokyo: Hyōronsha.

1970b   Préférence pour le mariage non-mixte parmi les Amidistes "Shin" du bouddhisme japonais. *Social Compass*, 17: 1, 9–20.

1970c   The Impact of Suburbanization on Shinto Belief and Behavior. *Social Compass*, 17: 1, 37–65.

1970d   "Ie" tono Kanren deno Shakaigaku-teki Bunseki (A Sociological Analysis of Japanese Religion in Terms of the Household). In *Nihonjin no Shūkyō* (Religions of the Japanese), ed. IKADO, Fujio, and YOSHIDA, Mitsukuni, pp. 143–159. Kyoto: Tankōsha.

1972a   The Changing Family and Buddhism in Post-War Japan. *East Asian Cultural Studies*, 11:1–4, 83–96.

1972b   Hōkatsu Shūkyō Hōjin no okonau Jigyō (Sects' Institutionalized Activities in Non-Religious Spheres). *Shūmu Jihō*, 29, 51–71.

1972c   Gairai Shūkyō no Dochakuka o meguru Gainen-teki Seiri (A Conceptual Examination of the Indigenization of Foreign-Born Religions). *Shichō*, Otsuka Shigakkai, 109, 52–57.

1973   Kisei Bukkyo-Kei Ichi-Shō-Kyōdan Dokuritsu no Shin'i to Ronri (Grounds and Process of the Separation of a Small Local Buddhist Body from an Established Sect). In *Sonraku Kōzō to Shinzoku Soshiki* (Village Social Structure and Kinship Organization), pp. 511–548. Tokyo: Miraisha.

MORIOKA, Kiyomi, and HANASHIMA, Masazaburō
1968   Kinkōka ni yoru Jinja Shinkō no Henbō (Suburbanization and Transfiguration of Worship in Shrine Shinto). *Nihon Bunka Kenkyūjo Kiyō*, Kokugakuin University, 22, 71–136.

MORIOKA, Kiyomi, and KUMAGAI, Sonoko
1966   Impact of Population Mobility on Christian Churches. *Contemporary Religions in Japan*, 7, 274–296.

MORIOKA, Kiyomi, and NEWELL, William H.
1968   (eds.) *The Sociology of Japanese Religion*. Leiden: E. J. Brill.

MOROTO, Motozumi
1972   *Sosen Sūhai no Shukyōgaku-teki Kenkyū* (Ancestor Worship: An Approach from the Science of Religion). Kyoto: Jōdō Kaishū 800 nen Kinenkai.

MUNAKATA, Iwao
1968   *Shūkyō Shakaigaku* (trans. of O'DEA, Thomas F., *The Sociology of Religion*, 1966). Tokyo: Shiseidō.

MURAKAMI, Shigeyoshi
1963   *Kindai Minshū Shūkyō-Shi no Kenkyū* (A Historical Study of Modern Popular Religions). Kyoto: Hōzōkan.

1965   *Sōka Gakkai to Kōmeitō* (Sōka Gakkai and Kōmeitō Party). Tokyo: Nihon Bunkasha.

1966   Sengo ni okeru Bukkyōkai no Dōkō (Postwar Trends in the Buddhist World). *Shūmu Jihō*, 11, 35–45.

1967   Tenkanki o mukaeta Kōmeitō (Kōmeitō Party in Transition). *Sekai*, 257, 47–57.

1970a   *Kokka Shinto* (State Shinto). Tokyo: Iwanami-shoten.

1970b   Les religions nouvelles au Japon. *Social Compass*, 17:1, 137–151.

1970c   Soka Gakkai no Shisō to Kōdō (Sōka Gakkai: Its Ideology and Behavior). *Rekishi Hyōron*, Hazekura-shobō, 69–77.

1972a   *Konkō Daijin no Shōgai* (A Biography of the Founder of Konkōkyō). Tokyo: Kōdansha.

204 RELIGION IN CHANGING JAPANESE SOCIETY

1972b   New Religions in Japan. *East Asian Cultural Studies*, 11:1-4, 17-27.
NAITŌ, Kanji
1941   Shūkyō to Keizai-Rinri—Jōdo Shinshū to Omi Shōnin (Religion
        and Business Ethics—Shin Buddhism and Omi Merchants).
        Shakaigaku, 8, 243-286.
1943   *Shūkyō-Kō no Mondai—Shakaigaku-teki Shiron* (The Religious *Kō*:
        A Sociological Approach). Tokyo: Report of the Japanese Research
        Institute of Religion, No. 3.
1954   Hokuriku Nembutsu Kō Chōsa-Ki (Notes on Field Study of
        Nembutsu Kō in the Hokuriku Region). *Tetsugaku Nempō*, Kyūshū
        University, 15, 65-102.
1968   Catholic-Jima no Sōzoku Kankō (Inheritance Customs in a
        Catholic Island). *Shūkyō Kenkyū*, 195, 1-24.
1970   Inheritance Practices on a Catholic Island: Youngest-Son In-
        heritance (Ultimogeniture) on Kuroshima, Nagasaki Prefecture.
        Social Compass, 17:1, 21-36.
1971   *Sei naru monono Shakaigaku* (trans. of CAILLOIS, Roger, *Quatre
        essais de sociologie contemporaine*, 1951). Tokyo: Kōbundō.
NAKAMATSU, Hisahide, et al.
1973   Sonraku Kōzō to Saishi Sekai (Social Structure and Religious Rites
        in the Village). In *Okinawa no Minzokugaku-teki Kenkyū* (An Eth-
        nological Study of Okinawa), eds. Japanese Society of Ethnology,
        pp. 1-168. Tokyo: Minzokugaku Shinkōkai.
NAKANO, Takashi
1964   *Shōka Dōzokudan no Kenkyū* (A Study of the *Dōzoku* Group among
        Merchant Households). Tokyo: Miraisha.
1972a   Musashi Sōsha Rokushogū o meguru Meiji Shoki no Kyū-Shinkan
        to Jinin Jun-Jinin (The Hereditary Priesthood of the Musashi
        Grand Shrine in the Early Meiji Period). *Fuchūshi-Shi Kindai-Hen
        Shiryōshū*, Fuchū City Office, 9, 2-113.
1972b   Meiji Shoki Ogawa Yoshiyasu rano Fuchū Dendō to sono Hamon
        (Christian Mission Work in the Fuchū Area by Y. Ogawa and his
        Associates in the Early Meiji Period). *Fuchū-shi-Shi Kindai-Hen
        Shiryōshū*, Fuchū City Office, 9, 175-193.
1973   Rokushogū Saishi Soshiki no Hendō (Changes in the Priestly
        Organization of the Rokushogū Shrine). In *Sonraku Kōzō to Shin-
        zoku Soshiki* (Village Social Structure and Kinship Organization),
        pp. 459-510. Tokyo: Miraisha.
NAKAYAMA, Tarō
1924   Miyaza no Kenkyū (A Study of the *Miyaza* System). *Shakaigaku
        Zasshi*, 6, 1-32.
NAKAZAWA, Kiichi
1938   *Kami, Hito, Dōbutsu* (God, Man, and Besast). Tokyo: Hokuryūkan.
NAOE, Hiroji
1966   *Yashiki-Gami no Kenkyū* (A Study of House-Site Gods). Tokyo:
        Yoshikawa Kōbunkan.
NARA, Tsuyoshi
1973   Indo no Hitotsu no Shūkyō Kaikaku (The New Buddhist Move-

ment: One Religious Revolution in India). *Asia Review*, 4:4, 168–174.

NEWELL, William H., and DOBASHI, Fumiko
1968　Some Problems of Classification in Religious Sociology as Shown in the History of Tenri Kyōkai. *Journal of Asian and African Studies*, 3:1–2, 84–100.

NIHON BUKKYŌ KENKYŪKAI
1970　(eds.) *Nihon Shūkyō no Genze Riyaku* (Worldly Benefits in Japanese Buddhism). Tokyo: Ōkura-shuppan.

NIHON SHŪKYŌ GAKKAI
1967　(eds.) *Shūkyō Kenkyū*, 191, Special Issue on "Method of Religious Studies."

NISHIGAKI, Haruji
1970　Jinja Saishi (Shinto Rites in Shrines). In *Tsugaru no Minzoku* (Folkways in the Tsugaru Province), ed. WAKAMORI, Tarō, pp. 368–378. Tokyo: Yoshikawa Kōbunkan.

NISHIHIRA, Shigeki
1972　Seiyōjin wa Shūkyō ni tsuite dō kangaete iruka (Westerners' Conceptions of Religion). *Shūmu Jihō*, 29, 2–21.

NISHINA, Yoshinori
1967　Sonraku Saishi no Kakaku-teki Kōsei (Family Status in Neighborhood Festival). *Shakai to Denshō*, 10:3, 21–37.

NISHIYAMA, Matsunosuke
1959　*Iemoto no Kenkyū* (A Study of the *Iemoto*). Tokyo: Hazekura-shobō.

NISHIYAMA, Shigeru
1972　Meiji Kōhanki ni okeru Fuchū Sei Maka Kyōkai no Dōkō (Fuchū St. Mark Episcopal Church in the Latter Part of the Meiji Period). *Fuchūshi-Shi Kindai-Hen Shiryōshū*, Fuchū City Office, 9, 194–250.
1972–73　Shimo-osa Fukuda Seikōkai no Keisei to Tenkai (Shimo-osa Fukuda Episcopal Church: Its Establishment and Development). *Shingaku no Koe*, Theological Seminary of the Episcopal Church, 18:2, 10–27; 19:2, 21–39.

NOGUCHI, Takenori
1973　Okinawa ni okeru Funadama Shinkō no Dempan to Juyō (Diffusion and Acceptance of the Belief in Ship Spirits in Okinawa). *Jinrui Kagaku*, 25, 23–26.

NOMURA, Nobukiyo
1962　Mawatari-Jima Shūdan Catholic no Kenkyū (A Study of a Catholic Settlement in Mawatari Island). *Tetsugaku Nempō*, Kyūshū University, 24, 51–86.
1968　Nagasaki-ken Sotome-cho Kurosaki Chiiki no Kirishitan Catholic no Kenkyū (A Study of Kirishitan Catholics in Kurosaki District, Sotome-cho, Nagasaki Prefecture). *Tetsugaku Nempō*, Kyūshū University, 27, 25–66.
1972a　Kirishitan Catholic Sonraku no Religious Cultural Mentality no Kenkyū (A Study of Religious Cultural Mentality in a Kirishitan Catholic Village). *Tetsugaku Nempō*, Kyūshū University, 31, 1–36.
1972b　Shūkyō-teki Tōgō no Seikaku no Free Association ni yoru Kenkyū

(A Study of Religious Integration by Free Association). *Nishi Nihon Shūkyōgaku Zasshi*, 2, 15–33.

NOZAKI, Kiyotaka
1969   Mie-ken Watarai-gun Kumano-nada Engan no Kamagata Ujiko Shūdan (A Shrine-Worshipping Group in Kumano District, Mie Prefecture). *Chihōshi Kenkyū*, 99, 2–18.

NUMA, Gishō
1953   Kāsuto to Indo no Shūkyō—Weber Shūkyō-Shakaigaku no Ichi-Mondai (Caste and Indian Religion—A Problem in Weber's Sociology of Religion). *Shakaigaku Hyōron*, 11, 3–26.
1954   Nichiren Kyōdan no Shakaigaku-teki Chōsa Kenkyū (A Sociological Study of the Nichiren Sect). *Bungakubu Ronsō*, Risshō University, 3, 3–26.

NUMA, Kenkichi
1961   Buraku Kaihō Undō no Sakigake—Meiji no Catholic no Ichi Yakuwari (Predecessors of the Movement for the Emancipation of Outcasts—A Role Played by Catholics in Early Meiji). *Rekishi Hyōron* (Historical Review), 125, 45–59.
1965   Meiji Zenki ni okeru Girisha Seikyō Junan-shi—Hachiōji Sōgi Jiken o meguru Tatakai (Persecution of the Greek Orthodox Christians in the Early Meiji Period—Struggle over the "Funeral Incident" in Hachiōji). *Jinbun Shizen Kagaku Ronshū*, Tokyo College of Economics, 8–9, 35–63.

OGUCHI, Iichi
1935   Doitsu Shūkyō-Shakaigaku no Hatten (Development of the Sociology of Religion in Germany). *Shūkyō Kenkyū* (New Edition), 12:5, 112–114; 12:6, 89–98.
1951   Shin Shūkyō Shūdan no Keisei to sono Kiban (The Formation of New Religious Groups and Their Basis). *Shisō*, 327, 29–34.
1954   *Nihon Shūkyō no Shakai-teki Seikaku* (Social Character of Japanese Religions). Tokyo: University of Tokyo Press.
1955a   *Shūkyō Shakaigaku* (Sociology of Religion). Tokyo: University of Tokyo Press.
1955b   Shinkō Shūkyō no Tokushitsu (Characteristics of the New Religions). *Gendai Shūkyō Kōza*, V, 191–199. Tokyo: Sōbunsha.
1956   Shūkyōgaku Gojūnen no Ayumi (Fifty Years of Religious Studies in Japan). *Shūkyō Kenkyū*, 147, 4–5.
1957   Jujutsu-teki Shūkyō (Magical Religion). *Tōyō Bunka Kenkyūjo Kiyō*, University of Tokyo, 12, 27–47.
1959   Noro to Yuta (*Noro* and *Yuta*). *Jinrui Kagaku*, 11, 120–124.
1960   Oki no Kitōshi (The Diviner in the Oki Islands). *Kokugakuin Zasshi*, Kokugakuin University, 61:2–3, 41–43.

OGUCHI, Ichi, and SAKI, Akio
1956   *Kyōso* (The Founder of New Religions). Tokyo: Aoki-shoten.
1957   *Sōka Gakkai*. Tokyo: Aoki-shoten.

OGURA, Manabu
1964   Noto Chihō no Saishi Soshiki (The Organization for Shinto Rituals in the Noto Province). *Shakai to Denshō*, 8:1, 20–32.

1972   Detsukuri-Chi no Shinkō Jittai (Religious Life in a New Settle-
        ment). *Shakai to Denshō*, 13:2, 1–17.
OGURI, Junko
1968   Tenrikyō ni okeru Fukyōsha to Minshū tono Taiwa (Confronta-
        tion of Tenrikyo Missionaries and People). *Nihon Shūkyōshi Kenkyū*,
        2, 223–235.
1969a   Tenrikyō no Hatten to Kisei Shūkyō tono Masatsu (Development
        of Tenrikyo and Its Conflict with Other Established Orders).
        Nihon Bukkyō, 30, 17–46.
1969b   *Nihon no Kindai Shakai to Tenrikyō* (Development of Tenrikyō in
        the Modern Society of Japan). Tokyo: Hyōronsha.
ŌHAMA, Tetsuya
1963   Meiji Zenki Nishi Jōshū ni okeru Kirisuto-Kyōkai no Keisei (The
        Formation of a Christian Church in the Western Jōshū Region in
        the Early Meiji Period). *Shichō*, Otsuka Shigakkai, 82–83, 52–73.
1965   Kirisuto-kyō Dendō no Tenkai o meguru Bōgyo to Kōsō (Defense
        and Conflict in Development of Christian Proselytization). *Chihōshi
        Kenkyū*, 77, 2–19.
1966   Meiji Zenki ni okeru Kirisuto-Kyōkai no Sonzai Keitai (Actual
        Status of Christian Churches in Early Meiji). *Nihon Rekishi*, 222,
        34–55; 223, 54–71.
1968   Kirisutosha to Minshū no Kakushitsu (Conflicts between Christians
        and Non-Christians in the Early Meiji Period). *Nihon Shūkyōshi
        Kenkyū*, 2, 186–211.
1969   Kirisutokyō no Dochakuka (Indigenization of Christianity). *Nihon
        Shūkyōshi Kenkyū*, 3, 181–197.
1973   Eirei Shūhai to Tennōsei (Worship of the War Dead and the
        Emperor System). In *Kindai tono Kaigō* (Confrontation with the
        Modern Age), cds. TAMARU, Noriyoshi, et al., pp. 113–178.
        Tokyo: Kōsei-shuppan.
OIKAWA, Hiroshi
1941   Iwayuru "Mairi no Hotoke" no Zokushin ni tsuite (*Mairi no
        Hotoke*: A Local Folk Belief). *Minzokugaku Nempō* (Annual Report
        of the Institute of Ethnology), 3, 141–159.
OJIMA, Akira
1954   Sonraku Keisei ni taisuru Shaji no Yakuwari (The Role of Shrines
        and Temples in the Making of a Village). *Seikō Bunka*, 7, 54–56.
OKADA, Akio
1956   *Kirishitan Bateren* (Jesuit Missionaries). Tokyo: Shinbundō.
OKADA, Jun'ichi
1965   (ed.) *Nihon no Fūdo to Kirisutokyō* (Japan's Natural Features and
        Christianity). Tokyo: Risōsha.
OKADA, Shigekiyo
1955   Ijū to Shūkyō (Migration and Religion). *Jinrui Kagaku*, 7, 52–77.
OKADA, Yoneo
1964   *Jinja Un'ei Hō* (How to Manage a Shinto Shrine), No. 2: *Kindai
        Shakai o Ikinuku tameno* (To Survive in Modern Society). Tokyo:
        Jinja Honchō Chosabu (Research Department of the National
        Union of Shinto Shrines).

OKADA, Yuzuru
  1931   Max Weber no Shūkyō-Shakaigaku—Tokuni Kare no Jukyō-
          Dokyō-Ron (Max Weber's Sociology of Religion—His View of
          Confucianism and Taoism). Risō, 21, 71-89; and 23, 115-131.
OKADA, Yuzuru, and KAMIYA, Keiji
  1960   (eds.) Nihon Nōgyō Kikaika no Bunseki (Analyses of Farm Mecha-
          nization in Japan). Tokyo: Sōbunsha.
OKO, Kin'ichi
  1973   Sorei-Kan to Shinzoku Kankō (A View of Ancestral Spirits and
          Kinship Practices). In Okinawa no Minzokugaku-teki Ken kyū (An Eth-
          nological Study of Okinawa), ed. Japanese Society of Ethology, pp.
          169-205. Tokyo: Minzokugaku Shinkōkai.
ŌMIYA, Shōsaku
  1972-73 Jinja no Hō-teki Seishitsu (The Legal Quality of the Shinto Shrine).
          Kiyō, Yamagata University, 4:1, 1-96; 4:2, 27-85.
ŌMOTO 70-NEN SHI HENSAN-KAI
  1964   Ōmoto 70-Nen Shi (70 Years of Ōmoto), 1. Kameoka: Ōmoto
          Headquarters.
  1967   Ōmoto 70-Nen Shi (70 Years of Ōmoto), 2. Kameoka: Ōmoto
          Headquarters.
ŌNO, Michikuni
  1971   Symbol to Shakai (Symbol and Society with Reference to Durk-
          heim's Theory of Punishment and Religion). Shakaigaku Hyōron,
          22:1, 17-35.
ONO, Yasuhiro
  1973   Jinkaku Henkan no Shinri to Hyōe Taiken (Psychology of Per-
          sonality Change and Possession Experiences). Nempō, Sankō
          Research Institute for the Studies of Buddhism, 4-5, 51-100.
OOMS, Herman
  1967   The Religion of the Household: A Case Study of Ancestor Worship
          in Japan. Contemporary Religions in Japan, 8, 201-333.
ŌTSUKA, Hisao
  1950   Shūkyō Kaikaku to Kindai Shakai (Reformation and Modern Society).
          Tokyo: Misuzu-shobō.
  1963   Gendai Nihon no Shakai ni okeru Ningen-teki Jōkyō (The Human
          Situation in Japanese Society Today). Sekai, 212, 73-80.
ŌTSUKA, Hisao, and IKUMATSU, Keizō
  1972   Shūkyō Shakaigaku Ronsen (trans. of parts of WEBER, Max, Gesam-
          melte Aufsätze zur Religionssoziologie, 3 vols., 1920-21), Tokyo:
          Misuzu-shobō.
ŌYAMA, Hikoichi
  1973   Okinawa no Saishi to Kazokusei (Religious Rites and the Family
          System in Okinawa). In Sonraku Kōzō to Shinzoku Soshiki (Village
          Social Structure and Kinship Organization), pp. 49-72. Tokyo:
          Miraisha.
OZAWA, Hiroshi
  1969   Kindai Minshū Shūkyō ni okeru Hitei no Ronri no Tenkai (De-
          velopment of the Logic of "Negation" in Modern Popular Reli-
          gions). Nihon Shūkyōshi Kenkyū, 3, 198-214.

RAHNER, Karl
1971   Kyōkai no Shakai Hihan-teki Kinō (The Church as a Critic of Society). *Catholic Theology*, 19, 1–21.
RYU, Tong-Shik
1972a   Religion and Changing Society of Korea. *East Asian Cultural Studies*, 11:1–4, 6–16.
1972b   A Bibliography on Family and Religion in Korea. *East Asian Cultural Studies*, 11:1–4, Appendix.
SAKAI, Nobuo
1971   Amish no Ji-Bunka Undō (Perpetuative Nativistic Movements of the Old Order Amish). *Shūkyō Kenkyū*, 208, 53–74.
1972a   Amish Personality no Ichi Kenkyū (A Study of the Amish Personality). *Nishi Nihon Shūkyōgaku Zasshi*, 2, 34–55.
1972b   Amish ni okeru Kyōiku no Mondai (Education in the Amish Community). *Nishi Nihon Shūkyōgaku Zasshi*, 2, 108–112.
1973   *Amish no Bunka to Shakai* (Culture and Society of the Amish). Tokyo: Yorudansha.
SAKAI, Tatsurō
1969   Ujiko Sōdai no Seikaku to Sonraku Kōzō (Nature of the Office of Shrine Community Representatives and Social Structure of a Neighborhood). *Bungaku Ronsō*, Aichi University, 40, 69–104.
SAKI, Akio
1964   *Shinkō Shūkyō* (New Religions). Tokyo: Aoki-shoten.
SAKI, Akio, et al.
1970   *Godai Kyōso no Jitsuzō* (The Reality of Five Great Founders of New Religious Sects). Tokyo: Yakumoi-shoin.
SAKURAI, Shūyū
1972   Sōtōshū Jiin no Keizai-teki Haikei (Economic Background of Sōtō Buddhist Temples). *Bukkyō Keizai Kenkyū*, Komazawa University, 4, 101–115.
SAKURAI, Tokutarō
1955   Shinkyū Bunka no Sesshoku (Contact of New Culture with Old Culture). In *Noto—Shizen, Bunka, Shakai* (Noto: Its Nature, Culture, and Society), pp. 144–155. Tokyo: Heibonsha.
1958   *Nihon Minkan Sinkō Ron* (On Japanese Folk Beliefs). Tokyo: Yūzankaku.
1960   Jinja Saishi to Shinkō (Shinto Ceremonies and Beliefs). In *Kunisaki —Nishi Nihon Bunka ni okeru Chii* (Kunisaki—Its Position in the Culture of Western Japan), ed. WAKAMORI, Tarō, pp. 198–217. Tokyo: Yoshikawa Kōbunkan.
1962a   *Kō Shūdan Seiritsu Katei no Kenkyū* (A Study of the Formation of the Kō Group). Tokyo: Yoshikawa Kōbunkan.
1962b   Gairai Shinkō no Juyō to Shūzoku no Henyō (Acceptance of Foreign Belief and Change in Indigeneous Customs). *Jinrui Kagaku*, 14, 94–106.
1962c   Sinkyū Shinkō no Sesshoku to Shūzoku no Henyō (Contact of Old and New Religions and Change in Customs). In *Nishi Iwami no Minzoku* (Folklore in the West Iwami Region), ed. WAKAMORI, Tarō, pp. 227–272. Tokyo: Yoshikawa Kōbunkan.

1962d   Saiki Shūzoku no Kaitai Katei (Dissolution of Purification Customs). In *Kokumin-Seikatsu-Shi Kenkyū* (Historical Studies of Japanese Life), ed. ITŌ, Tasaburō, pp. 355–388. Tokyo: Yoshikawa Kōbunkan.

1963a   Bunka Henyō (Acculturation). In *Mimasaku no Minzoku* (Folklore in the Mimasaku Region), ed. WAKAMORI, Tarō, pp. 311–352. Tokyo: Yoshikawa Kōbunkan.

1963b   Zairai Shinkō to Bukkyō Shinkō tono Sesshoku Henyō (Contact of Indigeneous Beliefs with Buddhism and Subsequent Changes). In *Nihon Rekishi Ronkyū* (Studies of Japanese History), Collection of Papers in Archeology and Folklore, pp. 105–133. Tokyo: Bungadō Ginkōsha.

1964   Sonraku ni okeru Bukkyō no Kinō (Functions of Buddhism in the Village). In *Awaji-shima no Minzoku* (Folklore in the Awaji Island), ed. WAKAMORI, Tarō, pp. 250–264. Tokyo: Yoshikawa Kōbunkan.

1966a   *Minkan Shinkō* (Folk Beliefs). Tokyo: Hanawa-shobō.

1966b   Hachijō-Kojima no Buraku Saishi (Village Rituals in the Hachijō Minor Island). *Nihon Minzokugaku Kaihō*, 48, 19–41.

1966c   Jiin no Kinō (Functions of the Buddhist Temple). In *Wakasa no Minzoku* (Folklore in the Wakasa Region), ed. WAKAMORI, Tarō, pp. 289–311. Tokyo: Yoshikawa Kōbunkan.

1966d   Miko to Shaman (Medium and Shaman). *Nihon Minzokugaku*, 43, 1–28.

1966e   Sonraku ni okeru Shūzoku Henka no Katei to Yōin (Process and Factors of Change in Country Folkways). *Jinrui Kagaku*, 18, 14–29.

1968a   Kuchiyose Fuzoku no Shūkyō-Minzokugaku-teki Kōsatsu (A Religio-Folkloristic Study of the Female Shaman System in Japan). *Shūkyō Kenkyū*, 196, 1–24.

1968b   The Major Features and Characteristics of Japanese Folk Beliefs. *Journal of Asian and African Studies*, 3:1–2, 13–24.

1968c   *Shinbutsu Kōshōshi Kenkyū* (A Historical Study of Contacts between Shinto and Buddhism). Tokyo: Yoshikawa Kōbunkan.

1969a   Sanchū Takai-Kan no Seiritsu to Tenkai (Emergence and Development of the Other-World-in-the-Mountain View). *Nihon Rekishi*, 249, 1–20.

1969b   Shūkyō Kōshō-Shi Kenkyū no Kaiko to Tenbō (Retrospect and Prospect of Studies in the History of Contacts of Religions). *Nihon Shūkyōshi Kenkyū*, 3, 7–19.

1969c   Minkan Fuzoku to Shirei-Kan (Popular Necromancy and Accompanying View of the Dead). *Bungaku*, 37:9, 72–91; and 37:10, 55–77.

1969d   Kuchiyose Miko no Seitai (Necromancers in Yamagata). *Nihon Minzokugaku Kaihō*, 64, 1–25.

1969e   Minkan Fuzoku no Seikaku (Nature of Popular Necromancy). In *Nihon Minzoku Shakaishi Kenkyū* (Historical Studies in Japanese Folklore and Society), ed. Higo Sensei Koki Kinen Rombun Kankō Kai, pp. 17–62. Tokyo: Kōbundō.

1969f   Minkan Fuzoku no Keitai to Kinō (Forms and Functions of Popu-

lar Necromancy). In *Rikuzen Hokubu no Minzoku* (Folklore in the Northern Rikuzen), ed. WAKAMORI, Tarō, pp. 291–340. Tokyo: Yoshikawa Kōbunkan.
1970 Tsugaru Itako to Fuzoku (Folkways Surrounding the Female Shaman in the Tsugaru Province). In *Tsugaru no Minzoku* (Folkways in the Tsugaru Province), ed. WAKAMORI, Tarō, pp. 297–330. Tokyo: Yoshikawa-Kōbunkan.
1973 *Okinawa no Shamanism* (Shamanism in Okinawa). Tokyo: Kōbundō.
SAKURAI, Tokutarō, and OZAWA, Hiroshi
1971 Gairai Shūkyō no Dochakuka o meguru Mondai (Issues Concerning the Indigenization of Foreign-Born Religions). *Shichō*, Otsuka Shigakkai, 108, 68–82.
SASAKI, Kōkan
1972 Sōrei no Shūkyō-teki Imi ni kansuru Ichi Kōsatsu (Religious Meanings of the Funeral Service). *Kyōka Kenshū*, Komazawa University, 15, 28–35.
1973 Shamanic Trance no Shōchō-teki Naiyō ni tsuite (Symbolic Contents of Shamanic Trance). *Shūkyōgaku Ronshū*, Komazawa University, 6, 29–47.
SASAKI, Kōkan, and ŌMORI, Motoyoshi
1967 Shūkyō Jinruigaku no Kiso-Riron (trans. of EVANS-PRITCHARD, E. E., *Theories of Primitive Religion*, 1965). Tokyo: Sekaishoin.
SATŌ, Seijin
1958 Miyagi Kempoku Chihō no Miko (Mediums in the Northern Region of Miyagi Prefecture). *Shakai to Denshō*, 2:1, 35–38.
SATŌ, Yoneji
1971 *Sōsō Girei no Kenkyū* (A Study of Burial Rites). Tokyo: Iwasaki-shoten.
SAWA, Masahiko
1973 Kankoku Kyōkai to Minzoku-shugi (The Christian Church in Korea and Nationalism). *Shingaku*, Tokyo Theological Seminary, 34–35, 1–59.
SCHIFFER, Wilhelm, S. J.
1967 Necromancers in the Tōhoku. *Contemporary Religions in Japan*, 8, 177–185.
SCHULL, William J.
1953 The Effect of Christianity on Consanguinity in Nagasaki. *American Anthropologist*, 55, 74–88.
SEKI, Keigo
1965 Miyaza Kenkyū no Hitotsu no Mondaiten (One Problem in the Study of the *Miyaza*). *Kyōdōtai no Hikaku Kenkyū*, 2, 1–6.
SETO, Mikio
1968 Kindai ni okeru Shūkyōsha to Minshū tono Taiwa (Confrontation of a Founder of Religion and People in the Modern Period). *Nihon Shūkyōshi Kenkyū*, 2, 212–222.
SHIBATA, Minoru
1951 Ikezuki no Kyū-Kirishitan (The Hidden Christians in the Ikezuki Island). In *Hirado Sōgō Chōsa Hōkoku* (Report of Interdisciplinary

Research of Hirado), pp. 139–168. Kyoto: Kyoto University Hirado Gakujutsu Chōsadan.

1964   Minkan Shinkō Ron (On Folk Beliefs). In *Iwanami Kōza Nihon Rekishi*, vol. 23, pp. 257–297. Tokyo: Iwanami-shoten.

SHIBUSAWA, Keizō
1958   (ed.) *Japanese Life and Culture in the Meiji Era* (trans. TERRY, C. S.). Century Cultural Council Series, V. Tokyo: Ōbunsha.

SHIMAMOTO, Hikojirō, et al.
1957   Hazemura Monograph—Hitotsu no Monto-Mura (Haze-mura: Monograph of a Shinshū-Dominated Village). *Sōgō Kyōdo Kenkyūjo Kiyō*, Aichi University, 3, 1–62.

SHIMAZAKI, Minoru
1953   Geinō Shakai to Iemoto Seido—Ryūha ni okeru Shitei Ketsugō no Tokushitsu (The *Iemoto* System in Artistic Society with Special Reference to Characteristics of Master-Disciple Relationships). *Shakaigaku Hyōron*, 3:4, 131–156; 4:1–2, 101–134.

SHIMIZU, Akitoshi
1970   Ie no Nai-teki Kōzō to Sonraku Kyōdōtai (The Inner Structure of the Household and the Village Community). *Minzokugaku Kenkyū*, 35:3, 177–215.

SHIMPO, Mitsuru
1962   Ōmi ni okeru Shinshū Kyōdan to Kirisuto Kyōdan no Taiketsu (Conflict between the Christian Church and the Shin Buddhist Order in the Omi Region). *Shakai Kagaku Journal*, International Christian University, 3, 203–228.

1968   Impact, Congruence, and New Equilibrium: A Case Study of Annaka Church, Gumma Prefecture. *Journal of Asian and African Studies*, 3:1–2, 54–72.

SHINNO, Toshikazu
1972   Mura no Matsuri to Shakai Kankei (Social Relations as Manifested in Village Festivals). *Minzokugaku Hyōron*, Otsuka Folklore Society, 8, 34–51.

SHINOHARA, Eiju, KITAKŌJI, Zuikō, and SUZUKI, Eijō
1970   Toshika ni taiō shita Shūkyō no arikata to Dendō (How to Proceed with Mission Work in Response to Urbanization). *Kyōka Kenshū*, Komazawa University, 13, 39–48.

SHINOHARA, Eiju, KITAKŌJI, Zuikō, SUZUKI, Eijō, and HYAKU-TAKE, Seigi
1971   Toshika to Kyōka (Urbanization and Mission Work). *Kyōka Kenshū*, Komazawa University, 14, 37–57.

SHINSHŪREN CHŌSASHITSU
1963   (eds.) *Sengo Shūkyō Kaisō-Roku* (Recollection of Religions after the War). Tokyo: PL-shuppan.

SHIOYA, Masanori
1972   Fuchū-shi ni okeru Jiin no Genkyō (Present Status of Buddhist Temples in Fuchū City). *Fuchūshi-Shi Kindai-Hen Shiryōshū*, Fuchū City Office, 9, 114–174.

SHIRAI, Nobuaki
1972   M. Weber "Shūkyō Shakaigaku" ni okeru Charisma to Higōrisei

(Chrisma and Irrationality in Max Weber's Sociology of Religion). *Shūkyō Kenkyū*, 212, 1–23.

SHU, Kyung-Soo
1972   The Present Situation of Korean Buddhism. *East Asian Cultural Studies*, 11:1–4, 97–105.

SONODA, Minoru
1967   Matsuri Sanka no Sho-Sō to Kaisō (Various Forms of Participation in a Shinto Festival and Social Class). *Jinrui Kagaku*, 19, 27–57.
1969   Matsuri to Toshi Shakai (Shinto Festival and Urban Community). *Nihon Bunka Kenkyūjo Kiyō*, Kokugakuin University, 23, 63–125.

SŌTŌSHŪ KYŌKA-KENSHŪJO
1970   Kumagai-shi ni okeru Shūkyō Ishiki Chōsa Hōkoku (Data from a Survey of Religious Consciousness in Kumagai City). *Kyōka Kenshū*, Komazawa University, 13, 173–179.
1971   Chichibu Shinai ni okeru Shūkyō Ishiki Chōsa Hōkoku (Data from a Survey of Religious Consciousness in Chichibu City). *Kyōka Kenshū*, Komazawa University, 14, 101–107.

SPAE, Joseph J.
1964   *Catholicism in Japan—A Sociological Study*. Tokyo: International Institute for the Study of Religions.
1965   *Christian Corridors to Japan*. Tokyo: Oriens Institute for Religious Research.
1966   Toward a Sociology of Religion for Japan. *Japan Missionary Bulletin*, 20, 404–425.
1968   *Christianity Encounters Japan*. Tokyo: Oriens Institute for Religious Research.
1971   *Japanese Religiosity*. Tokyo: Oriens Institute for Religious Research.

SUENARI, Michio
1972   Yearly Rituals within the Household—A Case Study from a Hamlet in Northeastern Japan. *East Asian Cultural Studies*, 11:1–4, 77–82.

SUGIURA, Hiroshi
1946   *Amerika Shihon-shugi to Kirisutokyō* (trans. of WEBER, M., *Die protestantischen Sekten und der Geist des Kapitalismus*). Tokyo: Kikuya-shoten.
1953   *Sekai Shūkyō no Keizai-Rinri* (trans. of WEBER, M., *Hinduismus und Buddhismus*, II). Tokyo: Misuzu-shobō.

SUGIURA, Ken'ichi
1935a   Chien Shūdan no Kami to Ketsuen Shūdan no Kami (Gods of Locality Groups and Gods of Consanguineous Groups). *Minzokugaku Kenkyū*, 1:2, 122–132.
1935b   Yama no Kami Shinkō—Kinō-teki Hōhō ni yoru Kami-Kannen no Kenkyū (Worship of Mountain Gods: Functional Approach to Study of the Concept of Gods). *Shūkyō Kenkyū* (New Edition), 12:3, 89–107.

SUGIYAMA, Kōichi
1972   Changing Agrarian Rites—In a Rice-Growing Village in Northeast Japan. *East Asian Cultural Studies*, 11:1–4, 58–76.

SUMIYA, Kazuhiko
1963   Amami-Ōshima Kuninao no Kami-Matsuri (Shinto Rituals in the Amami Oshima Island). *Shakai to Denshō*, 7:1, 22–42.

SUMIYA, Mikio
1950   *Kindai Nippon no Keisei to Kirisutokyō* (The Formation of Modern Japan and Christianity). Tokyo: Shinkyō-shuppan.
1965   (ed.) *Nihon Kindaika no Sho-Sokumen* (Some Aspects of Modernization of Japan). Tokyo: Nihon YMCA Dōmei Press.

SUZUKI, Eitarō
1935   Yashiki-Gami Kō (A Study of House-Site Gods). *Minzokugaku Kenkyū*, 1:2, 72–87.
1938   Ujiko Shūdan no Kenkyū (A Study of the Shinto Shrine-Worshiping Groups). *Shakaigaku*, 5, 251–258.
1940   *Nihon Nōson Shakaigaku Genri* (Principles of Japanese Rural Sociology). Tokyo: Nihon Hyōronsha.

SUZUKI, Hiroshi
1963–64 Toshi Kasō no Shūkyō Shūdan—Fukuoka-shi ni okeru Sōka Gakkai (Religious Group and Urban Lower Class: Sōka Gakkai in Fukuoka City). *Shakaigaku Kenkyū*, 22, 81–102; 24–25, 50–90.
1970   Sōka Gakkai to Toshi-teki Sekai (Sōka Gakkai and the Urban World). In *Toshi-teki Sekai* (Urban World), pp. 259–335. Tokyo: Seishin-shobō.

SUZUKI, Mitsuo
1965   Ōsumi Hantō Sanchi Sonraku no Saishi Kōzō (Social Organization for Festivals in Mountain Villages in the Ōsumi Peninsula). *Kyōdōtai no Hikaku Kenkyū*, 2, 7–36.

SUZUKI, Norihisa, and SPAE, Joseph J.
1968   (eds.) *Nihonjin no mita Kirisutokyō* (Christianity Seen through Japanese Eyes). Tokyo: Oriens Institute for Religious Research.

SUZUKI, Shuken
1956   Gendai Nihon Chūkan Shimin-Sō no Shūkyō—Seichō no Ie no Shūkyō Shakaigaku-teki Kōsatsu (Religion of the Contemporary Japanese Middle Class: A Sociological Analysis of *Seichō no Ie*). *Ritsumeikan Bungaku*, Ritsumeikan University, 130, 181–199.
1959   Bukkyō Kyōdan no Kiso Kōzō (The Basic Structure of Buddhist Orders). *Nihon Shūkyōshi Kōza*, 4, 159–201.
1964   *Nihon no Kindaika to On no Shisō* (Modernization of Japan and the Concept of "On"). Kyoto: Hōritsu Bunkasha.
1970   Noto ni okeru Shinshū no Kō (The Shin Buddhist Kō in the Noto Peninsula). *Shakaigaku Hyōron*, 21:1, 63–77.

SUZUKI, Takeshi
1973   Nizam al-Din Auliya Byō deno Shūkyō Shūkai ni tsuite (A Religious Meeting at the Dargah of Nizam al-Din Auliya). *Toyō Bunka Kenkyūjo Kiyō*, University of Tokyo, 59, 89–115.

TACHIKAWA, Musashi
1970   America ni okeru Hari-Krisna Kyōdan ni tsuite (The Hari Krisna Movement in the United States). *Kokusai Shūkyō News*, 11:6, 22–30.

TAGITA, Kōya
1953   Kyū-Kirishitan no Nando-Gami to sono Yurai (The Origin of
        Closet God of the Old Kirishitans). *Shūkyō Kenkyū*, 135, 27–61.
1954a   *Shōwa Jidai no Sempuku Kirishitan* (The Hidden Kirishitans in
        the Showa Period). Tokyo: Japan Society for the Promotion of
        Science.
1954b   Nihon no Ichi Nōson ni okeru Kirisuto-kyō no Henyō (Transforma-
        tion of Christianity in a Japanese Farming Village). *Minzokugaku
        Kenkyū*, 18:3, 1–32.
1956   Sempuku Kirishitan ni okeru Kyōkai Soshiki oyobi Tenrei no
        Henyō (Transformation of Church Organization and Sacraments
        among the Underground Kirishitans). *Kirisutokyō Shigaku*, 7,
        30–42.
1958   Kirisutokyō no Nihon-teki Bunka Henyō (Acculturation of Chris-
        tianity in Japan). *Shūkyō Kenkyū*, 155, 65–88.

TAKAGI, Hiroo
1954   Shūkyō Kyōdan no Seiritsu Katei—Tenrikyō no Baai (The Process
        of Formation of a Religious Organization—A Case of Tenrikyo).
        Tōyō Bunka Kenkyūjo Kiyō, University of Tokyo, 6, 265–338.
1955   Nihonjin no Shūkyō Seikatsu no Jittai (Religious Life of the
        Japanese). *Gendai Shūkyō Kōza*, V, 211–256. Tokyo: Sōbunsha.
1956   Shūkyō-teki Kō no Kinō—Kyōdan no Seiritsu Katei to shiteno
        (The Function of the *Kō* as the Basis of a Religious Organization).
        Tōyō Bunka Kenkyūjo Kiyō, University of Tokyo, 11, 213–235.
1957   Amami-Ōshima no Yuta ni tsuite (*Yuta* in the Amami Oshima
        Island). *Jinrui Kagaku*, 9, 188–193.
1958   *Shinkō Shūkyō* (New Religions). Tokyo: Kōdansha.
1959a   *Nihon no Shinkō Shūkyō* (New Religions in Japan). Tokyo: Iwanami-
        shoten.
1959b   Minkan Shinkō to Shinkō Shūkyō (Folk Beliefs and New Religions).
        Nihon Minzokugaku Taikei, VIII, 407–419. Tokyo: Heibonsha.

TAKAHASHI, Hiroshi
1971   Meijiki ni okeru Jinja Hi-Shūkyō-ka no Igi (The Significance of
        the Governmental Conception of the Shinto Shrine in the Meiji
        Period). *Seishin Bunka Kenkyūjo Kiyō*, Nihon University, 5, 59–108.

TAKAHASHI, Kenshō
1962   Jōdo Kyōdan no Hitotsu no Seikaku (One Charactersitic of the
        Jōdo Sect). *Soshioroji*, 30, 57–65.
1969   Kyōdan no Shakaigaku-teki Bunseki (A Sociological Analysis of
        Religious Groups). *Shūkyō Kyōkagaku Kenkyūkai Kiyō*, Otani Uni-
        versity, 3, 132–138.

TAKAHASHI, Tōichi
1970   Miyaza-Sei Oboegaki (Notes on the *Miyaza* System). In *Minzoku-
        gaku kara mita Nihon* (Ethnology Looks at Japan), pp. 77–97. Tokyo:
        Kawadeshobō-Shinsha.

TAKANO, Tomoharu
1968   Tenrikyō to Tashū tono Sesshoku (Contacts of Tenrikyo and Other
        Religions). *Shakai to Denshō*, 11:1, 1–9.
1970   Nihon Shūkyō Bumpu no Kenkyū (Jo) (An Introductory Study

of the Geographical Distribution of Religions in Japan). *Gakuhō,*
Tenri University, 65, 1–19.

TAKASE, Hiroi
1962   *Daisan Bunmei no Shūkyō* (Religion of the Third Civilization).
       Tokyo: Kōbundō.
1964   *Kōmeitō* (The Komei Political Party). Tokyo: Gakushū Kenkyūsha.

TAKEDA, Chōshū
1951   Bukkyō-teki Dōzoku-Shin (Tutelary Deities of the *Dōzoku* in a
       Buddhist Appearance). *Bukkyō Shigaku,* 2:3, 47–58.
1954   Onsen o meguru Ichizoku Miyaza (A Clan *Miyaza* Organized
       around the Title to a Hot Spa). *Hisutoria,* 9, 35–52.
1955   Tamba no Sanson ni okeru Danka Shūdan to Dōzoku Ketsugō
       (Buddhist Parish and *Dōzoku* Group in a Mountain Village of
       Tamba). *Gakuhō,* Buddhist College, 30, 28–42.
1957a *Sosen Sūhai—Minzoku to Rekishi* (Ancestor Worship—Folklore and
       History). Kyoto: Heirakuji-shoten.
1957b Dōzoku-shin no Honshitsu ni tsuite (On Essential Qualities of
       Tutelary Deities of the *Dōzoku*). *Nihon Minzokugaku,* 4:2, 100–106.
1958a Aru Mumei Sonraku Jiin no Keidai Butsudō to sono Zensei (A
       Country Minor Temple and Its Historical Background). *Bukkyō
       Shigaku,* 6:2, 93–112.
1958b Hi-Chomei Jiin no Kaisō Denshō—Jōdo-shū no Baai (Legend
       Concerning Establishment of Ordinary Temples: As Observed
       in the Jōdo Sect). In *Uozumi Sensei Koki Kinen Ronsō* (Historical
       Studies Presented in Commemoration of the Seventieth Birthday
       of Dr. Uozumi), pp. 428–442. Suita: Kansai University Depart-
       ment of Japanese History.
1959a Mura no Minzoku to Tera no Keizai—Aru Mumei Sonraku Jiin
       no Baai (Village Folkways and Temple Finance—A Case of a
       Small Country Temple). In *Dokushikai Sōritsu 50-Nen Kinen Ronshū*
       (Collection of Papers in Commemoration of the 50th Anniversary
       of the Establishment of Dokushi-Kai), pp. 1445–1462. Kyoto:
       Kyoto University Dokushi-Kai.
1959b Gōshi Matsuei no Ujigami Matsuri (The Festival of Clan Gods
       among Descendants of the Samurai Class). *Bunkagaku Nempō,*
       Dōshisha University, 9, 108–137.
1960   Kusawake Hyakushō no Ujigami Matsuri to sono Engi Denshō
       (The Festival of Clan Gods among Descendants of Village Found-
       ers), *Kiyō,* Human Science Research Institute, Dōshisha University,
       3, 67–126.
1964   Kakusō Dōzoku Saishi to sono Suii (*Dōzoku* Rites and Their
       Transition). In *Kinki Gōshi Sonraku no Kenkyū* (A Study of a War-
       rior-led Village in the Tamba Province), pp. 153–246. Kyoto:
       Dōshisha University Press.
1971a *Minzoku Bukkyō to Sosen Shinkō* (Folk Buddhism and Ancestor
       Veneration). Tokyo: University of Tokyo Press.
1971b Jian to Sōdō (Private Temple and Communal Temple). *Nihon
       Minzokugaku,* 75, 54–58.

TAKEDA, Chōshū, and TAKATORI, Masao
1957   Nihonjin no Shinkō (Religious Beliefs of the Japanese People).
        Tokyo: Sōgensha.
TAKEDA, Hitoyoshi
1943   Nōson no Nenchū Gyōji (Annual Events of the Rural Society). Tokyo:
        Ryūseikaku.
TAKENAKA, Masao
1959   Okayama-ken ni okeru Shoki no Kyōkai Keisei (Early Stage of
        Church Formation in Okayama Prefecture). Kirisutokyō Shakai
        Mondai Kenkyū, Dōshisha University, 3, 1–32.
TAKENAKA, Shinjō
1971   Gendai ni okeru Shūkyō no Yakuwari (The Role of Religion
        Today). Shūmu Jihō, 27, 2–15.
TAKEUCHI, Toshimi
1941   Ujiko Soshiki to sono Hensen—Shinshū Kami-Ina Kawashima-
        mura ni okeru (The Ujiko Organization and Its Development in
        Kawashima Village, Kami-Ina, Shinano Province). Minzokugaku
        Kenkyū, 7:1, 39–79.
1943   Kō Shūdan no Soshiki Keitai—Matsumoto Daira no Kōshinkō ni
        tsuite (Patterns of the Kō Group Organization: A Study of the
        Kōshin-kō in the Matsumoto Basin). Minzokugaku Kenkyū, 8:3,
        34–84.
1958–59 Oshira-sama no Matsuri (Rites of Oshira-sama). Shakai to Denshō,
        3:1, 1–8; and 3:2, 11–17.
TAMAMURO, Taijō
1963   Sōshiki Bukkyō (Buddhism for Funeral Services). Tokyo: Daihōrin-
        kaku.
TANABE, Hisatoshi
1926   Durkheim-Ha no Shūkyō Shakaigaku (Sociology of Religion of
        the Durkheimian School). Minzoku, 1:2, 103–122; 1:3, 129–140;
        1:4, 109–120; and 1:5, 113–124.
1928   Shūkyō-Genshō no Shakai-Keitaigaku-teki Setsumei (Socio-
        morphological Analysis of Religious Phenomena). Shūkyō Kenkyū,
        6:1, 81–100.
TANASE, Jōji
1951   Wach no Shūkyō Shakaigaku (Wach's Sociology of Religion).
        Shūkyō Kenkyū, 125, 48–53.
1958   Daitoshijin no Shūkyō Ishiki (Religious Consciousness of Metro-
        politans). Kyoto: Headquarters of Shin Honganji Sect.
TANGE, Ryūichi
1970   Durkheim Shakaigaku ni okeru Semiology-teki Shikō ni tsuite
        (Semiology in the Work of Durkheim). Soshioroji, 16:1, 26–46.
TANIOKA, Haruo, and MORIYASU, Hitoshi
1971   Jinja Gappei to Mura Matsuri no Henka (Shrine Mergers and
        Changes in Village Festivals). Shakai to Denshō, 12:4, 45–50.
TERAKAWA, Shunshō
1957   Kyōdan Saikō (Revival of the Shin Buddhist Order). In Kiyozawa
        Manshi no Kenkyū (A Study of Manshi Kiyozawa), pp. 407–456.
        Kyoto: Research Institute of Shin Ōtani Sect.

TERAKAWA, Shunshō, RYŌSE, Masao, and SATAKE, Onchi
1954   Nōson to Jiin (Rural Society and the Buddhist Temple). Kyoto: Research Institute of Shin Ōtani Sect.

TODA, Yoshio
1952   Tsushima ni okeru Shinshū Kyōdan (The Shin Buddhist Temples in the Tsushima Island). Jinrui Kagaku, 4, 116–126.
1955   Noto ni okeru Shinshū Dempan (The Spread of Shin Buddhism in the Noto Region). Jinrui Kagaku, 7, 110–117.

TOGAWA, Anshō
1943   Haguro-yama no Kasumiba to Dannaba ni tsuite (Two Kinds of Parishes of the Haguro Mountain Priests). Shūkyō Kenkyū, 5:2, 95–120.
1949   Haguro Yamabushi no Shūdan Soshiki (Social Organization of Haguro Mountain Priests). In Nihon Minzokugaku no tameni (Toward Development of Japanese Folklore Studies), VIII, 87–108. Tokyo: Minkan-Denshō-no-Kai.
1954   Shōnai Chihō ni okeru Miko to Okonai-Gami (Mediums and Okonai-gami in the Shōnai Region). Minzokugaku Kenkyū, 18:4, 97–105.
1964   "Ōdera" to Shugenja (Large Buddhist Temples and Mountain Priests). Shakai to Denshō, 8:4, 1–21.
1967   Suginoo Jinja Chōsa Hōkoku (A Case Report on a Shinto Shrine in Tsuruoka). Nihon Bunka Kenkyūjo Kiyō, Kokugakuin University, 21, 115–186.

TŌKEI SŪRI KENKYŪJO
1961   (eds.) Nihonjin no Kokuminsei (National Character of the Japanese People). Tokyo: Shiseidō.
1970   (eds.) Daini Nihonjin no Kokuminsei (The National Character of the Japanese People, II). Tokyo: Shiseidō.

TOKORO, Shigemoto
1966   Kindai Nihon no Shūkyō to Nationalism (Religion and Nationalism in Modern Japan). Tokyo: Fuzanbō.

TOYODA, Takeshi
1938   Nihon Shūkyō Seidoshi no Kenkyū (Historical Study of Japanese Religious Institutions). Tokyo: Kōseikaku.

TOYOSHIMA, Kakujō
1964   Doitsu Shūkyō-Shakaigaku no Kihon-teki Tokuchō to Gendai no Dōkō (The Core Characteristics of German Sociology of Religion and Its Present Trend). Soshioroji, 35–36, 112–118.

TSUBOI, Hirobumi
1964   Nishi-Nihon ni okeru Tōya Saishi no Girei-teki Tokushitsu (Ritual Characteristics of Tōya Rites in the Western Part of Japan). Kokugakuin Zasshi, Kokugakuin University, 65:2–3, 31–64.
1970   Nihonjin no Seishikan (The Japanese View of Life and Death). In Minzokugaku kara mita Nihon (Ethnology Looks at Japan), pp. 7–34. Tokyo: Kawade-shobō-Shinsha.

TSUBOUCHI, Yoshihiro
1973   Kelantan no Nōson ni okeru Pondok (A Pondok School in Kelan-

tan, Malaysia). *Tōnan Asia Kenkyū*, Kyoto University, 11:2, 223–237.

UCHIDA, Yoshiaki
1962–64 *Kodai Yudayakyō* (trans. of WEBER, M., *Das antike Judentum*). Tokyo: Misuzu-shobō.

UEHARA, Senroku, et al.
1971 *Honganji Kyōdan* (The Honganji Sects). Tokyo: Gakugei-shorin.

UMEDA, Yoshihiko
1951 Ishizuchi-yama o meguru Kyōdan (The Religious Body with Mt. Ishizuchi at Its Center). *Shintō Kenkyū*, 3, 34–39.
1962 *Nihon Shūkyō Seidoshi* (History of Religious Institutions in Japan). Kyoto: Hyakkaen.

UNO, Enkū
1936 Nihon Minkan Shinkō no Minzokugaku-teki Seikaku (Folkloristic Characteristics of Japanese Folk Beliefs). *Shisō*, 169, 62–76.
1946 Mura no Saishi to Ie no Saishi (Rituals of the Village and Rituals of the Household). *Tōyō Bunka Kenkyū*, 2, 11–22.

UNO, Mitsuo
1957 Max Weber "Kodai Yudayakyō" ni okeru Gōrisei no Mondai (On Rationality in Max Weber's *Das antike Judentum*). *Shūkyō Kenkyū*, 153: 39–59.

USHIJIMA, Iwao
1966 "Ihai" Saishi to Nihon no Kazoku, Shinzoku ("Ihai" Cult in Relation to Japanese Kinship and Family). *Minzokugaku Kenkyū*, 31:3, 169–178.

VAN HECKEN, J.
1963 *The Catholic Church in Japan since 1859*. Tokyo: Enderle.

VAN STRAELEN, Henry
1957 *The Religion of Divine Wisdom*. Kyoto: Veritas-shoin.

WACH, Joachim
1944 *Sociology of Religion*. Chicago: University of Chicago Press.

WAKAMORI, Tarō
1947 *Nihon Minzoku Ron* (On Japanese Folklore). Tokyo: Chiyoda-shobō.
1952 Miyaza no Kaishō Katei (Dissolution of the *Miyaza* System: A Case in the Deep Noto Province). *Nihon Minzokugaku*, 1:2, 1–17.
1965 *Shomin no Seishinshi* (History of Thought of the Common People). Tokyo: Kawade-shobō.

WAKIMOTO, Tsuneya
1967 *Kindai no Bukkyōsha* (Modern Buddhists). Tokyo: Chikuma-shobō.
1968a Manshi Kiyozawa and the Otani Sect of Shinshu Buddhism: A Study of His Early Life. *Journal of Asian and African Studies*, 3: 1–2, 73–83.
1968b Shūkyō no Jisshō-teki Kenkyū (Empirical Study of Religion). In *Shūkyō to Dōtoku* (Religion and Morality, Iwanami Lectures on Philosophy, No. 15), pp. 77–99. Tokyo: Iwanami-shoten.

WATANABE, Baiyū
1950 *Gendai Nihon no Shūkyō* (Religions in Modern Mapan). Tokyo: Daitō-shuppan.

WATANABE, Eimi
1968   Risshō Kōsei Kai: A Sociological Observation of Its Members,
        Their Conversion and Their Activities. *Contemporary Religions in
        Japan*, 9, 75–151.

YAMAGUCHI, Motomitsu
1960   Review of HOULT, T. F., *The Sociology of Religion. Soshioroji*, 23,
        85–92.
1961   Sonraku to Shūkyō Kō (The Village and the Religious *Kō*). Ibid.
        26, 29–56.

YAMAORI, Tetsuo
1970   Jujutsu to Hōetsu—Max Weber no Indo Shūkyō-Ron (Magic
        and Bliss—Religions in India by Max Weber). *Shūkyō Kenkyū*,
        203, 1–29.
1973   Charisma to Kinyoku (Charisma and Asceticism). *Bunka*, Tohoku
        University, 37:3–4, 146–169.

YAMAZAKI, Mie
1972   Shūkyō Jinruigaku ni okeru Yōjutsu Kenkyū (An Anthropological
        Study of Witchcraft). *Kokusai Shūkyō News*, 13:3, 21–34.

YANAGAWA, Keiichi
1955   Sonraku ni okeru Sangaku Shinkō no Soshiki (The Organization
        for Mountain Worship in the Village). *Shūkyō Kenkyū*, 143, 41–64.
1958   Iwaki-yama Mairi (Pilgrimage to the Top of Mt. Iwaki). *Shakai
        to Denshō*, 2:4, 1–6.
1959   Dewa Sanzan Shinkō to Rōnensō (Worship of the Dewa Sanzan
        Mountains and the Old People). *Jinrui Kagaku*, 11, 51–59.
1960   Shūkyō Chōsa no Genjō (Review of Field Studies in Religion). In
        Sengo ni okeru Shūkyō Chōsa no Jitsujō (Survey of Postwar Field
        Studies in Religion), pp. 15–66. Tokyo: Ministry of Education,
        Section for Religious Affairs.
1960–61 Shūkyō Shakaigaku ni okeru Kinōshugi Riron (Functional Theory
        in the Sociology of Religion). *Shūkyō Kenkyū*, 161, 53–67; and 166,
        70–90.
1966   Saikin no Shūkyō Chōsa ni okeru Shūkyō to Shakai Hendō no
        Mondai (The Problem of Religion and Social Change in Recent
        Field Studies in Religion). *Shūmu Jihō*, Ministry of Education,
        10, 2–17.
1971   Matsuri no Shingaku to Matsuri no Kagaku (Theological and
        Scientific Thinking about Festivals). *Shisō*, 569, 57–72.
1972   The Family, the Town, and Festivals. *East Asian Cultural Studies*,
        11:1–4, 125–131.

YANAGAWA, Keiichi, and NAKAMAKI, Hiromitsu
1973   Shūkyō Hendō no Kaishaku o megutte (Interpretations of Reli-
        gious Changes). *Shisō*, 591, 92–103.

YANAGITA, Kunio
1914   Kebōzu Kō (On Lay Priests). *Kyōdo Kenkyū*, 2:1, 1–10.
1946   *Senzo no Hanashi* (Notes on Ancestors). Tokyo: Chikuma-shobō.
1962–64 *Teihon Yanagita Kunio Shū* (Collected Works of Yanagita Kunio).
        35 vols. Tokyo: Chikuma-shobō.

YONEJI, Minoru
1963   Sonraku ni okeru Kō to Ie Rengō (*Kō* and *Ie* Groups in the Village). *Shakaigaku Kenkyūka Kiyō*, Keiō University, 1, 29–37.
1970a   Meiji Shoki ni okeru Sonraku Shozai Jinja to Kokka Tōsei (Village Shrines and Governmental Controls over Them in the Early Meiji Period). *Kiyō*, Nihon Women's University, 19, 51–95.
1970b   Kyūson Gappei to Rengō Saiji (Village Amalgamation and Collective Festival). *Shakai to Denshō*, 12:3, 25–35.
1970–71 Kō no Sonzai Keitai to Shugoshin Shinkō (The *Kō* and Guardian Deity Beliefs). *Tōyō Gakujutsu Kenkyū*, Oriental Philosophy Research Institute, 9:2, 124–139; 9:3, 98–109.
1971   Ujigami Chinju to Shakai Kōzō no Kanren ni kansuru Ichi Kōsatsu (Relationships of Local Shinto Shrines and the Social Structure of a Hamlet). *Hōgaku Kenkyū*, Keiō University, 44:5, 57–80; 44:6, 40–72.
1972   Sonraku ni okeru Ie no Gojo Shūdan to Shugoshin (The Mutual Aid Group of Households and Its Guardian Deities in a Hamlet). *Kiyō*, Nihon Women's University, 21, 144–187.
YONEMURA, Shōji
1962   Saishi Soshiki to Sonraku Kōzō (The Organization for Shinto Rituals and the Village Structure). *Shakai to Denshō*, 6:2, 1–19.
1963   Kyū Kajinami-Shō no Saishi Soshiki (The Organization for Shinto Rituals in the Kajinami District). *Shakai to Denshō*, 7:1, 17–54.
1967   Chūsei ni okeru Shinshoku-Sō Shihai (Medieval Control over Priesthood). *Shakai to Denshō*, 10:4, 48–63.
1970   Saishi Soshiki to Sonraku Kōzō (Organization for Shrine Rites and the Social Structure of a Hamlet). *Sonraku Shakai Kenkyū*, 6, 73–119.
YONEMURA, Shōji, and INOUE, Keimi
1971   Saishi Soshiki to Sonraku Kōzō (The Organization for Shrine Rites and the Social Structure of a Hamlet). *Kyōikugakubu Kenkyū*, Okayama University, 31, 91–117.
YOSHIDA, Teigo
1970   *Jujutsu—Sono Gendai ni ikiru Kinō* (Magic—Its Modern Functions). Tokyo: Kōdansha.
1972a   *Nihon no Tsukimono* (Phenomena of Possession in Japan). Tokyo: Chūō Kōronsha.
1972b   Tsukimono to Shakai (Possession and Society). In *Gendai Sho Minzoku no Shūkyō to Bunka* (Religion and Culture of People in the Contemporary World), pp. 421–438. Tokyo: Shakai-Shisōsha.
1972c   Spirit Possession and Kinship System. *East Asian Cultural Studies*, 11:1–4, 44–57.
YOUNG, C. K.
1961   *Religion in Chinese Society*. Berkeley: University of California Press.
YUASA, Yoshio
1932   (ed.) *Jirō Yuasa* (Biography of Jirō Yuasa). Annaka: Aritaya.

List of Major Periodicals in Japan
which published one or more articles listed in the Bibliography.

Asia Review
The Asahi Asia Review, edited and published by Asahi Press, Tokyo.

Bukkyō Shigaku
The Historical Study of Buddhism, edited and published by Bukkyō Shigakkai, Kyoto.

Chihōshi Kenkyū
The Study of Local Histories, edited and published by Chihōshi Kenkyū Kyōgikai, Tokyo (1951–).

Contemporary Religions in Japan
Edited and published by the International Institute for the Study of Religions, Tokyo (1960–1970).

East Asian Cultural Studies
Edited and published by the Centre for East Asian Cultural Studies, Tokyo (1962–).

Jinrui Kagaku
The Scientific Study of Man, edited and published by Kyū Gakkai Rengō, Tokyo, (1949–).

Kirisutokyō Shigaku
The Journal of History of Christianity, edited and published by the Society of Historical Study of Christianity, Yokohama.

Kokusai Shūkyō News
International Religious News, edited and published by the International Institute for the Study of Religions, Tokyo (1959–).

Kyōdo Kenkyū
Home Town Studies, edited and published by Kyōdokai, Tokyo (1913–1917).

Minzokugaku Kenkyū
Japanese Journal of Ethnology, edited and published by the Japanese Society of Ethonology, Tokyo.

Nihon Bukkyō
Journal of Japanese Buddhism, edited and published by Nihon Bukkyō Kenkyūkai, Tokyo (1958–).

Nihon Minzokugaku
Bulletin of the Folklore Society of Japan, edited and published by the Folklore Society of Japan, Tokyo (1970–).

Nihon Minzokugaku Kaihō
Bulletin of the Folklore Society of Japan, edited and published by the Folklore Society of Japan, Tokyo (1958–1969).

hon Rekishi
Ni Journal of Japanese History, edited by Nihon Rekishigakkai and published by Yoshikawa Kōbunkan, Tokyo.

Risō
Ideals, edited and published by Risōsha, Tokyo.

Sekai
World, edited and published by Iwanami-shoten, Tokyo.
Shakaigaku
Annals of Sociology, edited by the Japan Sociological Society and published by Iwanami-shoten, Tokyo (1933–1943).
Shakaigaku Hyōron
Japanese Sociological Review, edited and published by the Japan Sociological Society, Tokyo (1950–).
Shakaigaku Kenkyū
The Sociological Review, edited by the Japan Sociological Society and published by Takayama-shoten and Kokuritsu-shoin, Tokyo (1947–1948).
Shakaigaku Zasshi
Journal of Sociology, edited and published by the Japan Sociological Society, Tokyo (1924–30).
Shakai to Denshō
Society and Folklore, edited and published by HARADA, Toshiaki (1956–).
Shinto Kenkyū
Shinto Studies, edited and published by Shinto Kenkyūkai, Ise.
Shinto Shūkyō
Journal of Shinto Studies, edited and published by the Society of Shinto Studies, Tokyo.
Shisō
Thoughts, edited and published by Iwanami-shoten, Tokyo.
Shūkyō Kenkyū
Journal of Religious Studies, edited and published by the Japanese Association for Religious Studies, Tokyo.
Shūmu Jihō
Religious Affairs News, edited and published by the Ministry of Education (1964–1968) and later by the Agency for Cultural Affairs (1968–).
Sonraku Shakai Kenkyū
Annals of Rural Sociology, edited by Sonraku Shakai Kenkyūkai and published by Hanawa-shobo, Tokyo (1965–).
Soshioroji
Sociology, edited and published by Shakaigaku Kenkyūkai, Kyoto (1952–).

INDEX

A

adopted son: 91
Agency for Cultural Affairs (Bunka-chō): 4
Akamatsu, Chijō: 172, 177
Akiba, Takashi: 177
American Episcopal Church: 117
American Methodist Episcopal Church: 122
Amida Buddha: 109, 110, 156, 163
ancestor veneration: 36

ancestral cult: 177
Anezaki, Masaharu: 171
Annaka Church: 119–121, 126, 129, 132, 133
annual religious events: classification of, 17
annual religious functions: 85, 87
anomie: 182
Anzai, Shin: 80
Aruga, Kizaemon: 174

B

Bastide, R.: 173
Bellah, R. N.: 173
Bishamonten: 27, 29
bodai-ji (funeral temple): 7, 99
Bon: 32, 33, 59, 128, 129, 130, 131
Bon dana: 59
Bonten: 27
Buddha. SEE Amida Buddha

bunke (branch family or household): 64, 91, 122
bureaucratization: 94
butsudan (family or household Buddhist altar): 7, 15, 32, 36, 59, 105, 125, 128, 129
butsuji kinshu: 132, 133

C

Canadian Methodist Church: 123
Catholic Church. SEE Roman Catholic Church
Catholicism: 180, 181
charismatic leader: 118
charismatic ruler: 173
chōkai (community council): 40, 42, 61

chōnai-kai. SEE *chōkai*
chūhonji (district temple): 93
church type: 182
civil code: 96, 101, 102, 103, 162
class endogamy: 79, 86, 87
community religion: 124
conjugal family: 161, 162, 165
conjugal family system: 96, 101, 105

D

Daikaku-sama: 19

daimyō: 93

daisan-kō: 63
democratization: postwar, and effects on temples, 103, 104
denomination type: 182
deviant behavior: 118, 119, 121, 122, 124, 125, 126, 128, 129, 133
diffused religion: 155, 156
diviner: 178

dormant parishioner: 50, 51, 68, 107, 117, 160
Dōsoshin: 130, 131
downtown church: 150
dōzoku: 32, 81, 91, 93, 177
dual religious membership: 4, 5, 7
Durkheim, E.: 171, 172, 174

E

ecological change: 183
Embree, J. F.: 6
emperor cult: 4

established religion: 164, 165
expressive values: 165
extended-family household: 106

F

family: continuity of, 100, 107; cycle of, and religious events, 36
father-son relation: in temple groups, 91, 95
Federation of Shin Sects (Shinshū Kyōdan Rengō): 111
festival parishioner: 46–47, 51
Fichter, J. H.: 50, 117, 173
filial piety: 100, 125

formal organizations: participation in, 61–63, 65–67
Fujii, Masao: 183
Fukuzawa, Yukichi: 120
functional approach: to study of religion, 175
funeral rites: 60
Furuno, Kiyoto: 172, 175, 180

G

gempuku: 95
gempuku-oya: 5
gradient pattern: 54, 58, 59, 63, 65,

67, 68, 69, 70, 143
Greek Orthodox Church: 181
group conversion: 180

H

Hagiwara, Tatsuo: 176
Hanashima, Masazaburō: 183
Harada, Toshiaki: 175, 176, 179
Haruna-kō: 62
hatsumōde: 53
Hayashi, Masataka: 180
Hayashi, Megumi: 173
Higo, Kazuo: 174
Hirai, Naofusa: 177
Hirayama, Binjirō: 83

Hommon Hokke sect: 26
Hongan-ji: 82, 84
honke (main family or household): 64, 91, 122
honke-bunke relation: 95
hon-matsu relation: 93, 94, 95, 96, 97
hon-matsu seido: 93, 95, 96
honzan (main, head, or central temple): 90, 92, 93, 94, 96, 97, 102, 103, 104, 109, 113, 178

honzan-matsuji
institution. SEE *hon-matsu seido*
relation. SEE *hon-matsu* relation
Hōonkō: 85, 87
Hori, Ichirō: 177, 178, 179, 180, 181
hotoke-okuri: 33
Hoult, T. F.: 173

household
altar. SEE *butsudan* and *kamidana*
line: 89, 100
religion: 99, 110, 111, 124, 126, 156
religious events: 30–35
house-site guardian deities. SEE *ya-shikigami*

I

ie (Japanese family or household): 14, 90, 91, 99, 100, 101, 103, 107, 108, 109, 113, 155, 161–162, 177, 178, 179, 181
ie no kami: 180
ie religion: 109
ie system: 89, 92, 97, 102, 103
Ikado, Fujio: 180, 182
Ikeda, Akira: 176
Ikeda, Giyū: 177
Ikegami, Hiromasa: 177
immediate family: 106, 161

industrialization: 109, 166, 167, 183
industrial society: 182
informal relationships: participation in, 61, 64–66
instrumental values: 165
interfaith marriage: 75
Ise Grand Shrine: 8, 42, 52
Ishizuka, Takatoshi: 178
Itō, Mikiharu: 176, 178, 183
Iwai, Fumio: 180
Iwasaki, Toshio: 179
Izumo Grand Shrine: 28, 29

J

Japanese Association for Religious Studies: 151
Japanese Buddhism: 89–90, 99; modernization of, 109, 112–113
Japanese Buddhists: 74
Japanese family. SEE *ie* and *ie* system
Japanese National Character Survey: 4
Japanization: of Buddhism, 177
Jishin-matsuri (land god festival): 17, 19, 24
Jizō: 130
Jōdo sect: 179

K

kakure kirishitan: 180, 181
kamidana (family or household Shinto altar): 7, 15, 32, 36, 51, 52, 125, 128
kanki-kō: 19
Kawasaki, Eshō: 178
Kirishitanism: 180
Kishimojin: 26
Kishimoto, Hideo: 182
kitō-ji (prayer temple): 7, 8, 99
Kiyozawa, Manshi: 113, 179
kō: 62, 177, 178

Kobugahara-kō: 63
Kogi Shingon sects: 76
Konkōkyo: 28
Korean oneiromancy: 177
koseki: 95
kōshin-kō: 174
Kudō, Eiichi: 180
Kumagi, Sonoko: 40, 183
Kurata, Washio: 180
Kurube, Nobuo: 108
Kusakabe Church: 123–124, 126,

128, 132, 133

L

land reform: 79, 104, 105, 109
lay leader: 111
layman evangelism: 165
Le Bras, G.: 173
Linton, R.: 14
local

endogamy: 78, 82, 86, 87
exogamy: 78
group: 155, 156, 166, 167, 176, 179
involvement: 69
long-term "pseudo-observation":
    16–17

M

mago bunke: 93
mago matsuji: 93
main family. SEE honke
main temple. SEE honzan
mairi no hotoke: 174
makke: 91
Malinowski, B.: 172, 173
marginal parishioner: 50, 51, 68, 107,
    117
mass movement: relation of, to new
    religions, 181
matsuji (subordinate temple): 91, 92,
    93, 94, 96, 97, 103, 104, 178
Mauss, Marcel: 172
mediums: studies on, 178
Meiji Restoration: 90, 94, 95, 97
Meiji Shrine: 53, 59, 70
Meiroku Zasshi: 120
mikoshi: 159
minority group: 117, 118

missionary area: 147, 148
Mitake-kō: 62
mixed marriage: 76, 78, 80, 85
Miyake, Hitoshi: 177
Miyata, Noboru: 177
miyaza: 174, 176. SEE ALSO oza
modal behavior: 118, 119, 127, 128,
    129, 133
model parishioner: 50, 51, 68
modernization: 95
monogamy: 129
Mori, Tōgo: 173
Morioka, Kiyomi: 176, 178, 179, 180,
    182, 183
mountain priest (shugen): 174–175
mountain worship: 177
mukae-bi: 59
mura-gitō (neighborhood prayer): 17–
    18, 23–24
Myōken sect: 28

N

Naito, Kanji: 173, 177
Narita-san: 6
National Union of Shrine Shinto
    (Jinja Honchō): 5
neighborhood religious events: 17–25
new religions: 112, 164–165, 166,
    167, 181, 182
Nichiren-sama (Saint Nichiren festi-
    val): 17, 19, 24
Nichiren sect: 19, 26, 27, 179

Niejima, Joseph: 120
Nijūhachinichi-kō: 84
Nomura, Nobukiyo: 180
non-mixed marriages: 85, 87
noro (necromancers): 178
nuclear family household: 101, 104,
    106, 181
nuclear parishioner: 50, 51, 68, 160
Numa, Kenkichi: 180, 181

O

occupational endogamy: 80
Oguchi, Iichi: 173, 181
Ōhama, Tetsuya: 180
Oikawa, Hiroshi: 174
Okada, Yoneo: 46, 47, 51
Okada, Yuzuru: 173
okuri-bi: 59n.

omandara: 20
ordinary temple: 102, 103, 105
Ōtsuka, Hisao: 173
outcasts: 81, 180
oyabun-kobun relation: 95
oza: 83, 84. SEE ALSO *miyaza*

P

parishioners: types of, 46–47, 50
Parsons, T.: 173
population: movements of, and effects
 on religious groups, 39, 159
possession: 178

preferential marriage: 79, 83
primogeniture: 103, 162
prostitution: 132
Protestantism: 117, 179
Pure Land Buddhism: 87

R

real parishioners: 46, 51
Reiyūkai Kyōdan: 118
religion
 as a social institution: 172
 ecology of: 135
 sociology of: 135, 172
religious
 behavior: 13–15, 47–48
 commitment: 69, 77
 endogamy: 76, 78, 79–82, 84–86, 87

 exogamy: 76, 78
 homogamy: 75, 79, 86
 practices: 135
 segregation: 84
Rennyo: 82, 83, 84, 87
residential zone: 163
Risshō Kōsei Kai: 9, 10, 165
Roman Catholic Church: 75, 76, 117,
 180

S

Saijō Inarikyo: 28
Sakurai, Tokutarō: 177, 178, 179
samurai: 119, 120, 180
Sanjūbanshin: 26
Sectarian Shinto: 8
secularization: 37
Segaki: 26
Seichō no Ie: 118, 181
Seki, Keigo: 82–83
Shakai to Denshō: 176
shaman: 178
shamanism: 177, 181
shanichi: 19
Shibata, Minoru: 180

Shimamoto, Hikojirō: 178
Shimamura Church: 122–123, 126,
 129, 132
shime-kazari: 6
Shimpo, Mitsuru: 180
Shin Buddhism: 5, 76, 84, 97, 103,
 108, 109, 110, 111, 113, 163, 173,
 178, 179; customs of, 85, 179; sects
 of, 19, 75, 87, 92, 94, 97, 101, 102,
 103, 179
 Bukkōji sect: 108
 Honganji sect: 104, 108
 Kōshō sect: 108
 Ōtani sect: 76, 102, 103, 105, 108–

112, 113, 163; Brotherhood Movement in, 108–112, 113; and *Kaishin* Problem, 112
Shingon sect: 108
Shinjin-sha: 108
Shinran: 75, 84, 85, 92, 108, 109, 110, 111
Shinto: delocalization of, 70, 71
Shinto parishioner: types of, 46. SEE ALSO *ujiko*
Shinto shrine: functions of, 6, 41; reasons for importance of, 56–58
shōgun: 93
shrine: 5
Shrine Shinto: 3, 4, 6, 51, 155
Shugen: 6
Simmel, Georg: 171, 172
social change: 182
Sōka Gakkai: 4, 9, 10, 165, 181

Sonoda, Minoru: 176
spectator parishioner: 47, 51
spiritualism: 179
stem family: 89, 96, 162
stem family system: 96, 101
structural-functional analysis: of religion, 182
subordinate temple. SEE *matsuji*
suburban area: 163, 182
suburbanization: 41, 69
Sugiura, Ken'ichi: 174
Suijin: 130, 131
Sumiya, Kazuhiko: 176
Suzuki, Eitarō: 174
Suzuki, Hiroshi: 181
Suzuki, Shūken: 179, 181
syncretic religious beliefs: 166, 167
syncretism: 181

T

Tagita, Kōya: 180
Taishakuten: 27
Takagi, Hiroo: 181
Takeda, Chōshū: 176, 177, 178
Takenaka, Masao: 180
Takeuchi, Toshimi: 174, 177
Tanabe, Hisatoshi: 172
tatami: 67
temple (*tera*): 5, 90–91; types of, 7, 99
Tenjin: 130
Tenrikyo: 8, 28, 118, 130, 181

Tensokyo: 3
tera. SEE temple
Terakawa, Shunshō: 178, 179
time-budget: 15–17
Toda, Yoshio: 179
Togawa, Anshō: 174, 177
tokudo (ordination ceremony): 94, 95
Tokugawa Shogunate: 7, 93, 95, 117, 125, 180
Toshigami: 130, 131
tsukinami-kanki (monthly sutra-chanting): 17, 19–20, 22–23

U

ubusunagami: 45, 131
ujibito: 71
ujigami: 45, 71
ujiko: 45, 71, 182
Umeda, Yoshihiko: 177

unions (*kumiai*): 63
United Church of Christ in Japan: 135, 138
Uno, Enkū: 175
urbanization: 71, 109, 182, 183

W

Wach, Joachim: 5, 173
Wakimoto, Tsuneya: 179

Weber, Max: 100, 173

Y

Yakushi: 131
Yanagawa, Keiichi: 177, 182
Yanagita, Kunio: 175
yashikigami (house-site guardian dei-

ties): 51–52, 128, 130, 131
Yonemura, Shōji: 176
Yuasa, Jirō: 120–121, 133
yuta (necromancers): 178

Z

za: 174